£1·00

D1437103

History of **Military Aviation**

hamlyn
History of **Military Aviation**

Bill Gunston

1 PIONEERS

2 TECHNOLOGY TAKES OVER

3 BETWEEN THE WARS

4 WORLD WAR II

Executive Editor: **Julian Brown**
Editor: **Tarda Davison-Aitkins**
Creative Director: **Keith Martin**
Executive Art Editor: **Geoff Fennell**
Design: **Martin Topping**
Picture Research: **Zoe Holterman/TRH Pictures**
Production Controller: **Joanna Walker**

First published in Great Britain in 2000
by **Hamlyn,** an imprint of Octopus Publishing Group Limited
2–4 Heron Quays, London E14 2JP

Copyright © 2000 Octopus Publishing Group Limited

Distributed in the United States and Canada by
Sterling Publishing Co., Inc.
387 Park Avenue South
New York, NY 10016-8810

ISBN 0 600 60005 X

All rights reserved. No part of this publication may be reproduced, stored in a retrieval system, or transmitted in any form or by any means, mechanical, photocopying, recording or otherwise, without the permission of the copyright holders.

A catalogue record for this book is available from the British Library

Produced by Toppan
Printed in China

5 THE JET AGE

6 LIMITED WARS

7 EUROPEAN AIRCRAFT

8 RECENT CRISES

9 21ST CENTURY WARPLANES

Contents

1 PIONEERS

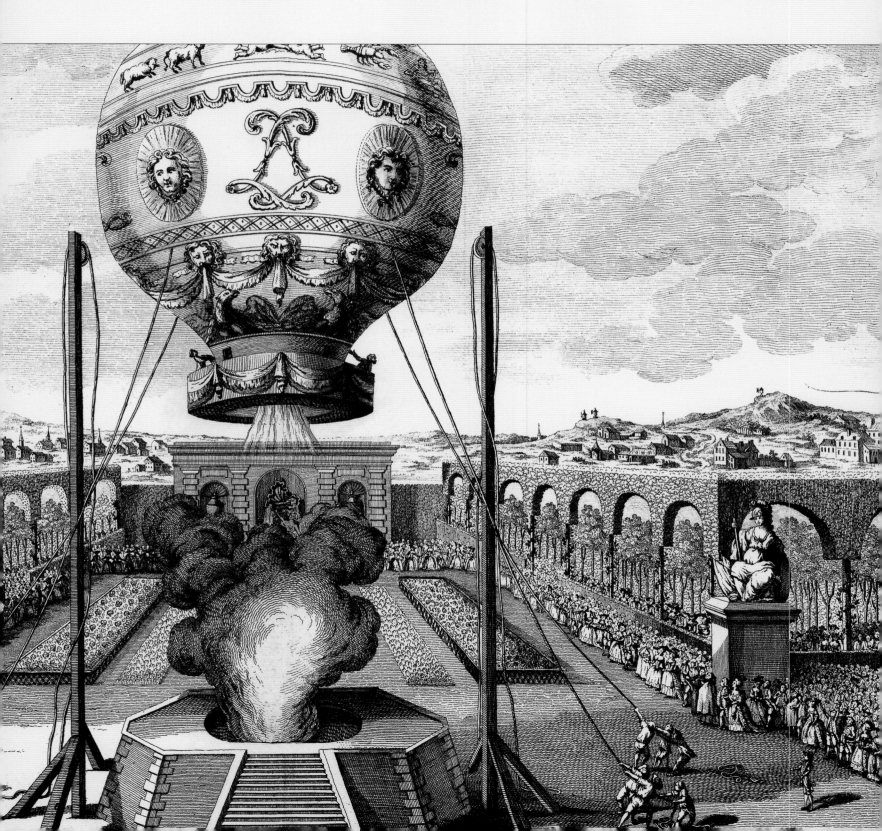

Myths and Legends

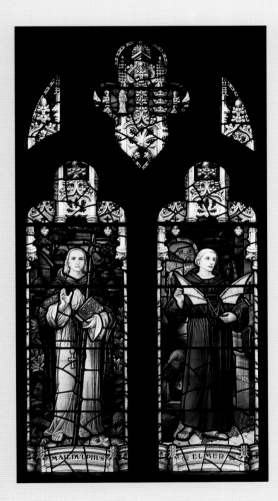

Above: This stained-glass window in Malmesbury Abbey depicts a stylised Eilmer with tiny wings. He actually had huge wings on his hands and feet.

Left: One of numerous paintings depicting the ascent of the first man-carrying aircraft, which flew on 21 November 1783.

From the most distant prehistoric times humans have watched the birds and tried to imagine how they could emulate their ability to fly. Myths and legends about would-be aviators are prolific. There are more than 200 such tales in the English language alone, as well as an even greater number of supposedly true narratives describing actual attempts at flight by real people.

Again considering only literature available in English, dozens of tales survive of men who either described how it should be possible to fly or who actually tried to do so. Set in Crete in c1700 BC, the story of Daedalus – who flew too near the Sun, so that his wax-bonded wings melted – is clearly apocryphal. On the other hand, the Celtic King Bladud, of c850 BC, probably has a basis in fact. In about 1010 the monk Eilmer, or Oliver, of Malmesbury, Wiltshire, certainly did try to glide from a high point on Malmesbury Abbey.

Another English monk, the Franciscan Roger Bacon, left writings which included suggestions dating from c1260 for two contrasting methods of flight. One was the usual method, by beating the air with wings. The other was what might (even at that late date) have been a new idea: a balloon. Bacon proposed making 'a large hollow globe of copper... wrought extremely thin to be as light as possible... filled with ethereal air or liquid fire... it will float like a vessel on the water'. It is easy to scorn this by asking what was meant by the phrase 'ethereal air', but in fact it was a huge leap by the human mind to imagine the possibility of a body with sufficiently low density for it to float in the atmosphere.

Over the next 500 years visionaries wrote about various ways of flying, almost all based on the flapping of wings. Many even fantasized about how airborne armies could invest a city, or rain down destruction on hostile fleets. But on 8 August 1709 a Brazilian priest, Laurenúo de Guzmão, lit a small fire under what we would today call a model hot-air balloon and released it in the crowded Hall of the Ambassadors in Lisbon. King John V was delighted, even though the balloon came up against curtains and set them on fire. This was probably the first demonstration of sustained flight by a human creation.

HYDROGEN 'DISCOVERED'

In 1766 Henry Cavendish, a Fellow of the Royal Society, discovered 'inflammable air'. Its density at atmospheric pressure was clearly much less than that of air. It was later named hydrogen. A Birmingham chemist, Dr Joseph Priestly, then experimented with gases, and in 1774 published his findings in a book. In 1776 this book was translated into French, to the intense interest of two young brothers, Joseph and Étienne Montgolfièr, who had a papermaking business at Annonay, near Lyons. Joseph tried filling paper and then silk balloons with hydrogen, but to no avail (with hindsight, the fabrics were porous). Then he mused on the fact that when paper is burned on a fire the charred fragments are whisked upwards. He had not heard of Guzmão.

The Montgolfièrs did not appreciate the crucial fact that hot air is less dense than the surrounding atmosphere. They wasted years trying to discover how the 'lifting gas' was created, investigating the burning of everything from paper to cow dung and old shoes. By 1782 they settled on wool clippings and damp straw, and incidentally wrote with passion how balloons could bring French and Spanish troops to overwhelm the British garrison which was then being attacked at Gibraltar (today that garrison is still holding out).

In November 1782 the brothers held a model balloon over a fire, let go and watched its majestic flight. They built a paper balloon with a diameter of 35 ft (10.6 m), and flew this on 25 April 1783. Five months later a bigger *Montgolfière* as they came to be known, lifted off with a sheep, a cock and a duck on board, and on 21 November 1783 a splendidly decorated balloon took off from the Château La Muette, Paris, manned by two men, Pilâtre de Rozier and the Marquis d'Arlandes. Just over a week later, on 1 December, Prof Jacques Charles and Noel Roberts made a flight in a balloon filled with hydrogen.

Balloons at War

A century ago the universal opinion was that flying machines were ridiculous. As we shall see, generals fought a bitter rearguard action against even considering whether they might be useful. It is therefore all the more remarkable that, a century earlier still, France set up the first official body using any kind of aircraft.

The date was 2 April 1794, and the place Avignon in the far south. For France this was, of course, a time of turmoil. The Revolution was not yet a year old, and the air was electric with every kind of new idea. Not least of these was to form an army unit equipped with balloons. The ruling body, called the Committee of Public Safety, decreed that there should be a *Compagnie d'Aérostiers* (company of balloonists), to number 30. At its head was scientist Capt. Coutelle. He chose to use hydrogen balloons.

Predictably, Coutelle and his company were regarded with disdain by most of the generals, but they were soon to have a chance to demonstrate their value. War broke out with Austria, and on 2 June 1794 Coutelle made the world's first operational flight when he ascended on a long tether and reported on the dispositions of the Austrian and Dutch forces threatening Maubeuge. Austrian artillery fired at him and missed. On 26 June the armies met at Fleurus, near Charleroi. Coutelle was there with a balloon called *l'Entreprenant* (enterprising). He ascended with General Morlot as an experienced observer. They stayed aloft throughout the ten-hour engagement, sending messages down in a bag. Not only did the balloon prove of immense value but its mere presence demoralized the Austrians, who considered that the French were 'in league with the devil'. They were routed.

Coutelle soon became a general, and his *aérostiers* were expanded to four companies. They did brilliantly at the siege of Mainz, but in 1797 they were annihilated by the British at Aboukir, Egypt. Having been on the receiving end, the empire of Austria began thinking about aerial warfare, and in its siege of Venice in 1849 constructed 200 small balloons each carrying 30 lb (13.6 kg) of explosive. On 22 June the armada was released, each with a smoking fuze. Unfortunately, the wind changed suddenly, and the Austrian troops had to try to avoid their own 'bombers'.

Left: On 8 August 1884 two French officers coaxed their airship from Chalais-Meudon to Villacoublay and back. This was the first human flight under control.

Above: During the Boer War in South Africa (1899–1902), the British Army used numerous hydrogen balloons to observe an elusive enemy, and when possible to direct artillery fire. Similar tasks had been carried out in several conflicts since 1794.

AVIATORS

By this time aeronautical terminology was taking shape. Would-be aviators were divided into aeronauts, who manned lighter-than-air craft called aerostats, and the smaller number who persisted in believing in heavier-than-air flying machines. The latter, technically called aerodynes, seemed as far away as ever, but balloons were soon being made all over the world. In 1858 one was over Melbourne, and a year later one carried four Americans an estimated 809 miles (1,302 km) from St Louis to upstate New York.

On 20 April 1861, a mere week after the clash at Fort Sumter had started the American Civil War, a New England balloonist, Thaddeus Lowe, was arrested by Confederate troops at Unionville, South Carolina. He was able to prove he was not 'a Yankee spy' but (a supposed imbecile) testing wind currents prior to trying to be carried across the Atlantic. In fact, he did join the Union cause, and on 31 May 1862 his tethered balloon reconnoitred Confederate positions at Fair Oaks, Virginia. His information saved Union forces from a crushing defeat. By this time John La Mountain and other aeronauts had joined Union forces, which in 1861 deployed seven balloons each equipped with five miles (8 km) of telegraph cable, a Morse heliograph and signal flags.

In the Franco-Prussian war of 1870 balloons played a major role, notably in the world's first airlift out of encircled Paris. By 28 January 1871 66 balloons had carried 100 passengers, 400 homing pigeons and ten tonnes of mail.

In 1878 the British Army spent £71 on a balloon, and appointed Capt. James Templer as Director of Balloons (because he owned his own balloon, *Crusader*). By this time, despite its probable lower costs, the hot-air balloon had been replaced by the gas balloon filled with hydrogen. Of course, all balloons are carried along by the surrounding atmosphere. From March 1784 many experimenters had tried to make a dirigible (steerable) balloon, by adding oars and a rudder, flapping wings or other ideas.

In 1852 Henri Giffard's airship had made the first dirigible flight, from Paris to Trappes, but it was too slow to be of practical use. However, the Franco-Prussian war accelerated such work, and on 8 August 1884 two French army captains, Charles Renard and Arthur Krebs, tested their *La France*. Despite the 704 lb (319 kg) of batteries feeding the 9-hp motor they made an out-and-return flight at about 14 mph (22.5 km/h).

Aerial Weapons

Above: Ely's arrival on USS *Pennsylvania* was arrested by 22 ropes stretched across the deck. These were removed for his departure from the ship on the same day, seen here.

We think of rockets as being a modern invention, but the Chinese were making gunpowder firecrackers before 200 BC, and rockets followed soon after. When Marco Polo visited China prior to 1300 he found another idea in common use: the man-lifting kite. By this time Chinese writings were linking the two, and describing how kitemen could throw bombs into enemy cities or ships. Proof of whether this was actually done is hard to find, and it may be that the Austrian bomb-carrying balloons of 1849 were the first aerial weapons actually used.

In 1858 Félix Tournachon (Nadar) took the first aerial photograph, showing the Paris Étoile, from a tethered balloon at about 1,640 ft (500 m). Gradually the idea was accepted that balloons or airships might have some value as reconnaissance platforms, and in the Boer War

in 1900 British balloons were used to direct artillery fire. In 1901, while that war was still going on, Sir Hiram Maxim addressed the Aeronautical Society (later given the prefix Royal) and discussed the use of flying machines for military purposes. In 1894 he had tested a gigantic biplane with 640 installed horsepower and more wing area than a B-52, and he was also famed for his machine gun.

PIVOTAL ROLE

In fact just such a gun was to play a pivotal role in aerial warfare. Before this, however, the attention of the British Army was to be diverted by the kite. This was because of the Texan Samuel F. Cody, who in 1901 pointed out how often it had been impossible for balloons in South Africa to become airborne (because of strong wind, lack of hydrogen and other factors), whereas his 'war kites' ought always to be ready. After such a kite was inspected at Leeds by Maj. F.C. Trollope, official trials followed. On 16 April 1903 Cody almost drowned when, on tow from HMS *Seahorse*, the captain turned the ship down-wind. In February 1905 Cody was appointed British Army kiting instructor, though such kites faded from the military scene. Their last appearance was as the Fa 330 rotary-wing gyro kite used by German submarines in World War II to spot distant targets.

When Cody got his official appointment in 1905 the Wright brothers had already become the world's first experienced aeroplane pilots. The world did not know this, and the centre of aeronautical activity was France, especially Paris, where there was frenzied effort to try to make successful flying machines. Europe was also the centre of intrigue and talk of war. It is therefore all the more astonishing that the pioneering achievements pointing the way to aerial warfare should all have taken place in the United States.

On 1 August 1907 the US Army Signal Corps created an Aeronautical Division. It comprised Capt. Charles de F. Chandler and two assistants, and they were charged to 'study the flying machine and the possibility of adapting it to war purposes'. On 23 December of the same year, the US Army issued a specification for a Signal Corps aeroplane and invited tenders. There were 41 bidders, 40 of whom eventually dropped out. The two-seat Wright Model A was duly delivered to Ft Myer, Virginia, on 20 August 1908.

The Signal Corps then bought two Wright Bs and seven Model Cs with full dual controls. On 27 July 1909 Orville Wright made 74 circuits of a course at Ft Myer, three days later flying out and back to Shooter's Hill to average 42.583 mph (68.53 km/h), earning the brothers US$30,000.

However, it was pure private enterprise that led to the first bombs and bullets from aeroplanes. On 30 June 1910 civilian Glenn Curtiss went aboard one of his own speedy biplanes and dropped 20 home-made bombs on a battleship-shaped target on Lake Keuka, NY. He scored 18 hits, watched grimly by officers headed by Admiral Kimball. Two months later an irrepressible Army officer took a gun aloft. The date was 20 August 1910, and the shots were fired from a Springfield '03 rifle aimed from a Curtiss biplane by Lt. Jacob E. Fickel. He made four passes over a 3 x 3-ft (roughly, 1-m²) target set up at Sheepshead Bay, NY. He scored two hits.

Last of the pioneer achievements was to operate an aeroplane from a ship. On 14 November 1910 Curtiss test pilot Eugene B. Ely made the first takeoff from a ship, using a ramp made of planks laid over the bows of the cruiser USS *Birmingham*, lying in Hampton Roads, Virginia. On 18 January 1911 he achieved the far more difficult task of landing on a similar platform on the stern of the *Pennsylvania* in San Francisco Bay.

Right: Samuel Cody's 'war kites' were tested from 20 November 1901, and improved versions were adopted by the British Army.

First Encounters

The very first use of aeroplanes in human conflict began on 1 February 1911, in the unlikely scenario of Mexico. In late 1910 a revolution had begun in that country. What was unusual was that the Mexican government hired a multinational US-managed troupe of daredevil flyers, which had been formed by the famed American John B. Moisant, who had crashed fatally a month earlier. They were asked to fly reconnaissance missions from El Paso, Texas, over rebel territory on the other side of the Rio Grande.

This was the start of a campaign which simmered for years, and was only ended by the transfer of US Air Service squadrons to France in 1917. It involved aircraft made by Burgess, Curtiss, Martin and Wright, the most numerous being the mass-produced Curtiss JN ('Jenny') family of two-seaters. While the prolonged campaign had a strong 'comic opera' element about it, its overtones were real and bloody. What it achieved was to teach the US military a great deal about how to design and operate aeroplanes in harsh front-line environments which embraced violent weather over everything from scorching desert to snow-capped mountains.

In 1911 the almost universal opinion among British 'gentlemen', especially generals, was that aeroplanes had no use in war whatsoever (a small minority conceded the possibility that they might be useful for reconnaissance). They generally ignored the fact that air warfare had already begun. Fighting had broken out between Italy and Turkey, both of which considered Libya part of their empire.

In October 1911 the Italians sent an expeditionary force, which included several aeroplanes. It quickly met fierce resistance from local Arabs, who (for their own purposes) were actively supported by Turkey. Within weeks the Italians had shipped a further six aeroplanes to North Africa, where they were rigged up with locally devised arrangements for carrying large plate cameras and, from October 1911, for dropping small bombs.

OVER THE LINES

On 22 October Capt. Carlo Piazza took off in his Blériot and flew the first reconnaissance

mission over Turkish positions around El Aziziya, Tripoli. He wrote his observations on a notepad. Further history was made on 1 November when Lt. Giulio Gavotti took off in his Etrich Taube (another monoplane), removed from a leather sack four 4.4-lb (2-kg) Cipelli grenades filled with potassium picrate, inserted detonators extracted from a pocket, and dropped them one by one on Turkish positions.

In 1899 a Hague Convention decree prohibited the dropping of bombs from balloons, but the Italian government pointed out that this could not apply to aeroplanes. Soon a type of vertical bomb tube, designed by Lt. Bailo, was being fitted to the Italian aircraft, even to a rather archaic Henry Farman pusher. By sliding down the tube the bomb left cleanly, with no

Above: Capt. Piazza of the Italian Air Flotilla pictured with the Blériot in which he made what can be described as the world's first combat mission by an aeroplane. The date was 22 October 1911.

chance of getting caught in fabric, struts or wires. By late 1911 the Italians were dropping Danish Aasen bombs, which were grenades fitted with a fabric stabilizing tail and a long cord which had to unwind before the safety pin was released.

On 24 November Capt. Moizo carried out the first artillery spotting mission (sending information on the disposition of targets and exactly where friendly shells were actually falling), and on 23 February 1912 Piazza flew the first photo-reconnaissance mission.

By early 1912 the Italian expeditionary force's land troops had become bogged down in trying to fight elusive enemies. They then received further air support in the form of two small non-rigid airships (a class of aircraft by now given the English word dirigible). Called P.2 and P.3, they were the creation of the versatile engineer Enrico Forlanini. Despite their fragility, and the fact that they presented a big target to the Arab marksmen, many of whom were brilliant shots, they survived (with much-patched envelopes) until towards the end of 1912 Turkey became committed to a war in the Balkans. The first reconnaissance mission by the airships was on 10 March 1912, and they made many further flights, on occasion dropping showers of Cipelli bomblets, large spherical mortar bombs and artillery shells fitted with tails. On 13 April both remained airborne for 13 hours, spotting for the Italian artillery.

The Balkan war was if anything more primitive. Five or six pilots were hired by the Turks, but the only effective air arm was that of Bulgaria, which gradually created a full air regiment. The first purpose-designed aerial bombs were dropped on Turkish targets at Adrianople (today Edirne) in October 1912. Bulgarian pilots also fired on Turkish troops with rifles and even pistols, though accurate aiming would have been impossible.

Below: Centre of attention at this US Army camp was this Wright Flyer in 1910. It was a Model B, Serial No 3 or 4.

No Practical Application

Hindsight is cheap, but it is difficult to avoid the conclusion that the British were astonishingly slow to recognize the importance of the aeroplane. On 25 July 1909 Blériot's arrival at Dover resulted in the *Daily Mail*'s headline next day being BRITAIN NO LONGER AN ISLAND. Two months later three young officers in the British Army risked damaging their careers by asking if they could fly reconnaissance missions *in their own aeroplanes* in the forthcoming manoeuvres. They were told this would frighten the horses.

Three oft-cited quotations from the 1909–11 period are: 'Their Lordships [of the British Admiralty] foresee no practical application for flying machines in naval service', 'We [the British military, expressed by the Secretary of State for War] do not consider that aeroplanes will be of

any possible use for war purposes', and 'We [this time the speaker was the Chief of the Imperial General Staff] have done very well without aeroplanes so far, we can do without them today'.

Thus, it was in the teeth of high-ranking opposition that the opposing armies – called Red and Blue – in the British manoeuvres on Salisbury plain in September 1910 did employ aeroplanes. They were hired. One was flown for the Red forces by one of the three officers who had offered to fly their own aircraft the previous year, former Capt. Bertram Dickson. Now employed by the British & Colonial Aeroplane Co. (forerunner of the great Bristol firm), he astonished the Red staff by providing a completely detailed account of the Blue army's movements, which the Red cavalry had been unable to do. Later Dickson landed in Blue

Below: One of several official plans of Cody's 1912 aeroplane built for the British Military trials on Salisbury Plain. Note the word 'SECRET' impressed in the top corner.

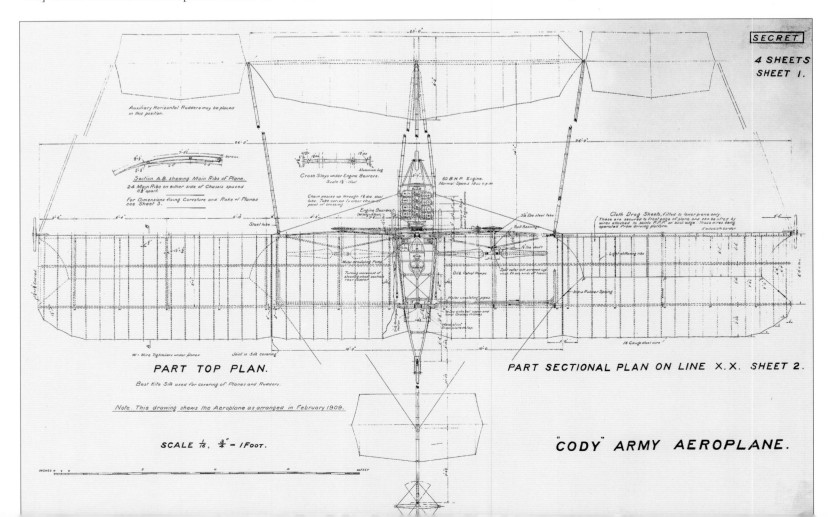

SECRET

4 SHEETS
SHEET 1.

PART TOP PLAN.

PART SECTIONAL PLAN ON LINE X.X. SHEET 2.

"CODY" ARMY AEROPLANE.

SCALE ⅟₁₆, ¾" = 1 FOOT.

Left: Cody's so-called *Cathedral* won the British Military Trials purely because of the 120-hp of its Austro-Daimler engine. Repeatedly modified, the machine itself was already obsolescent

territory in order to telephone his report but was captured! The story made the *Daily Mail*, prompting actor-aviator Robert Loraine to drive overnight from his London theatre to Salisbury, offer his services to the Blue army, take over Dickson's machine, fit it with radio and start providing reconnaissance information in real time.

FLYING CORPS FORMED

Public opinion forced the General Staff to take some action, and on 1 April 1911 an air battalion was formed as a unit in the Army's Royal Engineers. With a total strength of 190, it had four riding horses, 32 draught horses and five aeroplanes, none of which was in a flyable condition. Perhaps more motivated by what was

happening in France and Germany than by British public opinion, a Royal Flying Corps was set up on 13 May 1912. It was announced that 71 aircraft would be purchased. Absence of any previous orders meant that there was only an embryonic British aircraft industry, and matters were not helped when it was announced that virtually all the 71 machines would be purchased in France 'as French aeroplanes have been proved better'. As for pilots, anyone was welcome, provided of course that they previously learned to fly *at their own expense*.

In the summer of 1912 the British government decided to hold a grand Military Aeroplane Competition. Run by the War Office, it gave competitors just two months to

get their machines to the starting line, making it impossible for anyone to design a special military aeroplane. There were 31 entries, 25 aircraft took part and 21 actually got into the air, in some cases very briefly. The best aircraft by far was the B.E.2, designed by Geoffrey de Havilland and F. M. Green. It scored the highest marks in almost every section of the contest, but it could not win! This is because it had been designed at the Royal Aircraft Factory (previously the Army's balloon factory) at Farnborough, which was barred from officially taking part. Accordingly the winner was S. F. Cody's *Cathedral*, an archaic 'stick and string' creation which even Cody admitted would be a ridiculous choice for the Royal Flying Corps.

Progress was quicker on mainland Europe. While the British were organizing their abortive competition, the French were holding exercises with an air force already in being. Afterwards 72 of the aircraft which had taken part were flown direct from their *Aviation Militaire* bases to Villacoublay, where they were lined up for inspection by the war minister Alexandre Millerand. The Breguet, Caudron and Farman aircraft were biplanes, but other squadrons flew Blériot, Borel, Deperdussin, Hanriot, Morane, Nieuport, REP and Sommer monoplanes.

Sikorsky Bombers

Today the name Sikorsky means helicopters. In fact, Igor Sikorsky did begin his career trying to build helicopters – in 1909, aged 20 – but could not get them to fly. He turned to aeroplanes, and achieved fame and commercial success. Soon he was creating aeroplanes much larger than any others in the sky. Perhaps surprisingly, many were built, to play a major role in something few had previously considered: strategic bombing.

In spring 1912 M.V. Shidlovsky, chairman of the RBVZ (Russo-Baltic Wagon Factory), moved the main works to St Petersburg, to be closer to government contracts. He offered Sikorsky the post of aeroplane designer. Young Igor shut his Kiev works and brought his assistants with him. Within a week Sikorsky

landplanes and seaplanes, both monoplanes and biplanes, were back in production.

On 17 September 1912 Sikorsky suggested to his chairman that they should build a really large aeroplane. Ignoring the collective advice of all the experts, Shidlovsky said 'Start at once'. The result was called *Bolshoi Baltiskii* (big Baltic) or just *Grand*. Sikorsky flew it on 2 March (15 March in the old Julian calendar) 1913. Powered by two 100-hp Argus engines, it had a span of 88 ft 7 in (27 m). In the bow was a searchlight and a mount for a gun. Double doors then led through the two-pilot cockpit to a cabin with a sofa, table, camp stools, toilet (as made by RBVZ for trains), carpet and electric light.

On 10 May 1913 Sikorsky began flying the big Baltic with two more engines mounted as

pushers behind the first. Best of all was the final arrangement of July 1913 with all four engines in one row on the lower wing. Renamed *Russkii Vityaz* (Russian knight), it flew for almost two hours with seven passengers. The RBVZ was then given a contract for ten, for use as reconnaissance bombers. Sikorsky gave them the class name *Il'ya Muromets*, after a legendary hero of Kiev.

These ten IM aircraft were all slightly different, but all had a broadly similar design. Their biplane wings were much larger than those of the first giant, with a span typically 113 ft 2 in (34.5 m) and area of 2,369 sq ft (220 m²). Most had four engines, of various types including 125 or 140-hp Argus, 150 or 225-hp Sunbeam, 220-hp Renault or 200-hp Salmson radials.

Left: This was one of about 30 IM Type V bombers, powered by four British-supplied Sunbeam engines each of 150 or 225 hp. Fuel was housed in the two cylindrical tanks under the upper wing.

Their fuselages had a bluff nose hardly project-ing ahead of the wings, and maintained a roomy box section with large side windows. At the back was a simplified single-fin tail.

EPIC FLIGHT

The first IM even had an extra monoplane wing on the rear fuselage, but this was not a good idea. With this removed, Sikorsky began flight testing on 12 December 1913. This first IM even had an upper 'promenade deck' with a handrail. Sikorsky strolled on it in the course of an epic one-stop test flight to Kiev and back. Another long flight was made on 12 February 1914, with 12 men and a dog as passengers.

Unexpectedly, production continued until the RBVZ had delivered 80 of the monsters.

These equipped the world's first strategic aero-plane unit, the EVK (Squadron of Flying Ships). Shidlovsky was appointed commander, with the rank of major-general. Not least of the remarkable aspects of this story is that the EVK flew hundreds of long and tough missions. Seemingly frail – Sikorsky said 'It's better to fly cautiously with a design factor of two than stay on the ground with a factor of four' – many IMs came back after prolonged battles with German fighters. Only two were shot down, one on 15 February 1915 which made a forced landing and literally fell to pieces, and the sec-ond on 12 September 1916 after first shooting down three German fighters.

There were five principal sub-types. The EVK operated throughout the battle front. In

1916 the main base was Lida, but other main airfields included Gatchina, Pskov and, in the final stages, Vinnitsa. Crews usually numbered five or six. Bomb load varied with mission fuel but could reach 1 tonne (2,205 lb), in sizes up to 240 kg (529 lb), though a dummy of 410 kg (904 lb) was dropped. As many as six defensive guns were carried, including the Madsen, Maxim, Lewis, Colt-Browning and Hotchkiss. One ship even had a Hotchkiss of 37-mm (1.45-in) calibre.

Following the Russian Revolution, a few surviving EVKs were taken over undamaged by the Bolsheviks. The new owners were glad to use them throughout the 1920s as transports and also used them to train their pilots to fly large aircraft.

Western Front 1914

In 1913–14 the British House of Commons echoed to arguments about aeroplanes. On one occasion the Secretary of State for War claimed that the RFC had '101 aeroplanes... a great many being of the latest type', but a tiresome Member of Parliament, W. Joynson-Hicks, retorted that, in fact, 'No 2 Squadron has two B biplanes and three Farmans at Montrose, No 3 Squadron has one B and two Farmans at Larkhill and No 4 has two B and two Breguets at Farnborough'.

All these were obsolescent, and all were biplanes. On 15 September 1912 the War Office had forbidden any member of the RFC to fly a monoplane, even if he owned it! Monoplanes were described as 'not a good type'. Eventually this ridiculous order was rescinded, but its long-term effect was a deep prejudice in Britain against monoplanes which by the mid-1930s was to make British military aircraft design out of date.

The long-expected European war began in the summer of 1914. On 3 August, the day before Britain joined the fighting, the RFC's No 3 Squadron began its long move south from Montrose. Its pilots left most of their kit behind, because of the belief that the conflict would be over in a few weeks. On 13 August Nos 2 and 4 Squadrons began crossing to

France. They flew the B.E.2a, an improved form of the biplane that had scored best in the 1912 competition. Each pilot and observer was issued with an inflated inner tube, for use if he had to ditch in the Channel. One asked what he should do if he met a Zeppelin, to be told 'You should try to crash into it'.

By 1914 France's *Aviation Militaire* was a large and mature force. From July 1912 its aircraft had carried national insignia in the form of concentric red/white/blue rings. On 14 August one of its many Voisins took off from Verdun and set course for the German frontier. Lt. Cesari and Cpl. Prudhommeau managed to reach about 7,500 ft (2,300 metres) over the Zeppelin hangars at Metz. There they released two 155-mm (0.61-in) shells which had been fitted with fins, apparently scoring direct hits.

NEW MARKINGS

A week later RFC aircraft provided vital information which saved a French army from being caught in a pincer movement near Mons. By this time RFC aircraft had had large Union Jacks sewn under their wings, because they had been repeatedly fired at by Allied troops and their pilots had been arrested whenever they had landed to ask the way. Soon it was realized that at a distance the British flag could be

Above: Two of the RNAS Avro 504s that made the first strategic bombing raid on 21 November 1914. No 873 was flown by Flt. Lt. S. V. Sippe, and 875 by Flt. Cdr. J. T. Babington.

mistaken for a German iron cross, and in December 1914 it was decided to paint all British aircraft with blue/white/red roundels like the French but with the colours reversed, red in the centre.

The first aerial victories were gained on 25 August. Lt. C. W. Wilson closed on a Taube while his observer Lt. Rabagliati stood up and fired his rifle at it. The Taube promptly landed beside a British column near Le Quesnoy. On the same day three aircraft from No 2 Sqn. forced an enemy aircraft to land. The B. E. of Lts. Harvey-Kelly and Mansfield landed beside it. They chased the German pilot into a wood but then lost him, however, they set fire to his aircraft before flying back to their base at Le Cateau.

Above: One of the numerous variations on the graceful *Taube* (Dove) designed in 1910 by the Austrial Igo Etrich. Almost all had a water-cooled inline engine of 70 to 120 hp.

Top: Despite being fundamentally obsolete many thousands of Voisin pushers served with the Allies. This Voisin X (300-hp Renault) had a 37 mm (1.45-in) cannon.

On 30 August Parisians were amazed as a small monoplane, a Rumpler-built Taube, dropped three bombs on the Quai de Valmy, killing two people. It then released a shower of leaflets announcing that the Germans were 'at the gates of Paris'. The pilot was Lt. Ferdinand von Hiddesen.

On 5 October a German Aviatik became the first aircraft to be shot down by another. Sgt Joseph Frantz and his observer Cpl. Louis Quénault of Escadrille VB.24 took off in their Voisin to test its newly fitted Hotchkiss machine gun. Over Brimont they saw the enemy. As they drew near, the observer in the Aviatik opened fire, however, the Hotchkiss shot the Aviatik down in flames.

Before the end of the year the Royal Naval Air Service had made the first strategic bombing raids of the war, though with puny aircraft. On 8 October two Sopwith Tabloids took off from Antwerp. Sqn. Cdr. Grey bombed Cologne railway station, while Flt. Lt. Marix destroyed Zeppelin LZ.25 in its shed at Dusseldorf. On 21 November the RNAS struck again. Led by Sqn. Cdr. E. F. Briggs, three Avro 504s flew in sub-zero temperatures 125 miles (201 km) to bomb the Zeppelin factory at Friedrichshafen. They caused considerable damage and destroyed the hydrogen gas plant, but Briggs was shot down and captured.

2 TECHNOLOGY TAKES OVER

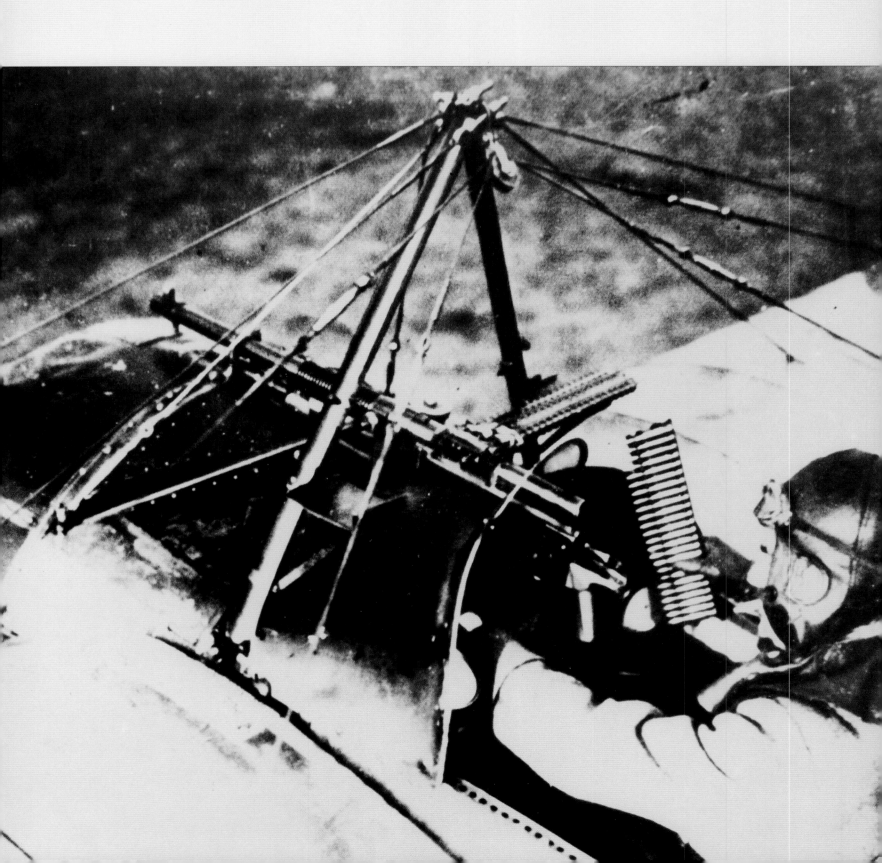

New Technology

Above: The Aviatik B.II was typical of a Central Powers aircraft of 1915. Almost all had a six-cylinder water-cooled engine, in this case a 120-hp Austro-Daimler. The observer had a rifle or pistol.

Left: Garros, test pilot of the Morane-Saulnier company, fitted his Type N monoplane with a 7.7-mm (.3-in) Hotchkiss firing straight ahead. He is holding a spare clip of ammunition.

At the outbreak of World War I in August 1914 two distinct types of aero engine existed. One was the air-cooled rotary, which took the world of aviation by storm when it was introduced by the French Gnome company in late 1907. Its crankshaft was fixed to the aircraft. The cylinders, arranged radially like spokes, rotated around it, carrying the propeller with them. Rotary engines were used in vast numbers, but suffered from high consumption of fuel and enormous consumption of castor-oil lubricant. It proved difficult to design them for high power settings and at the end of the war they disappeared from the factories.

The main alternative was the water-cooled engine with cylinders arranged in a row. This needed a long and heavy crankshaft and crankcase, and also required an equally heavy radiator and piping, all of which was vulnerable to enemy bullets. Despite this over 90 per cent of the aircraft of the Central Powers – Germany and Austria-Hungary – used water-cooled engines. All the most powerful engines were of this type. Italian firms made some with a single row of giant cylinders, but most of the high-power engines had two rows of cylinders forming a V when viewed end-on.

A few experimental propellers were made out of sheet steel or even the newly available aluminium, but the majority were beautifully carved from multiple laminations of hardwood, such as mahogany, walnut and ash. Often a metal strip was added to protect the leading edge of each blade from erosion by sand or stones. As the wood grain had to run from tip to tip, propellers had either two or four blades.

RIFLES AND PISTOLS

The obvious armament to be installed in aeroplanes was the machine gun, but in 1914 many pilots and observers had to make do with rifles and even pistols. Because governments had never even thought about such things, armament schemes were lash-ups, usually contrived at front-line squadron level. Sometimes individual brilliance made up for this. Capt. Lanoe G. Hawker of No 6 Sqn., RFC fixed a Martini carbine to his Bristol Scout so that it pointed diagonally out, just missing the propeller. On 25 July 1915, with this seemingly impossible arrangement, he took on three German aircraft, each carrying an observer armed with a machine gun, and shot down all three!

From 1911 at least 18 inventors had proposed ways of enabling a machine gun to fire ahead past the blades of a tractor propeller. This involved synchronizing the firing of each round with the speed of rotation of the propeller. Some were called 'interrupter gears' which suggests that the stream of bullets was interrupted to let each blade go past. In fact, typically from four to eight blades would go by between each shot and the next. All such ideas were ignored, so in desperation the test pilot of the French Morane-Saulnier firm, Roland Garros, fixed steel deflectors to the blades of his Type N monoplane fighter, so that it did not matter if the occasional bullet hit it. He soon shot down four German aircraft. Then, on 20 April 1915, he was himself shot down by ground fire.

Immediately the Germans took Garros' propeller to their top aircraft designer, Dutchman Anthony Fokker and said, 'Copy it'. Fokker said 'Why not use one of the synchronization systems?' In three days he was testing a Fokker M5K monoplane with a forward-firing gun, controlled by the system proposed to deaf ears by Franz Schneider in 1912. In turn this led to strident Allied demands that Fokker's scheme should be copied, to the chagrin of such ignored inventors as Challenger, Dibovsky, Kauper and Constantinesco. Their dusty patents were pulled from the archives, and it was Constantinesco's gear which became standard in the post-war RAF. It used hydraulic plungers driven by oil pressure from a cam on the propeller shaft.

Until such schemes were perfected the only way to make a fighter was to put the engine at the back. Thus, most had a two-seat nacelle with the observer/gunner sitting in the nose in front of the pilot. In July 1915 de Havilland's D.H.2 showed that a front gunner was not needed. The first D.H.2 had a Lewis gun aimed by the pilot, but soon it was realized that it was better to aim the whole aircraft.

The First Fighters

Aeroplanes intended to shoot down others are generally known as fighters. In the USA, until World War II they were called pursuits, apparently in the belief that their enemies would turn tail and run. During World War I they were called fighting scouts or just scouts, despite the fact that this term originally implied their mission was reconnaissance.

At the start of World War I a warplane was virtually any machine able to fly. The pilot – or, in a two-seater, the observer – would climb aboard with a gun he could carry and fire himself. A few tried dropping grenades on enemy aircraft, while another weapon was the fléchette, a steel dart usually carried in canisters of 250 (these were dropped mainly on troops on the ground). A few pilots even went to war

trailing grappling hooks or weights on long cables to snare the propellers of enemy aircraft.

Fokker showed the way to go with the M5K. More generally known as the E-type (E for *Eindecker*, meaning monoplane), this was a simple aeroplane with a rotary engine of only 80 or 100 hp, so it was hardly a sparkling performer. The crucial facts were that it could overhaul the many Allied aircraft that were even slower, it was outstandingly agile, and its pilot could aim it (and its fixed forward-firing gun) with deadly accuracy.

By far the most common British aircraft were the B.E. family. These were specially designed to be so stable that the pilot could take his hands off the stick and write reconnaissance information in a notebook. When the Fokker monoplanes appeared this stability was instantly turned into a death-trap. The RFC became what newspapers called 'Fokker fodder'. In the second half of 1915 the British, and to a lesser degree the French, were almost driven from the skies. An official report says 'Britain was nearer to losing the war than at any other time'.

MONOPLANES DEVELOP

Even though scores of Allied pilots were shot down and killed on their first combat mission, morale never cracked. Several French aircraft, notably the little Nieuports, were faster and more agile than the Fokkers. The Allies also had monoplanes, of which the most numerous were the French Morane-Saulniers. These came in

Above: All the Fokker E-types looked very similar, and all were fitted with an Oberursel rotary engine of 80 or 100 hp. The example illustrated is an E.II. Most were pale reddish-brown, the colour of the fabric varnish.

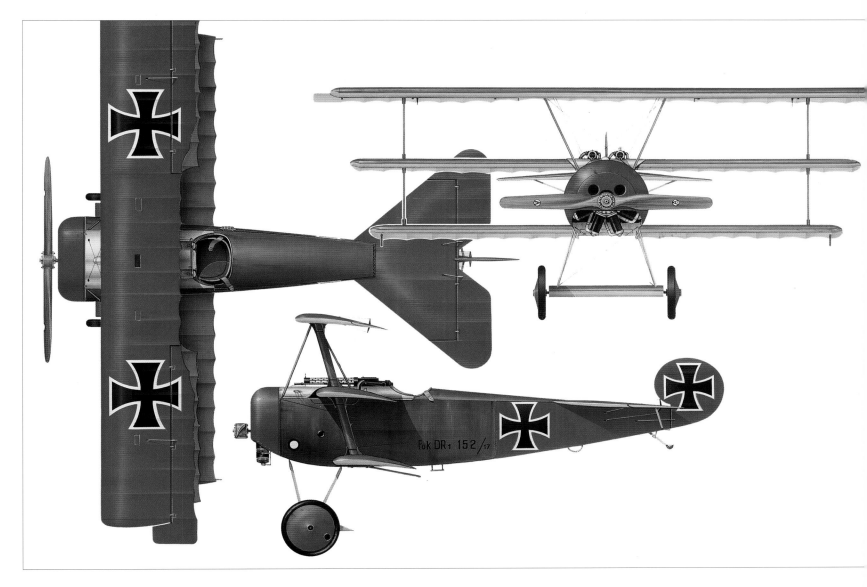

Fokker Dr. I

Type: single-seat triplane fighter

Powerplant: one 110-hp (82-kW) Oberursel Ur.II nine-cylinder rotary piston engine

Performance: maximum speed 115 mph (185 km/h) at sea level; climb to 3,280 ft (1000 m) in 2 minutes 55 seconds; service ceiling 20,015 ft (6100 m); range 186 miles (300 km)

Weights: empty 894 lb (406 kg); maximum take-off 1,291 lb (586 kg)

Dimensions: wing span upper 23 ft 7 in (7.12 m), centre 20 ft 5.25 in (6.23 m), lower 18 ft 8.5 in (5.70 m); length 18 ft 11 in (5.77 m); height 9 ft 8 in (2.95 m); wing area, including axle fairing 200.85 sq ft (18.66 m²)

Armament: two fixed synchronized 0.31-in (7.92-mm) LMG 08/15 machine-guns, each with 500 rounds

two families, the Type L, with the wing above the fuselage (so-called parasol configuration) and the Type N. The latter was faster, but the wing blocked the pilot's downward vision.

Perhaps the most agile aircraft in the sky was the Bristol Scout, though only the final batches had a synchronized gun. Apart from the *Eindeckers* nearly all the German and Austro-Hungarian aircraft were robust biplanes with heavy water-cooled engines. Hansa-Brandenburg built fighter seaplanes, and in Austria Lohner built neat flying boats with a single pusher engine mounted between the wings high above the hull.

Early in the war the Italians captured a Lohner, and a copy was put into production by the Macchi company. Gradually the Macchi boats were made faster, until in the M.5 the Italians had a flying boat which could 'mix it' in a dogfight with other fighters. Powered by an engine of 160 hp, it had a speed of 117 mph (188 km/h), which few other aircraft could equal. An incidental advantage of the configuration was that machine guns could be put in the bows with no need for any synchronization gear.

One of the problems facing designers was how to give the scout pilot a better view. The British Sopwith company reasoned that if you used three wings their chord (distance across the wing from leading to trailing edge) could be reduced, so the Sopwith Triplane appeared in May 1916. In fact there was no magic in having three narrow wings, but this machine made a huge impact on its enemies. Within three months seven companies in the Central Powers were making copies. One, the Fokker Dr.I (Dr from *Dreidecker*, three wings), became one of the most famous aircraft of the entire conflict, not least because top-scorer Manfred von Richthofen was killed in one on 21 April 1918.

Airships

In 1784 the only way aviators could think of making a dirigible was to replace the basket with a rowing boat, but rowing through the sky is ineffectual. By 1852 Giffard had adopted the engine-driven screw propeller and 150 years later we have never thought of anything better.

In Germany Count Ferdinand von Zeppelin had a distinguished army career, reaching the rank of general. From 1870 he sketched designs for airships. In 1893 he submitted such a design to the War Ministry, but it was rejected. Accordingly, he formed his own company and on 2 July 1900 made the first test flight of LZ.1 (*Luftschiff Zeppelin* 1, airship Zeppelin No 1). The gasbags were contained inside a huge tubular framework of aluminium, with pointed ends, covered in fabric and with a light girder structure underneath for engines, fuel and, on later tests, a weight on a looped cable for adjusting the fore/aft trim.

Before long Zeppelin had a rival: the Schütte-Lanz company which built airships with fabric-covered frameworks, mainly out of plywood. Gradually experience was gained. While it was recognized that these huge craft were rather fragile and to a considerable degree at the mercy of the wind, provided that strict rules were adhered to and no flame or spark allowed near the huge fabric cells filled with hydrogen, the airship was a practical vehicle. In 1910 Zeppelin formed an airline, called DELAG, which was soon serving five-course dinners to passengers over a kilometre above the ground.

In 1914 puny aeroplanes were regarded as insignificant compared with the formidable Zeppelins. However, the first to drop bombs,

Left: Rigid No 33, of Britain's RNAS (later RAF), was based on the German L33 and was shot down in 1916. It was 643 ft (196 m) long and had five 250-hp Sunbeam engines.

the German Army's Z.6, was hit by ground fire over Liège on 6 August, and damaged beyond repair in a forced landing in a forest near Bonn. Flown mainly by the German Navy, increasing numbers of ever-larger Zeppelins were soon roaming far over the North Sea. The Kaiser was haunted by the thought that airship bombs might fall on his cousins in Buckingham Palace, but by 1915 he gave permission for attacks on British coastal targets, and on 19 January Zeppelins bombed Yarmouth and King's Lynn

SHOESTRING DEFENCE

Gradually Britain organized a primitive air-defence system. Aircraft designers created anti-Zeppelin aircraft, such as the Armstrong Whitworth F.K.12 and Supermarine P.B.31E. It was soon recognized that such slow 'battleships of the sky' were useless. So also were radical kinds of armament, such as the 'fiery grapnel'. By sheer chance, on 9 June 1915 Flight Sub-Lt. Reginald Warneford, flying a tiny Morane

parasol of the RNAS, saw LZ 37 as he was on his way to bomb Zeppelin sheds near Bruges. He decided to go for the ship in the air, and managed to destroy it with one of his six small bombs.

By 1916 England was under quite serious attack, by German heavy bombers as well as the Navy Zeppelins and Army Schütte-Lanzes. On 2 September 1916 no fewer than 16 of the biggest airships set out and 14 crossed the coast. The morale of the defenders was raised by the sight – watched by many Londoners – of SL.11 making a fiery plunge to earth. She was the first ship to be shot down by air-to-air gunfire, in this particular case from the Lewis of Lt. Leefe-Robinson's puny B.E.2c.

Despite heavy casualties, by no means all caused by enemy action, Capt. Peter Strasser doggedly continued leading the German Naval Airship Division. He was convinced that even bigger ships, carrying heavier loads and flying higher, could prove decisive. On 1 May 1916 he

had accepted L31, the first 'Super-Zeppelin' capable of carrying five tonnes of bombs and ten defensive machine guns at 60 mph (96 km/h) at over 13,000 ft (4,000 m). Yet on 24 September L31 was to be the only one of three of the new giants to return from operations. And on 5 August 1918 Strasser himself was to die, with his crew, even though their L 70 was flying at over 20,000 ft (over 6,000 m) at 80 mph (129 km/h). This was effectively the end of the airship in warfare.

Below: Zeppelin Z.IX (Z.9) was brand new when war started in 1914. On 25 August she bombed Antwerp, but was herself destroyed on 8 October 1914 by the British RNAS raid on her shed at Dusseldorf.

Air-war at Sea

Like generals on land, the admirals at sea took time to appreciate that flying machines should be taken seriously and that they might have a role in both naval offence and defence. However, successful airships had been around longer, so the naval staff were more ready to accept the participation of lighter-than-air machines.

Though the German navy was the chief user of giant rigid airships, Britain's Royal Naval Air Service ran it a close second. Throughout World War I the RNAS used airships for reconnaissance whereas they could have been used for bombing. Designated from R.9 to R.32 (R for rigid), they were constructed by Armstrong Whitworth, Beardmore, Vickers and Short Brothers. They accomplished little apart from R.23's demonstration that airships could carry defensive fighters (Sopwith 2F.1 Camels in this case) slung underneath and released if enemy aircraft should appear.

Much more important in the war at sea were non-rigids, whose main task was looking out for hostile submarines. These were naturally smaller, with the car suspended under a fabric envelope of from 60,000 to 400,000 cu ft (1,700–11,300 m³). In 1915–18 the RNAS took delivery of nearly 400, ranging from the S.S. (Sea Scout) type up to the 360,000 cu ft (10194 m³) N. S. (North Sea) pattern. These flew 2,400,000 miles (over 3,862,000 km), often in foul weather, in over 60,000 hours, with the loss of only 48 crew members. On the small S.S. the car was basically the fuselage, with engine and propeller, of a B.E. or similar aeroplane. The N.S. had two 250-hp engines and a crew of ten, split into two watches, in an enclosed gondola. Just after the war N.S.11 flew 4,000 miles (6,440 km) nonstop in 101 hours.

The only weapon really feared by large warships was the torpedo, and so aircraft were soon developed to carry it. Just before the war a flimsy Short seaplane had dropped a 14-in (356-mm) Whitehead torpedo weighing 810 lb (367 kg), and the RNAS later took delivery of no fewer than 936 Short 184 seaplanes, one of which quickly sank two ships in

the Dardanelles. From the 184 Short Brothers developed the Type 320, with a 320-hp Sunbeam engine, able to carry the 1,000-lb (454-kg) 18-in (457-mm) torpedo. Well over 100 were delivered, but bad weather and other factors limited their achievements.

FIRST CARRIER LAUNCH

In 1916 the infant Fairey company produced the Campania, the first aircraft designed to operate from an aircraft carrier (after which it was named). Powered by engines of 250 or 345 hp, they were seaplanes which took off from a wheeled trolley, before landing alongside the *Campania* and being fished out by her derrick.

For reconnaissance over the open ocean the preferred choice was a flying boat. The pioneer here was the American Curtiss, one of whose boats Englishman John Porte selected in a 1913 attempt to fly the Atlantic. In August 1914 Porte rejoined the RNAS, and he persuaded the Admiralty to buy the Curtiss H.4, with a crew of four, a bow machine gun and light bombs or depth charges. Though underpowered, with two engines of 90-110 hp, 54 H.4s were supplied and eight were made in England. They saw much war service.

From the H.4 Porte developed improved flying boats, notably the Felixstowe F.2A of which

Above: Seen at Seemoos after being rebuilt with engines outside the hull, Dornier Rs I was a giant flying boat completed in October 1915. However, the German navy preferred airships and smaller seaplanes.

Below: Laid down as a battle-cruiser, HMS *Furious* was completed in 1916 as a 22,450-ton carrier. Repeatedly rebuilt, she was finally scrapped in 1945.

100 had been built by the end of the war. Powered by two 345-hp Rolls-Royce engines, they carried two 230-lb (104-kg) bombs and had up to seven machine guns. On 4 June 1918 three F.2As were patrolling near the German coast, over three hours away from their bases at Felixstowe and Yarmouth, when they were set upon by 14 German seaplanes. One F.2A was forced down with a broken fuel pipe, but this was repaired and it eventually returned with the others after they had shot down six of the German aircraft.

Several types of flying boat were operated by France, notably the Tellier T.3. Powered by a 200-hp Hispano-Suiza engine, some were fitted with 47-mm (1.85-in) cannon. Meanwhile, Curtiss developed a series of outstanding machines. In the final year of the war the company built 673 HS boats powered by a 360-hp Liberty engine and other firms added a further 417. The H.4 was developed into the H.12 with two 275-hp Rolls-Royce engines and the H.16 with either 345-hp Rolls-Royce or 400-hp Liberty engines. The combined total of these large machines was 270.

Early Warplane Design

At the start of World War I aeroplane design was embryonic. Designers generally followed established practice. Not many had real knowledge of aerodynamics or the strength of materials and a lot was done by eye, on the sole basis of what looked right and had worked before.

Structurally, almost all aircraft had a strong skeleton braced with wires and covered with fabric. The skeleton was usually made of hardwood, such as spruce or ash, carefully selected for straight grain and an absence of knot-holes. A very few aircraft used welded steel tubing, airships generally used girders built up from standard rolled sections of aluminium, while in Germany Hugo Junkers boldly made aeroplanes almost entirely out of metal. Initially he was forced to use thin sheet iron, but from 1916 he was able to use the new aluminium/copper alloy which was called duralumin.

Aerodynamics rather took a back seat, because at speeds generally below 100 mph (161 km/h) streamlining was a secondary consideration. Monoplanes appeared to be more streamlined, but their wings either had to be braced by a forest of wires, often to king-posts projecting above and below the fuselage, or else had to be very thick, increasing drag to about the same level as that of strut-braced biplanes.

A few designers made triplanes or even quadruplanes, but by 1918 these were no longer in production. In general aircraft were fitted with a simple tail comprising a horizontal tailplane (sometimes with an irreversible pivoting mechanism for longitudinal trimming, but usually fixed) carrying hinged elevators, and a vertical fin and rudder. Many aircraft did not even have a fixed fin, just a rudder, while large multi-engined aircraft often had a complicated tail with twin fins and rudders between biplane tailplanes and elevators.

Below: The Sopwith 1½-Strutter served in large numbers with eight Allied air forces. It was one of the first aircraft to have the layout that became standard, with a tractor propeller, synchronized fixed gun and a pivoted gun in the rear cockpit.

Above: Built in small numbers, the Armstrong Whitworth F.K.10 was one of several wartime quadruplane. Indeed, the F.K.11 was to have had 15 slender wings! In World War I nobody could have guessed the future actually lay with the monoplane.

PUSHERS OR PULLERS?

At the start of the war aircraft could be visibly divided into two classes. One group had a conventional fuselage. If they were single-engined, the propeller was on the nose, though in one or two experimental types it was on a ring round the rear fuselage or even behind the tail. The others had a short central nacelle, often with the single engine driving a pusher propeller at the rear. In such machines the tail was usually carried on a framework of struts, and thousands of Voisin aircraft were made to this formula even after it had begun to appear archaic.

Some designers achieved a more modern appearance by carrying the tail on two booms. In Italy over 600 powerful bombers were made to a Caproni design with this configuration, powered by one pusher engine at the back of the nacelle and two tractor engines at the front of each tail boom. A few designers created monsters, in both senses of the word. The British Tarrant Tabor had six 450-hp engines, and when the two top ones were opened up on its first takeoff they pulled the giant over so that its nose was crushed into the ground. In the

USA the Barling Bomber had a cruising speed just 6 mph (9.6 km/h) higher than the landing speed. The German SSW R.VIII had its propellers driven by six huge water-cooled engines all mounted in marine fashion in an engine room filling most of the fuselage, so that near deafened mechanics were able to repair faults in the air.

To end on a positive note, the Sopwith 1½-Strutter was regarded as an example of how an aeroplane should be designed. First flown in December 1915, it was a totally conventional biplane, usually powered by a Clerget or Le Rhône rotary engine of 110 or 130 hp. Most had two seats, and a synchronized Vickers gun for the pilot and another gun (usually a Lewis or Hotchkiss) for the observer, who sat in the rear cockpit. Up to 130 lb (59 kg) of bombs could be carried, or as a single-seater up to 224 lb (102 kg). This aircraft had no vices, could easily exceed 100 mph (161 km/h) and was very manoeuvrable. Over 1,500 were made in Britain, and about 4,500 under licence in France. Hundreds served foreign air forces after the November 1918 Armistice.

Heavy Bombers

It was Igor Sikorsky who showed the world how to create a force of large bombers (pp 16–17). In contrast, a Scot named Kennedy who had worked in Russia convinced the British War Office he could do the same, but his Kennedy Giant took over two years to build (at Northolt) and never flew, though test pilot Frank Courtney did once get the main wheels off the ground.

Chronologically the next large bombers were designed by Count Gianni Caproni in Italy (p. 29). Most were biplanes, with a loaded weight of around 7,000 lb (about 3.5 tonnes), but the Ca 40 family were huge triplanes more than twice as heavy. The Ca 43 series were seaplane torpedo-bombers, but the others had 16 main wheels and carried 3,913 lb (1,775 kg) of bombs in a container under the bottom wing. After the Armistice Caproni built a few derivatives with 17 passenger seats.

In December 1914 the British Admiralty issued a specification for an aircraft to carry six 112-lb (50.8-kg) bombs. Mr F. Handley Page responded, to be told that what was wanted was 'a bloody paralyser of an aeroplane'. Upgraded with two 250-hp Rolls-Royce Eagle engines, the resulting O/100 flew on 18 December 1915. By November 1916 improved versions were entering service and it was unfortunate that the third to reach the RNAS landed by mistake behind the German front line. By the Armistice 46 had been delivered, followed by 400 more powerful O/400s, plus 100 O/400s made in the USA.

From 1 April 1918 the RNAS O/100 squadrons were formed into an Independent Force, pending absorption into the newly created Royal Air Force, and it was to Independent (RAF) squadrons that the O/400s were delivered. A few flew out to bomb Turkish targets, but most carried out a damaging campaign against German targets, mainly in the Rhineland, dropping bombs of up to 1,650 lb (748 kg). In August 1917 an order was placed for the even larger Handley Page V/1500, powered by four 375-hp Eagle VIII engines in tandem push/pull pairs. With a loaded weight of 24,700 lb (11,204 kg), the V/1500 could carry a

bomb load of up to 7,500 lb (3.4 tonnes). It was specifically intended to raid Berlin, but the Armistice was signed about a week before the first mission.

MIGHTY STAAKENS

Greatest of all the early bombers were those of Germany. Most raids against England were flown by the Gotha G.IV and G.V, which were modest aircraft in the 4-tonne class with two 260-hp engines. Other units flew aircraft in the R (*Riesenflugzeug*, giant aeroplane) category, made by the Zeppelin-Werke at Staaken. Of many Staaken R-types the only version put into service in quantity was the R.VI, which first flew in late 1916. Most had four 260-hp Mercedes D.IVa water-cooled engines in push/pull tandem pairs. These impressive machines had up to seven defensive machine guns, and the normal maximum bomb load comprised 18 bombs of 220.5 lb (100 kg).

Like the Sikorskys, the Staakens lacked nothing. Full night lighting and powerful landing lights were installed, as well as two-way radio and exceptionally comprehensive instrumenta-

tion in the cockpit. An intercom system for use by the crew worked by means of displays of small light bulbs and messages sent along pneumatic tubes. Some aircraft were fitted with oxygen and in late 1918 a radio navigation aid was installed which, by means of repeated bearings, provided a fix.

Several other manufacturers constructed aircraft in the R class. The SSW R.VIII was mentioned on p.29, and Schütte-Lanz also followed

Above: Loading up to 1,000 lb (454 kg) of bombs under a Gotha G.V, one of the principal types which raided London from autumn 1916. The engines were two 260-hp Mercedes, driving pusher propellers.

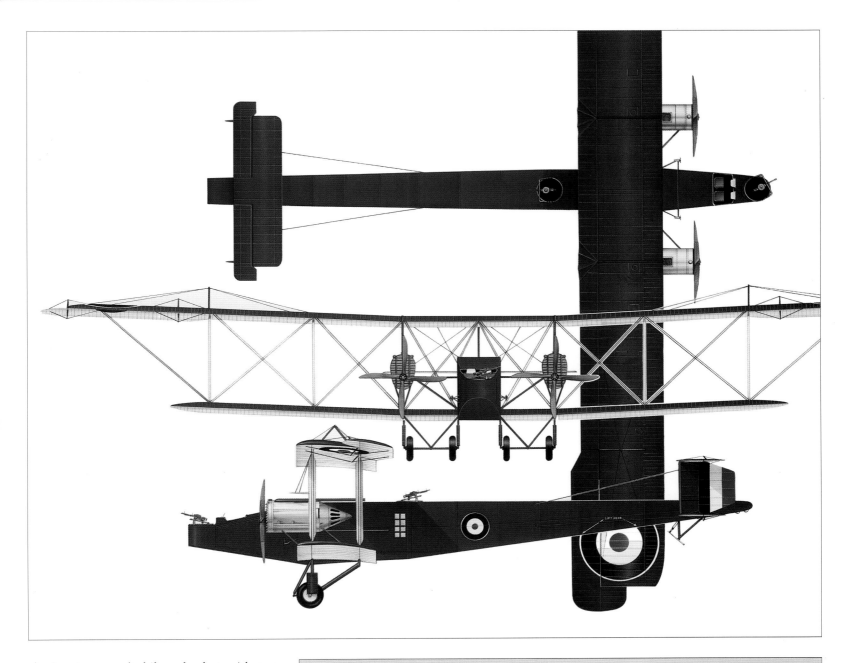

the 'engine room' philosophy, but with two pairs of enormous engines driving shafting geared to outboard tractor propellers and engines Nos 5 and 6 driving a pusher propeller at the rear of the central nacelle.

Perhaps the most startling of all World War I giant bombers was the Linke-Hoffman R.II. Seen in a photograph, this could easily have been mistaken for a small fighting scout. In fact, it was a monster, with biplane wings spanning 138 ft 4 in (42.2 m) and a loaded weight of 33,070 lb (15 tonnes). In the nose were four 260-hp Mercedes D.IVa engines, all geared to a single propeller. With a diameter of 23 ft (7 m), this was the largest propeller ever fitted to an aeroplane.

SPECIFICATIONS

Handley Page O/400

Type: five-crew long-range biplane heavy bomber

Powerplant: two 330-hp (268-kW) Rolls-Royce Eagle VIII water-cooled V-12 piston engines

Performance: maximum speed (with full bomb load) 98 mph (157 km/h) at sea level; climb to 10,000 ft (3048 m) in 40 minutes; service ceiling 8,500 ft (2625 m); endurance 8 hours

Weights: empty 8,502 lb (3857 kg); loaded 13,360 lb (6060 kg)

Dimensions: wing span 100 ft (30.48 m); length 62 ft 10 in (19.17 m); height 22 ft 0.75 in (6.72 m); wing area 1,648 sq ft (153.1 m²)

Armament: bomb load varied but usually consisted of 16 112-lb (51-kg) bombs, with a single 1,650-lb (748-kg) weapon as an alternative; defensive guns also varied but usually one or two 7.7-mm (0.303-in) Lewis machine-guns on Scarff ring in nose, two single Lewis guns on side posts at mid-upper position, and single pin-mounted Lewis gun firing through lower rear trapdoor

Air Defence

Above: The single-seat SPAD VII was powered by a 180-hp Hispano-Suiza V-8 engine, while the SPAD XIII (seen here) had one of 250 hp. Production of these two models alone exceeded 14,500.

Even after the damaging Zeppelin attack on London on 8 September 1915, it took Britain virtually until the end of the war to organize a really effective defence against air attack. Special high-angle anti-aircraft guns had to be produced, together with searchlights, all-weather day/night aerodromes, observer posts to report on the presence and location of hostile aircraft, and an effective network of communications.

Generals and aircraft designers tried to decide what kind of aeroplane might be most useful in defending against airships. In 1914 it was thought that Zeppelins could reach an altitude of 5,000 ft (just over 1,500 m) and a speed of 40 mph (64 km/h). Dynamic British designer Noel Pemberton-Billing created two special Zeppelin destroyers. The second, the P.B.31E, also known as the Supermarine Night Hawk, was first flown in February 1917. In some ways it was impressive. A quadruplane (four superimposed wings), it had a main cabin with windows all round. The pilot sat at the front of this, with an open cockpit in the nose with a Lewis gun. Above the upper wing was a

second Lewis, as well as a big Davis recoilless cannon. It was also intended to drop incendiary flares 'every 20 feet, so that in straddling an airship of 65-feet diameter at least three would strike'. There was a vast amount of other equipment, and a bunk for use on 18-hour missions. The only problem was that it took an hour to climb to 10,000 ft (3,050 m), at which height the speed was about 52 mph (84 km/h), while later Zeppelins were much faster and flew twice as high.

By far the best defending fighters were those mass-produced for front-line use. Best of the British machines were the Farnborough-designed S.E.5A, usually with a Wolseley-made Hispano-Suiza V-8 engine of 200 or 240 hp, and the agile Sopwith Camel with a rotary engine of 100 to 150 hp. A bigger machine, which turned out to be unexpectedly brilliant, was the Bristol F.2B Fighter (a registered name), powered by a 250-hp Rolls-Royce V-12 later named the Falcon, which was unusual in having a backseater with one or two guns of his own.

In France the nimble Nieuports gradually gave way to the excellent SPAD series, with the

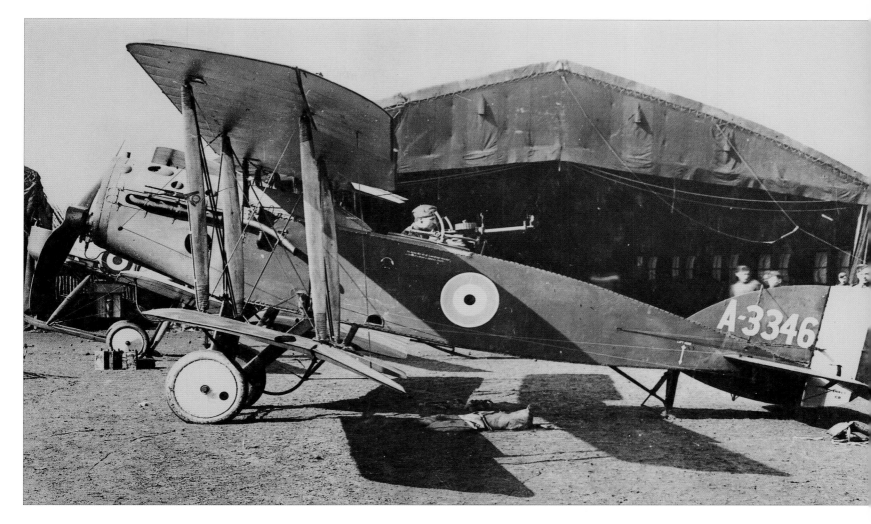

Above: The Bristol Fighter was the best of the early two-seat fighters, over 3,000 being built. An unusual feature of this plane was that the fuselage was mounted above the lower wing. This view of an early version, the F.2A (220-hp Falcon), shows the Scarff mounting for the observer's gun(s), which became standard on two-seaters of many countries.

V-8 Hispano, while the profusion of enemy fighters made by Albatros, Pfalz, Halberstadt, Austrian Aviatik, Hannover, Hansa-Brandenburg, LFG Roland, Phönix, Rumpler, Siemens-Schuckert and, above all, Fokker, tended to be serviceable rather than brilliant. Moreover, in almost every case they were burdened by the ponderous weight of a long water-cooled engine.

HIGHLY REGARDED

First tested at the start of 1918, the Fokker D.VII was regarded by many, on both sides of the conflict, as the best all-round fighter of the war. It was highly regarded even though it was an ordinary biplane fitted by one of the massive and not particularly powerful in-line engines. Early versions had the 160-hp Mercedes D.III, while by September 1918 some had the 185-hp BMW IIIa. With the new engine, speed increased only slightly, to perhaps 120 mph (193 km/h), which was no more than its opponents, but it reduced the time needed to climb to 16,400 ft (5,000 m) from 38 minutes to 14, and

also enhanced manoeuvrability. The D.VII was simply a good all-round dogfighter, many of which went into action painted in garish colours to frighten the enemy. After the war Fokker was told to hand them all over to the Allies. Instead he loaded them all into trains and steamed past the Allied Control Commission to set up a new factory in his native Holland.

Even in the final year of the war engines were unreliable, there were virtually no aids to navigation or to assist in flying at night, and even in friendly skies casualties were by any modern standard horrific. In the front line a significant proportion of pilots were shot down on their first mission and as virtually no flying personnel were issued with parachutes, the chances of survival were close to zero. Almost all aircrew however, carried a revolver. This was ostensibly for use after a forced landing behind the enemy lines, but Britain's top-scorer, Maj. Edward 'Mick' Mannock VC, was speaking for many (perhaps the majority) when he said that if he was shot down in flames he would put his gun to his own head.

New Technology II

By the Armistice of 11 November 1918 the engines of fighters and bombers had been developed to give powers up to 500 hp. The rotary was obsolescent and in its place was emerging the static radial. This looked similar, as its cylinders were again arranged like the spokes of a wheel, but the engine was attached to the aircraft and the crankshaft drove the propeller. A few engines (of whatever configuration) drove the propeller via a reduction gear, so that the crankshaft could revolve rapidly for high power while the propeller turned more slowly for higher efficiency. The V-type water-cooled engine looked more streamlined, but was usually heavier, and its cooling system was vulnerable to battle damage and to simple leaks.

Emergent technologies included superchargers and variable-pitch propellers. As aircraft climb into thinner atmosphere, the oxygen available for combustion with the fuel is reduced in proportion to the falling air density. Thus, the power that the engine can develop also falls, so that at 20,000 ft (about 6,100 m) its power has been cut by half. By 1918 designers were testing engines fitted with superchargers, which are pumps which suck in extra air and feed it to the cylinders under pressure to try to restore the conditions at sea level. Of course, superchargers could be used even at sea level to boost power (for example, for racing) but in military aircraft they were more important in maintaining power at high altitude.

Aero-engine superchargers are invariably centrifugal compressors in the form of a very rapidly spinning disc with radial vanes. Air is sucked in at the centre and flung off tangentially at the edge. It then reaches the cylinders via a diffuser, an expanding pipe where its high velocity is converted into pressure. Most superchargers are driven by step-up gears from the crankshaft, but an alternative scheme is the turbo-supercharger in which the compressor is driven by a turbine spun at high speed by the exhaust gas from the cylinders. Turbos make use of energy in the white-hot gas that would otherwise be wasted.

Left: Rolls-Royce produced high-power piston engines with 12 cylinders arranged in V formation. Dating from 1917, this Eagle VIII, of 20.32 litres (1,240 cu in) capacity, was rated at 375 hp at 2,000 rpm.

ADJUSTABLE BLADES

Variable-pitch propellers have blades which can be swivelled in their sockets in the hub. The blades are set to fine pitch (like a fine-pitch screwthread) for takeoff, for maximum engine rpm (revolutions per minute) and power, despite the low airspeed. As the aircraft flies faster, the blades are moved to the coarse position so that, while the aircraft travels at high speed, the engine rpm is reduced, for best fuel economy.

Whereas the first aeroplanes had no cockpit at all, the pilot sitting in the open air, by 1918 cockpits contained as many as a dozen instruments and as many switches. The basic cockpit of 1918 had dial instruments showing engine rpm, airspeed and altitude. There would also be a magnetic compass and probably an inclinometer (a liquid-filled tube showing for/aft or lateral inclination, or both). Possible additions included gauges showing fuel contents and oil pressure, a clock and, for water-cooled engines, water temperature.

As well as the obvious ignition switch(es) and throttle lever, some engines required extras, such as an ignition advance/retard lever, and a hand pump to pressurize the air above the fuel tank, this pressure being maintained in flight by a pump driven by a small windmill. Some aircraft carried oxygen in high-pressure containers, fed to a face mask to keep the pilot from feeling drowsy or even unconscious at heights around 20,000 ft (6,100 m).

An equally significant development, initially for airships and large aeroplanes, was airborne radio. Sometimes this was ground-to-air only, but the objective was to provide communications in both directions, especially when directing artillery fire or the guns of warships. Radio could be operated from batteries, but by 1918 heavy bombers often had electric generators. These were driven by small windmills, but the natural technological development was to make the engine(s) drive not only the propeller(s) but also ancillary devices. These eventually included an electric generator, air compressor, fuel pump(s), vacuum pump and, in the case of liquid-cooled engines, a pump to circulate coolant through the engine and the slipstream-cooled radiator.

Above: In the mass-produced B.E. family the rear cockpit was invariably the one occupied by the pilot. Here the pilot of a B.E.2c is reaching out to the externally mounted camera.

3 BETWEEN THE WARS

Policing Empires

Above: Powered by US-supplied 400-hp Liberty engines, the D.H.9A was a major RAF multi-role type from 1918 until well after 1930. By that time the same aircraft, with a 480 or 550-hp Bristol Jupiter radial engine, had become the mass-produced Westland Wapiti.

Left: To police the Empire the RAF wanted old-technology aircraft. Typical of the larger sizes was the Victoria (two 570-hp Napier Lions), used as a transport, bomber, ambulance and survey/mapping aircraft.

After the November 1918 Armistice nothing was less popular than funding for armaments. Armies and navies shrank to a tiny fraction of their wartime strength, while in Britain the Royal Air Force personnel appeared in new and distinctive grey-blue uniforms. It had been formed on 1 April 1918 by combining the Royal Flying Corps and Royal Naval Air Service, and throughout the 1920s it had to fight off attacks by the generals and admirals who resented its continued existence.

The fact that it did survive was largely because of one man, Hugh Trenchard, Chief of the Air Staff. He alone was able to stave off the opposition, make long-term plans (such as a great college for RAF officers at Cranwell, Lincolnshire) and fight for each miserly annual budget. He also realized that the RAF's first duty was 'to garrison the Empire'. The idea evoked scorn, but in one theatre, British Somaliland in tropical Africa, the RAF was allowed to try. That unhappy land had been devastated by 'the Mad Mullah'. Though no more than a bandit, he had taken over the country's forts, and prior to 1920 the lives of hundreds of British soldiers and millions of pounds had been thrown away trying to overcome him. In January 1920 a handful of RAF men and 12 small D.H.9 two-seaters arrived, with a few bombs. Seven days later the Mullah was fleeing, and on 9 February he was consigned to history.

KEEPING THE PEACE

The world watched while this tiny campaign became a blueprint for the use of military aircraft. For the next 20 years RAF aircraft kept the peace from Africa to the Far East, even quelling the endemic pastime on the North-West Frontier of warfare between different tribes. Other duties of the infant service included search and rescue by land and sea, the maintenance of communications and aerial photography and mapping. Occasionally conflict again reared its head, as at Christmas in 1928 on the far side of the North-West Frontier in rugged Afghanistan. Here the Kabibullah Khan and his rebel tribesmen surrounded the capital, Kabul. During January 1929 the eight Vickers Victoria transports of No 70 Sqn, RAF and a Handley Page Hinaidi bomber flew to and fro over the high mountains to evacuate 586 men, women and children. This was a genuine life-or-death operation, and it was carried out in textbook fashion.

For ten years after the Armistice, aircraft design made only modest progress, except in terms of engines. Their power remained in the region of 500 hp, but their reliability became far better, so that aircraft forced landings were no longer commonplace events. Most such engines were bolted on the front of two-seat biplanes with a traditional airframe of either wood or welded steel tube, covered in fabric. Important examples included the British Westland Wapiti (p.54), French Potez 25, Dutch Fokker C.V (C.5), American Douglas O-38, Russian Polikarpov R-5 and Japanese Kawasaki Type 88, all of which were made in large numbers.

After the Armistice, there seemed to be no demand for military aircraft, and many companies ceased aircraft construction altogether. Those who thought differently often did well. For example Breguet, one of the pioneer French manufacturers, followed over 8,000 Type XIV (14) by delivering 1,129 Type XIX (19) multi-role two-seaters in 1925-26 alone. They were bought by France, Argentina, Belgium, Bolivia, China, Greece, Persia, Poland, Serbia and Turkey, and licence fees poured in from examples manufactured elsewhere.

Many air forces and navies operated large seaplanes and flying boats. In order to stand up to the environment these had tough hulls, initially of varnished wood but increasingly made from duralumin, or of Alclad (duralumin coated with aluminium to avoid corrosion). A typical example was the US Navy's Type PN, a direct descendant of the wartime Curtiss H-16. On 1 September 1925 one of these, PN-9, took off from San Francisco Bay and headed for Hawaii, 2,400 miles (3,862 km) away. When still 559 miles (900 km) from the islands the two water-cooled Packard engines failed. The crew alighted on the sea and rigged up a sail.

Making Headlines

Unlike armies and navies, the flying services had no heritage of long traditions of service, and in Britain the RAF was a new service entirely. To a few, mainly young boys, flying seemed attractive and exciting, but to most Britons – and certainly to those with influence, the so-called 'Establishment' – the RAF was an inferior upstart. Accordingly, on 3 July 1920 it put on a show called The RAF Tournament. At Hendon airfield the public was treated to aerobatics, formation flying, crazy 'silly pupil' acts, and even mock bombing raids. Over 60,000 paid for admission, and even more watched from Mill Hill and other vantage points. This unprecedented display put the new service firmly on the map, got rave reviews in newspapers and became an annual event. Renamed the RAF Pageant, and ultimately Empire Air Day, it attracted huge crowds up to World War II.

In late 1917 the US Navy drew up plans for a large flying boat, the Navy Curtiss (NC), able to fly across the Atlantic and then enter the war against German submarines. They missed the conflict, but on 16 May 1919 three of them gathered at Trepassy Bay, Newfoundland, to fly to Europe. NC-1 was forced down and sank, NC-3 was forced down but taxied under its own power to the Portuguese Azores islands, and NC-4 flew 1,400 miles (2,253 km) to the Portuguese islands non-stop. NC-4 spent ten days at Horta, in the Azores, but on 27 May it took off again and flew to Lisbon. On 31 May it went on to Plymouth, England.

Left: Doped silver-grey, NC-4 is seen being readied for its attempt to cross the Atlantic. Powered by four 400-hp Liberty engines, the NC had a short central hull, the biplane tail being attached by struts and wires.

Above: The Douglas World Cruisers were doped olive-green, with polished metal back to the cockpits and bright yellow above the wings and tailplane. Here ship No 1 *Seattle* sees service as a seaplane.

ENCIRCLING THE GLOBE

On 17 March 1924 four Douglas World Cruisers of the US Air Service left Santa Monica (Los Angeles) and headed for Seattle, the official starting point for an attempt to fly Westbound round the world. The DWC was specially designed for this task by the infant Douglas company, with 536 gal (644 US gal, 2,438 litres) of fuel and interchangeable wheels or seaplane floats. Two were lost en route, but the other two arrived back in Seattle on 29 September. While the DWCs were airborne, on 23 June, Air Service Lieutenant Russell L. Maughan flew across the USA in 21 hours 48 minutes between dawn and dusk. He took off in his Curtiss PW-8 pursuit and finally made it to San Francisco, despite losing an hour at Dayton, Ohio, when the fuel filler cap was overtightened and stripped its thread.

On 1 July 1933 no fewer than 25 large Savoia-Marchetti S.55 twin-hull flying boats of the *Regia Aeronautica* (Italian Air Force) left Orbetello. Alighting at Amsterdam, one S.55 was damaged beyond repair. The other 24, led by General Italo Balbo, flew in stages to the Chicago World's Fair, arriving on 15 July. From that day, an impressive formation has been called a Balbo. On the 19th they flew in perfect formation to New York. A second S.55 was lost in the Azores, but on 12 August the remaining 23 returned to Ostia to a triumphant homecoming.

In 1937–38 the RAF and *Regia Aeronautica* competed to set new altitude records. On 30 June 1937 Flt. Lt. M. J. Adam reached 53,937 ft (16,440 m) in the Bristol 138A monoplane, but this was beaten on 27 October 1938 when Lt. Col. Mario Pezzi coaxed his Caproni 161 *bis* biplane to 56,046 ft (17,083 m). Both used radial engines of basically Bristol design, and similar engines were fitted to three Vickers Wellesley bombers of the RAF which took off from Ismailia, Egypt, on 5 November 1938. Arranged as a test of the newly developed 100-octane fuel, the three single-engined aircraft encountered bad weather and headwinds. One had to refuel on the island of Timor, but the other two went on to land on 7 November at Darwin, Australia. They had set a new distance record of 7,158 miles (11,519 km).

On 26 April 1939 Messerschmitt test pilot Fritz Wendel set a new world speed record at 469.225 mph (755.124 km/h). The German propaganda machine broadcast that it had been gained by 'the Me 109R', giving the world the impression that it had been achieved by a version of the Bf 109 fighter, then being supplied to the Luftwaffe. In fact the record had been gained by the Me 209, one of the most tricky and dangerous machines ever flown. It bore no relationship whatever to the Bf 109E, the maximum speed of which was 354 mph (570 km/h).

The Need for Speed

Above: The 1929 Schneider Trophy was contested at Calshot, England. Here the Italian team wheel out one of their all-red Macchi M.67s, but these planes suffered from dangerous faults, paving the way for another British win.

For two decades after World War I, while the speed of the fastest aeroplanes rose significantly each year, the speeds of the fighters and bombers actually in service rose less impressively. For example, in 1917 the Italian Ansaldo S.V.A.5 fighter could reach 143 mph (230 km/h) in full battle trim. By 1934 the fastest Italian fighter in service, the Fiat C.R.30, could reach 217 mph (349 km/h), while in the same year the Macchi M.C.72 seaplane set a record at 440.68 mph (709 km/h).

The M.C.72 had been designed to compete in the race for the Schneider Trophy. First flown in 1913, this was a speed race over many laps of a triangular course, and in the 1920s the high costs whittled entrants down to official military teams from France, Italy, the UK and USA. Each year the race was held in the country of the previous year's winning team, which in the 1920s was usually the USA or Italy. In 1927 it was decided that, instead of being an annual event, this race would be held every two years.

HISTORIC TROPHY WIN

In that year the huge trophy was won by the RAF, whose team flew the Supermarine S.5, powered by a Napier Lion engine specially boosted to about 900 hp. The winning speed was 281.65 mph (453.26 km/h). For the 1929 race the RAF team fielded the Supermarine S.6, powered by the Rolls-Royce R engine rated at 1,900 hp. Even though the S.6 was larger and heavier than the S.5, the winning speed went up to 328.63 mph (528.86 km/h). In 1931 the British government said that, in a time of economic slump and unemployment, it would not finance a British challenge. At the 'eleventh hour' a private individual, Lady Houston, said she was outraged by this feeble decision and would herself pay for a British entry. There was no time to produce a new aircraft, but the money enabled Rolls-Royce to power the S.6B with an R engine boosted to 2,350 hp, running on a special cocktail of fuels. As a result the RAF team won (in a mere walkover, at 340.08 mph, 547.3 km/h). Three wins in a row gave the UK the trophy in perpetuity. The government then said it would disband the High-Speed Flight, but engine-maker Sir Henry Royce pleaded for a few extra days in order to set a world speed record.

The government of the day appeared to have no interest in such matters, but it stayed its hand, and 16 days later, after further tinkering with fuels, the S.6B set a record at 407.5 mph (655.79 km/h). Supermarine designer Reginald Mitchell later went on to design the Spitfire fighter. In fact there was little similarity in design between the two aircraft, but the work done by Rolls-Royce and the Associated Ethyl fuel company was of immense importance in the development of future fighter engines.

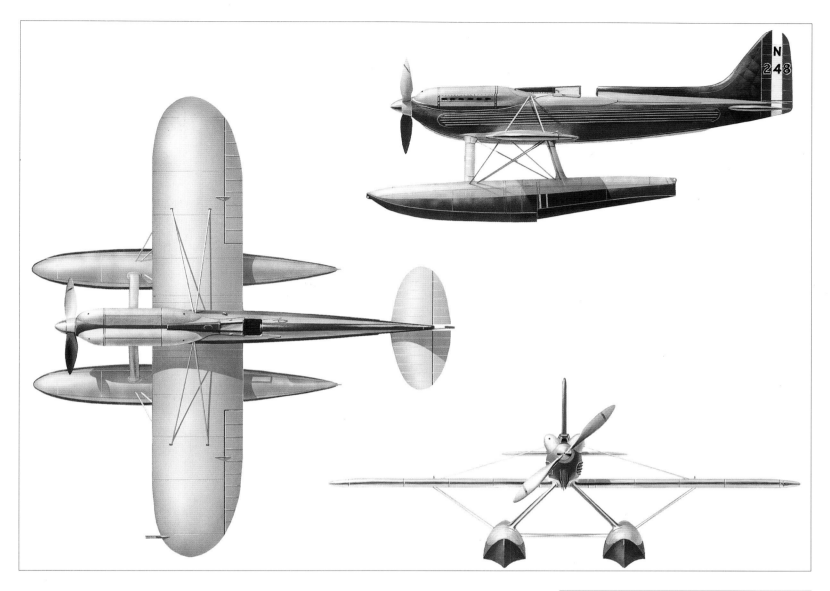

The United States had pulled out of the Schneider contests, but Army/Navy laboratories, the National Advisory Committee for Aeronautics (which had its own impressive research facilities) and the powerful American aircraft and engine industry all collaborated in pushing technology ahead, as described overleaf. Moreover, between the world wars many Army pilots participated in the US National Air Races, which provided a powerful spur in the quest for higher flight performance.

An unexpected result in the mid-1920s was the emergence of the Pratt & Whitney Wasp. The company had been started in 1925 by engineers formerly employed by Wright. The Wasp was simply a neat nine-cylinder radial whose power was developed from 400 hp to an eventual 600 hp. Though it looked less-streamlined than the long water-cooled engines, it significantly increased not only the manoeuvrability

but also the speed and rate of climb of Army and Navy aircraft.

In 1934 Australian interests organized the MacRobertson race from England to Melbourne, but this did not attract official military entrants. The winner was the specially designed de Havilland Comet, and second place was gained by a DC-2 airliner. Three years later military teams did enter for a race from Istres (near Marseilles) to Damascus and then back to Paris. Here a Comet was beaten into fourth place by three Savoia-Marchetti S.M.79 bombers of the *Regia Aeronautica*. In early 1938 three S.M.79s covered in stages the 6,116 miles (9,842 km) between Rome and Rio de Janeiro at an average speed of 251 mph (404 km/h), which was faster than the Comet's maximum. Such achievements made headlines, but in World War II the *Regia Aeronautica* would fail to live up to its reputation.

SPECIFICATIONS

Supermarine S.6B

Type: high-speed racing seaplane

Powerplant: one Rolls-Royce Type R V-12 liquid-cooled piston engine rated at 2,350 hp (1752 kW) with supercharging at sea level

Performance: maximum speed 408 mph (656 km/h) at sea level

Weights: empty 4,590 lb (2082 kg); loaded 6,086 lb (2760 kg)

Dimensions: wing span 30 ft (9.14 m); length overall including floats 28 ft 10 in (8.79 m); height 12 ft 3 in (3.73 m); wing area 145 sq ft (12.47 m²)

Monoplanes

In a comprehensive review of the Royal Air Force in 1935 virtually every machine in service was a biplane. Anyone looking below the fabric coverings would have found structure, and indeed systems, similar to those of World War I. This was partly because the tasks set the RAF were mainly to police the Empire. Other countries without such a commitment, made more rapid progress.

The few monoplanes that were built in Britain were burdened either by numerous struts and bracing wires (this applied even to the Schneider racers) or had extremely thick wings, which made high speeds impossible. But a few designers saw that if the fabric skin was replaced by aluminium, or the stronger alloy called duralumin, it became possible to make a wing as an unbraced cantilever, with no struts or wires, yet thin enough for it to fly at high speed. By 1935 virtually all the major US companies were producing such 'stressed skin' aircraft. So was Heinkel in Germany, but Junkers (a pioneer of duralumin in World War I) was slow to change over from corrugated skins, which increased drag.

In 1934–36 the speed of fighters doubled to 350 mph (563 km/h) and that of bombers and transports doubled to over 220 mph (354 km/h). This made it worthwhile retracting the landing gear inside the airframe, to reduce drag in cruising flight. Liquid-cooled engines and their radiators were designed much more carefully, while radial engines were tightly encased in drag-reducing cowlings with adjustable gills at the back to control the cooling airflow.

The much greater difference between cruising speed and takeoff or landing speed hastened the introduction of variable-pitch propellers (p.35), which were further improved by being controlled by a CSU (constant-speed unit) so that the pitch adjusted itself automatically to the best value. The wing loading (weight supported by unit area of wing) of the biplanes had seldom been much more than 10 lb/sq ft (49 kg/m^2), but the monoplanes of the late 1930s had a wing loading three to four times as great. This would have demanded longer takeoffs and much

faster landings, but designers added large hinged surfaces under the rear part of the wings, called flaps. These came in several versions, some intended mainly to increase lift and a few just to increase drag, but all were instrumental in enabling the new monoplanes to operate from the traditional small grass aerodromes.

AERODROMES EVERYWHERE

The writing was on the wall, however, and by World War II the world was being dotted with aerodromes with paved runways unlike anything seen before. Nearly all the runways were over 2,000 ft (600 m) long, and some were double this length. They were fitted with night lighting, and airfields were increasingly provided with radio navigation aids to help pilots in the worst weather. As war clouds gathered, navies commissioned new aircraft carriers

Above: The Martin Bomber was one of the classic leaps in technology. Powered by Hornet or Cyclone engines of around 700 hp, they introduced many new features (although this early YB-10 retained fixed-pitch propellers).

which increasingly became all-weather floating aerodromes at sea.

In 1926 the RAF, stung by the calculation that over 6,000 British pilots had died needlessly in World War I, at last issued parachutes to its flying personnel. Leslie Irvin opened a factory to make them. From 1932 he had competition from the GQ factory, where Gregory and Quilter predicted that parachutes would eventually be used to drop all kinds of supplies and weapons. They did not know that two years earlier a 'stick' of 12 troops had jumped from one aircraft over the Soviet city of Voronezh, but from 1932 the concept of airborne forces really 'took off' in that country and made headlines. In 1935 Soviet

aircraft, mainly TB-3 heavy bombers, dropped 1,200 paratroops and vast quantities of weapons and equipment near Kiev, followed a few weeks later by an exercise in Byelorussia involving 1,800 paras and 5,700 airlanded troops.

Soviet airborne forces went on to experiment with gliders. Even the R-5, a small two-seat biplane, was tested towing 'trains' of small gliders, and soon quite large gliders were on test. Designer Oleg K. Antonov even added wings to a T-60 light tank, but this was never put into production. Despite all this, the use of gliders in the German assault on Belgium in 1940 appeared to be a great shock to those on the receiving end.

Below: Soviet paras pour from a Tupolev TB-3 in 1935. Designed in 1929, these huge bombers were years ahead of the fabric-covered biplanes of other countries.

War Returns

In the early 1930s people in the developed countries were worried about air attack. Scare stories in the newspapers painted horrifying pictures of how, should there be a future major war, cities would be laid waste and thousands of innocent people killed. Then on 3 October 1935 the Italian dictator Mussolini sent 100,000 troops over the frontier from Italian Somaliland into Abyssinia and started bombing Abyssinian targets.

In the face of global condemnation, Italian aircraft not only bombed anything that appeared to be a worthwhile target, especially selecting hospitals, but also used poison gas against the defenceless population. As the only opposition came from poorly equipped tribesmen, the most remarkable feature of this campaign was that it took seven months to subjugate the country. Abyssinia was formally annexed by Italy on 9 May 1936.

The campaign, for all its obvious faults, appeared to confirm the absolute dominance of air power. Accordingly, the world watched apprehensively as, later in 1936, Spain slid towards civil war. Powerful elements were opposed to the democratically elected Socialist government, and their opposition became polarized around right-wing army officer General Francisco Franco. Calling themselves the Nationalists, on 19 July 1936 they flew Franco from the Canary Islands (where he had been exiled) to Spanish Morocco. Here there was a large army, which obeyed his orders.

The Spanish Navy remained loyal to the government, so Franco asked German Chancellor Adolf Hitler for transport aircraft. On 28 July the world's first large-scale military airlift began, as an average force of 40 Junkers Ju 52/3m transports began ferrying thousands of hardened soldiers and foreign legionnaires across the Strait of Gibraltar. Within days both Germany and Fascist Italy had begun building up the Nationalist air force, starting with Heinkel 51, Arado 68, Fiat C.R.32 and Meridionali Ro.37 fighters, and Ju 52/3m, Fiat B.R.20 and Savoia-Marchetti S.M.81 bombers.

FOREIGN AID

The fighting on the ground between the Nationalist invaders and the legitimate government (who became known as the Republicans) was especially bitter and without mercy. While modern weapons poured into the Nationalists from Germany and Italy, only individual volunteers from all over the world helped the government forces, until the Soviet Union decided to supply weapons (but no troops). Initially these took the form of ten Polikarpov I-15 biplane fighters, which went into action (very successfully) on 4 November 1936. But, whereas Hitler and Mussolini were delighted to test their latest weapons in Spain, Stalin demanded immediate payment in gold for everything. The only country that freely offered to help the Republican side was France, which supplied such aircraft as the Blériot-Spad S.510, Dewoitine D.371 and D.501 fighters and Potez 54 bombers.

As the terrible war moved into 1937 the number of aircraft involved multiplied. Always outnumbered, the Republican air force (whose insignia was the red/yellow/purple of Spain, with red bands across the wings) received Soviet I-16 fighters and Tupolev SB bombers, and managed to purchase a few other aircraft. Against them were ranged huge forces with the latest aircraft, all bearing the Nationalist insignia of a large X.

The Italians built up a strong *Aviazione Legionaria*, some of its later equipment including Fiat G.50 fighters, Breda Ba 65 attack aircraft, Cant multi-engined bomber seaplanes, and the new S.M.79 bomber. Germany formed an even stronger *Legion Kondor*. Among its bombers were the Heinkel He 111B, Dornier Do 17F, Junkers Ju 86D and Henschel Hs 123 and Ju 87 dive bombers. They were escorted by the newly developed Messerschmitt Bf 109 fighter, possibly the most formidable in the world at that time.

On 26 April 1937 the defenceless city of Guernica was totally destroyed during only four hours of bombing. The outcry from a shocked world was such that German propaganda minister Goebbels announced 'No German aeroplane took part', which was surprising news to Wolfram von Richthofen and his bomber crews in the *Kondor Legion*. At last the cruel war ended in Republican surrender on 28 March 1939. It served merely to tear Spain apart and set its economy back decades, but it also provided marvellous practice for Hitler's Luftwaffe. In contrast, though France supplied many aircraft at the start of the conflict, nothing was done in terms of studying their performance in battle and the government remained blissfully ignorant of their ineffectiveness.

Left: Among large quantities of weapons sent to the Spanish Nationalists in the 1930s were squadrons of Fiat C.R.32 fighters. Powered by a 600-hp water-cooled engine, these agile biplanes had two 0.5-in (12.7-mm) guns and could even carry bombs.

SPECIFICATIONS

Junkers Ju 52/3mg7e

Type: 18-seat military transport

Powerplant: three 830-hp (619-kW) BMW 132T-2 nine-cylinder air-cooled radial engines

Performance: maximum speed 183 mph (295 km/h) at sea level; initial climb rate 680 ft (208 m) per minute; service ceiling 18,045 ft (5500 m); range 802 miles (1290 km)

Weights: empty 14,462 lb (6560 kg); maximum take-off 23,180 lb (10515 kg)

Dimensions: wing span 95 ft 11.5 in (29.25 m); length 62 ft (18.80 m); height 14 ft 9 in (4.50 m); wing area 1,189.45 sq ft (110.50 m²)

Armament: (typical) one 0.31-in (7.92-mm) MG 15 machine-gun in dorsal position and two 0.31-in (7.92-mm) machine-guns mounted to fire abeam through side windows

Stalin's Armadas

From the bloody Civil War victory of the Bolsheviks in 1920 until Hitler's invasion of the Soviet Union in July 1941 the world's largest country was, to the outside world, a tightly controlled enigma. Suddenly given a huge ally, the British weekly *Aeroplane Spotter* on 31 July 1941 devoted a page to what it said was 'officially called The Red Air Fleet'. It listed 14 types of aeroplane, of which 11 were described as copies of Western designs. Two were labelled 'designer unknown', because they were not obviously copies of anything, and a great four-engined bomber was called, jokingly, 'most original'. In fact, seven of the 14 were not used by 'The Red Air Fleet' at all.

Instead of slavishly copying others, and under severe difficulties – not least the 'Terror' unleashed throughout the 1930s by paranoid dictator Stalin when anyone important, even aircraft designers, were likely to be either imprisoned or shot – the Soviet Union managed to build up an enormous and generally self-sufficient aircraft industry. To provide a foundation, it established laboratories and a large factory at Kolchug for the production of aluminium and its alloys. It also took the technology of wooden airframes further than any other country, achieving beautiful shapes in *shpon* and *delta* resin-bonded three-dimensional laminates. The Soviet designers were also world leaders in aircraft guns and air-launched rockets.

FULL STATE CONTROL

The elimination of capitalism meant that there were no companies. Instead there were State research institutes to develop improved technologies, design organizations to create designs and prototypes, and production factories (some among the largest in the world) where successful designs were built in quantity. The design organizations, called OKBs (from the Russian for experimental construction bureau), took their names from the head of the design team.

One, Grigorovich, had designed before the Revolution; he created fighters and, especially, flying boats. Polikarpov was the leading designer of fighters and the multi-role R-5 two-seater. In 1933 he designed a stumpy monoplane which went into production as the I-16. This was the world's first fighter with a cantilever monoplane wing, stressed-skin airframe and retractable landing gear. It was tricky to fly, and in 1941, like all 1933 fighters, it was completely outclassed by the Bf 109.

Tupolev was the pioneer of all-metal structures, initially (1922) basing his technology on that of Junkers, with corrugated skins. His sixth design, first flown in 1930, went into production as the TB-3. This was by far the best heavy bomber in the world, with four powerful engines along the leading edge of a cantilever monoplane wing, very heavy bomb load, and impressive defensive armament. Over 600 were still in use in 1941, but by this time they too were outclassed and vulnerable. His 40th design, of 1934, entered production as the SB. A sleek smooth-skinned twin-engined bomber, it was then the best fast tactical bomber in the world, but once again by 1941 it was extremely vulnerable.

Soviet high-power aero engines were initially derived from Western designs, notably the Hispano-Suiza V-12, BMW VI, Bristol Jupiter and Wright Cyclone. The Moscow research establishments worked on potentially outstanding new designs, including the world's best diesel aero engines which by 1940 were in production. In contrast, the M-11 five-cylinder radial of 100-140 hp was brutishly simple, so that unskilled people could service it at minus-50°C, and so 130,000 were produced, and some are still in use. To survive, Soviet hardware had to be tough and simple. On the other hand the cockpits, systems and equipment were better than in RAF aircraft, which would have amazed anyone in Britain.

Not only the design and production organization but also the whole of the Soviet aviation set-up was unique. There was one vast civil aviation organization, Aeroflot, and from 1932 the same name appeared on all civil aircraft. From 1925 a scheme had been worked out for military aviation. The air force, not actually called 'the Red Air Fleet' but the VVS, was divided into FA (frontal, or tactical, aviation, for close co-operation with the local theatre commander), DA (long-range aviation, for strategic bombing) and the VTA (military transport aviation). Totally separate were the PVO (air-defence forces, armed with interceptors, anti-aircraft guns and, later, missiles) and the AV-MF (naval aviation).

Left: Typical of the ideas that caught Stalin's attention were the *Zveno* (link) experiments in which fighters were launched from bombers. Here three Polikarpov I-5s are about to fly on top of a TB-3.

Below: Seen preserved in a Moscow park, this Polikarpov I-152 was an outstandingly agile fighter with a 750-hp M-25 engine and four machine guns. GAZ (State factory) No. 1 delivered 2,408 in 1938–39.

Italy's *Regia Aeronautica*

Left: Experience in Spain led to Fiat improving the B.R.20 into the B.R.20M seen here. First flown in 1939, this was a major type in World War II. Two 1,000-hp Fiat engines gave a speed of 273 mph (440 km/h).

After the Armistice in November 1918 Italy's air force, an integral part of the army, was the third-largest in the world. It was backed by a large aircraft industry, and though naturally it shrank in the first years of peace it was of great interest to the Fascist leader Benito Mussolini who seized power in 1922. He was one of many world leaders who were influenced by a classic 1921 book *Command of the Air* by Italian General Giulio Douhet. In March 1923 Mussolini proclaimed the *Regia Aeronautica* (Board of Aeronautics) to be a separate service. Impressive new airfields, factories and research centres were built, to support a strong air force which could also be an instrument of propaganda.

In the next 17 years the *Regia Aeronautica* fulfilled all expectations, and its morale was high. The wings of its aircraft bore a disc in which were the Fascist emblem: three *fasces* (bundles of faggots with protruding axe-heads). On the tail was the white cross of Savoy with the arms of Savoy in the centre. Italian aircraft, often painted entirely red, gained speed, distance and height records (two of which still stand).

Throughout the inter-war period the dominant builder of fighters was Fiat, and this huge industrial group was also the No 1 builder of engines. Until 1937 the fighters were all biplanes, noted for their unsurpassed agility and, because they were small and had large engines, for their good flight performance. A visual distinguishing feature was that their wings were braced by diagonal Warren-type struts (having a W form seen from the front). They switched to an aircooled radial (the 840-hp Fiat A74) in the C.R.42 of 1939, and this biplane was important in World War II – including a few bomber escorts over England in 1940. It continued in production alongside the uninspired G.50 monoplane.

MODEST ARMAMENT

The rival fighter firm was Macchi, whose C.200 of 1937 was not only a monoplane but also one of the first Italian all-metal stressed-skin warplanes. Powered by a Fiat A74 boosted to 870 hp, it was agile and tough, and soon reverted to having an open cockpit to meet the demands of the pilots. Its shortcomings were that it was slow and weakly armed, with the usual Italian fighter armament of two 12.7-mm (0.5-in) guns.

In 1940 the Italians began re-engining their fighters with Daimler-Benz engines of much greater power. At first the DB 601 of 1,175 hp was available, produced under licence by Alfa Romeo. By 1942 this was replaced by the 1,475-hp DB 605. The Fiat G.50 thus became the G.55, and the Macchi fighter became the C.202 with the DB 601 and the C.205 with the DB 605. Not only was flight performance utterly transformed, but armament was also enhanced, the two 12.7-mm (0.5-in) guns above the engine being supplemented by two or even three of the outstanding German Mauser MG 151/20 cannon.

The principal bomber constructor was Savoia-Marchetti, which adhered to traditional airframes with fuselages of welded steel tubing and wooden wings. The most important types were the S.M.81, with three engines and fixed landing gear, and the excellent S.M.79 with three (sometimes two) engines and retractable gear.

Fiat also produced one important bomber, the B.R.20. First flown in 1936, this looked adequate for the period, though it retained a traditional structure with a steel-tube fuselage and with almost the whole surface skinned in fabric. Repeatedly modified, with engines increased in power to 1,250 hp each by 1941, about 600 were delivered.

Caproni, famed between the wars for gigantic bombers with a huge lower wing and smaller upper wing, then built large numbers of pedestrian monoplanes with one, two or three engines for use as reconnaissance bombers and

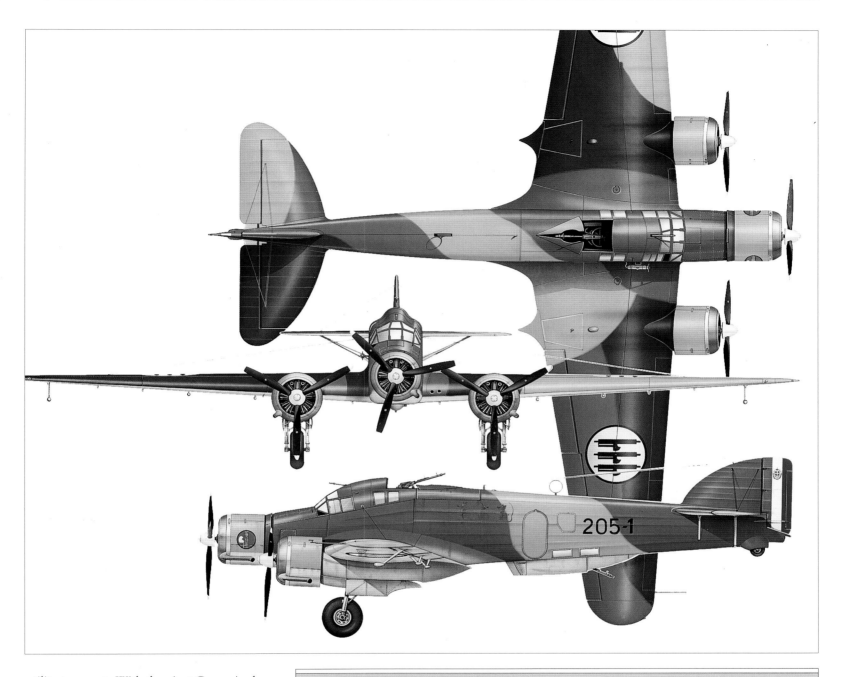

utility transports. With the giant Caproni obsolete, the only heavy bomber was the Piaggio P.108B with four 1,500-hp engines. One example had a massive 102-mm (4-in) gun for use against ships. The Cant firm supplied the Z.501 flying boat, the Z.506B three-engined seaplane and the Z.1007 landplane bomber. All were outstanding, despite being made of wood.

War against Abyssinia in 1935 demonstrated that Italian aircraft were good at dropping bombs, firing guns and releasing mustard gas against primitive enemies. A year later war in Spain provided a sterner test, but when Italy declared war against Britain in June 1940 it had no idea that it could possibly lose.

SPECIFICATIONS

Savoia-Marchetti S.M.79-II Sparviero

Type: four/five-crew medium bomber/torpedo bomber

Powerplant: three 1,000-hp (746-kW) Piaggio P.XI R.40 14-cylinder air-cooled radial piston engines

Performance: maximum speed 270 mph (435 km/h) at 12,000 ft (3658 m); climb to 16,400 ft (5000 m) in 14 minutes 30 seconds; service ceiling 22,966 ft (7000 m); range with 2755-lb (1250-kg)

Weights: empty 16,755 lb (7600 kg); maximum take-off 24,912 lb (11300 kg)

Dimensions: wing span 69 ft 6.5 in (21.20 m); length 53 ft 1.75 in (16.20 m); height 13 ft 5.5 in (4.10 m); wing area 656.60 sq ft (61.00 m²)

Armament: one pivoted and two pivoted 0.5-in (12.7-mm) Breda SAFAT machine-guns, and one pivoted 7.7-mm (0.303-in) Lewis machine-gun; internal bomb load two 1,100-lb (500-kg), five 550-lb (250-kg) or 12 220-lb (100-kg) bombs or two 17.7-in (450-mm) torpedoes

American Airpower

Above: In 1935, despite the rival Boeing 299, the US Army ordered the Douglas B-18 as its next bomber. Here improved B-18As of the 5th Bombardment Squadron fly over Manhattan in 1939.

stayed in business was Boeing, enabled to do so largely by a succession of contracts for improved versions of DH-4. The only other aircraft available in large numbers was the Curtiss JN family of trainers, popularly called the Jenny. Most of them were powered by the same maker's OX-5 engine of 90 hp, but later versions had the Wright-Hispano, likewise a water-cooled V-8 but rated at 150 or even 180 hp.

Between the wars Curtiss remained the largest planemaker, selling to both the Army and Navy. Martin did likewise, but from 1925 its heavy bombers were supplanted by the Huff-Daland/Keystone series. This changed in 1932 when Martin hit back. The breathtaking company-funded Martin 123 bomber was tested, and found to be faster than any of the Army's pursuits (fighters). Other companies providing competition were Douglas from 1922 and Lockheed from 1932.

RACING AND RECORDS

In the 1920s the Army, Navy and Marines all operated their own types of aircraft, and gained publicity through setting records and air racing (pp. 38–41). From 1926 the general level of flight performance was significantly enhanced by the Wasp engine (p.41), and the Martin 123 did the same for airframes. Apart from the novel idea of a gun turret, it featured a cantilever monoplane wing, stressed-skin structure, fully cowled engines, flaps and retractable landing gear.

However, no such aircraft were available when, on 19 February 1934, President Roosevelt cancelled 'corrupt' US Mail contracts, and ordered that the established mail routes be flown by the Air Corps. This was done for almost four months, but at the cost of 66 aircraft crashed and 11 pilots killed. This was a hard way to learn, but henceforth the Air Corps was a world leader in flying by day and night in the most severe weather.

In 1927 the Navy had commissioned two enormous 33,000-ton carriers, USS *Lexington* and *Saratoga*. From this time on the Navy never looked back, and it grew until in World War II it alone was bigger than all but three of the world's air forces. Almost the only error it made was to

When the United States entered World War I in April 1917 it had a large army and navy but few aircraft, and only a 'backyard' aircraft industry. Orders were quickly placed for thousands of aircraft, mostly of established European types. The most numerous was the British D.H.4, but powered by the US-developed Liberty water-cooled V-12 engine of 400 hp. By 1919 three companies had delivered 4,846, with the designation written as DH-4, and over 5,000 more were cancelled.

After the 1914–18 War, retrenchment was severe, and funding was tight. One firm that continue the commissioning of large rigid airships. Despite the destruction of the British-made R.38 before delivery, and of the *Shenandoah* in a storm in 1925, in 1926 the Navy was authorized to procure two airships 'for scouting purposes' larger than any previously built. The ZRS-4 *Akron* was commissioned in October 1931 and the ZRS-5 *Macon* in June 1933. Each could carry, launch and retrieve four specially designed Curtiss F9C-2 Sparrowhawk fighters. In April 1933 *Akron* was destroyed in a storm, with only three survivors from her crew of 60. In February 1935 *Macon* followed, but this time with only two deaths.

In the mid-1930s two prototypes pointed the way ahead for both Services. On 28 March 1935 Consolidated began testing the XP3Y flying boat. It was noteworthy for its long-span wing,

with stabilizing floats which folded up to form the wingtips. Redesignated PBY, and later named Catalina, it became the most important patrol flying boat of the Allies in World War II.

In 1934 the Air Corps issued a requirement for a new multi-engined bomber. It was taken for granted that this meant 'twin engined', but Boeing asked if a four-engined aircraft would be admissible. The result was the Model 299, first flown on 28 July 1935. Boeing picked four engines not so much for bomb load as for speed and high altitude, and the aircraft made headlines by flying from the Seattle factory to Wright Field, Ohio, at 252 mph (406 km/h). A newspaper called it a 'Flying Fortress'. Then, by carelessness, this remarkable machine was destroyed, but as the B-17 it was to become one of the most famous warplanes of all time.

Below: Grumman made their name with agile biplanes with retractable landing gear, to operate from Navy carriers. This beautiful F3F-2 replica has an original 950-hp Cyclone, and is based at the Chino Air Museum.

France's *Armée de l'Air*

At the 1918 Armistice France had over 20,000 warplanes, more than any other country except the UK. Its huge aircraft industry survived post-war cutbacks by exporting more military aircraft than any other country. In 1925 the naval air arm was reorganized as the *Aéronautique Navale*, while in 1933 the *Aviation Militaire* was itself reorganized as the *Armée de l'Air* (army of the air).

By this time the French aircraft and aero-engine industries were potentially among the most capable in the world, but there were problems. One was that the most powerful engines were rated at 900 hp or less, with no engine in the 2,000-hp class likely for many years. An even more serious problem was that in 1933, when the air force was reorganized, nearly all its equipment was obsolescent.

Air Minister Pierre Cot signed contracts for prototypes of impressive new fighters and bombers, such as the Dewoitine D.520, Bloch 150, Breguet 690, Potez 630, Lioré et Olivier 45 and Amiot 340. These new aircraft appeared from 1936 onwards, and were ideal for modernizing what was still a very large air force. By this time the emergence of Hitler's growing Luftwaffe scared the French, who decided drastic measures were needed in order to speed production of the new types. On 16 October 1936 Cot announced that all factories making aircraft and engines for the government were to be nationalized.

A great plan was drawn up in which all the famous old companies disappeared into vast State groupings. It was done in a brutal way, on a purely geographical basis. For example, part of Breguet was handed to the *Société Nationale de Constructions Aéronautiques du Nord* (the north group), some factories were handed to SNCAO (*Ouest*, west) and other Breguet plants came under SNCASO (*Sud-Ouest*, south-west). It was the same across France. Each factory was then handed enormously increased contracts for warplanes.

NATIONALIZED CHAOS

To say the entire vast aircraft industry was thrown into chaos is an understatement. Output, which was meant to double by 1938, dropped close to zero. Before long a further, and sinister, trend became manifest: sabotage. From a distance it is difficult to understand why workers in a national defence industry, facing a growing threat from the neighbouring Luftwaffe, should have done all they could to make sure that each aircraft, as it came off the assembly line, was actually lacking various vital items which made it unable to go into action and probably unable to fly.

For example, Amiot flew the prototype Amiot 340 on 6 December 1937. This beautiful high-speed bomber was used by the Chief of Air Staff, General Joseph Vuillemin, on an official visit to Berlin in August 1938. The aircraft was painted to look as if it was in regular service. In fact the first production Amiot 354 did not reach the *Armée de l'Air* until January 1940, and by 1 April 1940 only 21 had been received, instead of the planned 285. Moreover, all were deficient in equipment and, especially, in armament.

In July 1936 the Bloch (pronounced Blosh) company failed to get its MB.150 fighter airborne. It had to be redesigned, and at last flew in October 1937. Soon 475 were on order, but it was then discovered the aircraft had to be redesigned yet again, to make it simpler and easier to produce. The resulting MB.151 at last flew on 18 August 1938. Frantic orders were placed for hundreds, as well as for the MB.152 with the newly developed 1,050-hp Gnome-Rhône 14N

Above: In June 1932 the Dewoitine company flew the prototype D 500, a bold stressed-skin fighter with no wing struts or bracing wires. It led to hundreds of speedy monoplanes for many customers, including 360 for the *Armée de l'Air*. The picture shows No 47 (despite bearing '46'), the first production D 500, with 690-hp Hispano-Suiza engine. Later versions had a 0.78-in (20-mm) cannon firing through the propeller hub.

Above: The Farman F 221 heavy bomber was one of many French aircraft of astonishing ugliness. Powered by four 970-hp Gnome-Rhône engines, it led in 1936 to the F 222 which at least had retractable landing gear, enabling speed to increase to 199 mph (320 km/h).

engine. Most had four machine guns, but from late 1939 some had two of the small guns replaced by 0.78-in (20-mm) cannon.

Two huge factories strove to feed these very tough and useful machines to the waiting squadrons. By the outbreak of World War II 120 had been produced, however, 95 had no propeller and not one of the 120 had a gunsight. At the collapse on 20 June 1940 no fewer than 593 had been delivered, but only a fraction were ever able to go into action.

By far the most numerous fighter was the Morane-Saulnier M.S.406, of which 1,037 had been produced by 20 June 1940. Unfortunately it was an inferior and obsolescent design, no match for the Bf 109E. In fact, the most successful of all French fighters in May/June 1940 was the imported Curtiss Hawk 75. In November 1942 the Vichy (collaborative French) air force used them against the Allies.

The Royal Air Force

Above: The Handley Page Heyford was powered by two 525-hp Rolls-Royce Kestrel engines and carried up to 3,500 lb (1588 kg) of bombs in the thick centre section of the lower wing. Its technology was that of World War I, and it swiftly became outdated.

fabric-covered biplane. Despite having a Napier Lion engine of 570 hp the maximum speed of 120 mph (193 km/h) was no higher than that of aircraft of World War I. A total of 235 were built as two-seat day bombers for the RAF, and a further 352 as three-seat reconnaissance machines for the Fleet Air Arm. It was run close in numbers by the 517 Westland Wapitis, all for the RAF (see p.37).

In 1925 Richard Fairey shocked the Air Staff by demonstrating his Fox, a two-seat bomber in the same class, yet able to 'walk away' from any RAF fighter. Fairey's reward was an order for enough aircraft to equip just one squadron, but a longer-term result was to start Hawker Aircraft building two-seat biplanes that were even faster. In June 1928 the Hart, powered by the new 525-hp Rolls-Royce Kestrel engine, reached 184 mph (296 km/h). It led to the most varied family of inter-related warplanes in British aviation. With traditional light-alloy airframes covered in fabric, these two-seat biplanes served as day bombers, fighters, reconnaissance and training aircraft, and the RAF received no fewer than 2,603.

This was at least a small move in the right direction, and the speed and agility of fighters was dramatically improved by Bristol's improved radial engines. In the early 1930s the standard fighter was the Bulldog, whose 1,753 cu in (28.7 litres) Jupiter engine gave 490 hp and resulted in a speed of 174 mph (280 km/h). In 1934 the prototype Gloster Gladiator was fitted with a Bristol Mercury of only 1,520 cu in (24.9 litres), but it gave 840 hp and resulted in a speed of 255 mph. Unfortunately by the time the Gladiator reached the RAF in 1937 it was essentially obsolete, with no asset save manoeuvrability.

POOR PERFORMANCE

It was the same story with bombers. The lumbering (maximum speed 108 mph, 174 km/h) Vickers Virginia was still in use in 1937. Its replacement, the Handley Page Heyford, was still a fabric-covered biplane. Next came the same manufacturer's Harrow. This was at least a monoplane, with slatted wings, but it still had

O n pp. 36–37 it was explained how important aircraft were to policing empires and maintaining communications. In the 20 years from 1918 this was the main task of Britain's RAF, and most of its aircraft were designed accordingly. They were required to be tough and reliable in primitive environments, and most were designed with no thought that they might ever have to engage in aerial combat. In addition, the RAF was responsible for aircraft of the Fleet Air Arm, whose personnel were members of the Royal Navy.

In the 1920s the aircraft purchased in the largest numbers was the Fairey IIIF, a pedestrian

SPECIFICATIONS

Bristol Bulldog Mk IIA

Type: single-seat biplane interceptor

Powerplant: one 490-hp (366-kW) Bristol Jupiter VIIF air-cooled radial piston engine

Performance: maximum speed 178 mph (286 km/h) at 10,000 ft (3050 m); climb to 20,000 ft (6095 m) in 14 minutes 30 seconds; service ceiling 27,000 ft (8230 m); normal range 310 miles (499 km)

Weights: empty 2,222 lb (1008 kg); maximum take-off 3,660 lb (1660 kg)

Dimensions: wing span 33 ft 11 in (10.34 m); length 25 ft 2 in (7.67 m); height 9 ft 10 in (3.00 m); wing area 206.50 sq ft (28.47 m²)

Armament: two forward firing synchronized 7.7-mm (0.303-in) Vickers machine-guns on the sides of the nose, plus occasional provision for four 9-kg (20-lb) bombs

fabric covering, fixed landing gear and hand-aimed Lewis machine guns, and only managed to reach 200 mph (322 km/h) because of its 925-hp Bristol Pegasus engines.

Throughout the inter-war period flying boats (boat-type seaplanes) equipped many RAF squadrons engaged in what was called 'general reconnaissance'. The Supermarine Southampton simply carried on from World War I, with wooden wings with fabric covering but a hull made of non-corroding Alclad. Gradually the successors – Supermarine Scapa, Blackburn Perth, Saro London, Short Singapore and Supermarine Stranraer – became all-metal aircraft, with maximum speeds rising from 100 mph (161 km/h) to the Stranraer's 165 mph (266 km/h).

Then in 1933 the Air Ministry issued a specification for a totally new flying boat, to be a four-engined monoplane. The result was the Short Sunderland, which entered service in

1938. No fewer than 739 of these aerial battle-ships were built, and in World War II they patrolled the oceans of the world carrying radar, bombs, depth charges and a mass of other equipment. On one occasion a Sunderland was set upon by eight Ju 88s, shot down three and returned to base. Other German crews were to find the Sunderland to be no sitting duck.

It was not the same for the other new crop of monoplanes ordered in the mid-1930s. The Armstrong Whitworth Whitley, Handley Page Hampden and Vickers-Armstrongs Wellington bombers soon discovered they could survive only at night. The speedy Bristol Blenheim soon became a night fighter or was packed off to the the Western Desert and India. As for the Fairey Battle, this Merlin-engined three-seat monoplane replaced the Hawker Hind as a light day bomber. It carried twice the bomb load at 1½ times the speed, but in the Battle of France it was easy meat for Bf 109s.

Rise of the Luftwaffe

On 28 June 1919 the Treaty of Versailles was signed. The victorious Allies decreed, among other things, that all German military aircraft should be destroyed, and that a German air force was prohibited. Accordingly many experienced German pilots and designers worked for foreign governments, while a few constructors did likewise. For example, Hugo Junkers set up a factory at Linhamm in Sweden, and sent design engineers to Aviation Factory No 1 at Fili near Moscow, which produced a remarkable succession of all-metal monoplanes under its Soviet head Andrei N. Tupolev.

After 1930 the rise of the National Socialist (Nazi) party attracted people from all walks of life who saw in it a way out of economic depression and a restoration of German greatness. At the same time the Allies lost interest in suppression of German militarism, withdrew their occupying forces, and ignored developments which a child could see were ways of getting around the hated 1919 Treaty. For example, hundreds of flying and gliding clubs sprang up. By 1932 the *Luftsportverband* had over 50,000 members, resulting in thousands of young men becoming qualified pilots.

Moreover, it was increasingly self-evident that the massively expanding German aircraft industry was once more making warplanes. By 1933 the Junkers Ju 52/3m, a three-engined airliner notable for its corrugated metal skin, was also being produced as a bomber. At the Dornier factory at Altenrhein the Do 11C all-metal twin-engined monoplane was being delivered in surprising numbers to the 'traffic inspectorate of the State Railways', accompanied by crates of 'spare parts' which actually contained gun mountings, bomb sights and bomb racks. By 1935 Dornier was openly producing the improved Do 23 bomber. Nobody in the former Allied camp seemed to care.

BRILLIANT HEINKEL

In December 1932 the Heinkel He 70 set a new standard in both aerodynamic cleanliness and smooth stressed-skin construction. Later Rolls-Royce bought one as a high-speed engine testbed, because no such aircraft existed in Britain. They found that, with the same Kestrel engine as the RAF's fastest fighter, it was 20 mph (32 km/h) faster with a pilot and five passengers! As a reconnaissance-bomber, the He 70 saw service in the Spanish Civil War.

From early 1935 a further succession of advanced stressed-skin prototypes appeared which were clearly military, though some were described as sporting aircraft or airliners. In 1934 the newly formed RLM (air ministry) issued a requirement for an aeroplane to be used as either a fast 10-passenger transport or a bomber. From the He 70 Heinkel developed the twin-engined He 111, which predictably changed from a slim-bodied airliner into a bomber. Junkers produced the Ju 86, which was exported as an airliner and as a bomber.

The Dornier Do 17 was designed purely as a fast mailplane with a cramped six-seat cabin. Rejected by *Lufthansa*, a Do 17 prototype was flown by an important test pilot, and thus by genuine chance it went into production as a fast bomber.

The new Luftwaffe's first fighters were traditional fabric-covered biplanes. First came the Arado Ar 65, which in 1933 began equipping a *Reklame-Staffel* (publicity squadron). In March 1935 this unit revealed its true colours as JG 132 (JG, *Jagdgeschwader*, fighter wing), equipped with the superior He 51. On the 28th of the same month Messerschmitt test pilot 'Bubi' Knötsch made the first flight of the Bf 109. Temporarily powered by a British Kestrel engine, this rakish machine had a simple all-metal stressed-skin airframe with a small wing

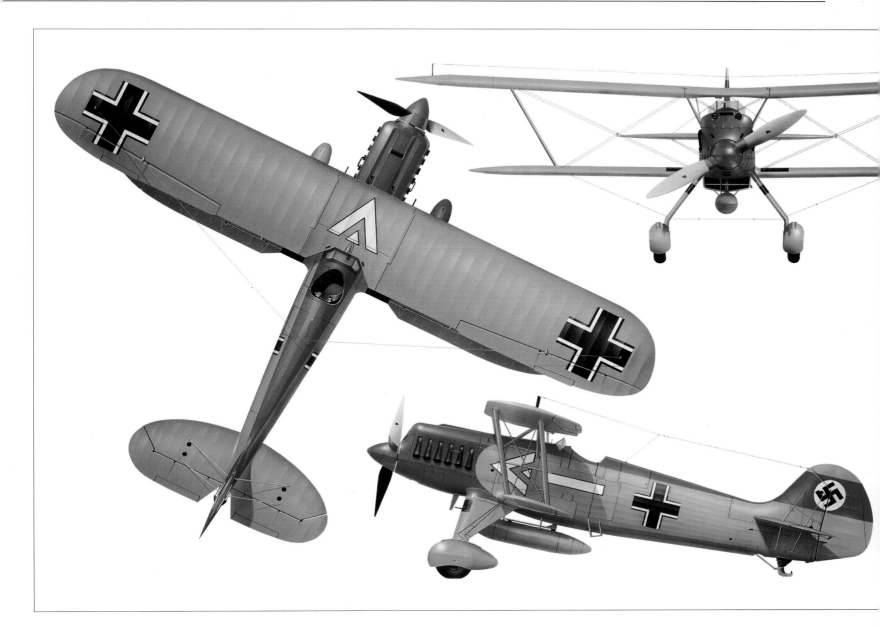

Left: Black-crossed rudders show that these Messerschmitt Bf 109E-1 fighters were serving with the *Legion Kondor*'s JG 88 in Spain. The Spanish Civil War was invaluable in teaching the Luftwaffe both technology and tactics.

fitted with slats, a rather narrow-track landing gear attached to the fuselage and retracting outwards into the wings and a slim fuselage with a sideways-hinged cockpit canopy.

Ernst Udet, later to be Luftwaffe procurement chief, exclaimed to Willy Messerschmitt 'This will never make a fighter!' Like most 1935 fighter pilots, he was convinced such aircraft had to be agile biplanes with open cockpits, so that the pilot could look in all directions. In fact, repeatedly fitted with a succession of high-power Junkers and Daimler-Benz engines, the Bf 109 was probably the best fighter in the world in the late 1930s. It was to remain in production until Germany's defeat in 1945, the final total of approximately 35,000 being exceeded only by the Russian Il-2 (p.84).

SPECIFICATIONS

Heinkel He 51B-1

Type: single-seat fighter

Powerplant: one 750-hp (559-kW) BMW VI 7,3Z 12-cylinder inverted-Vee piston engine

Performance: maximum speed 205 mph (330 km/h) at sea level; service ceiling 25,260 ft (7700 m); range 354 miles (570 km)

Weights: empty 3,219 lb (1460 kg); maximum take-off 4,178 lb (1895 kg)

Dimensions: wing span 36 ft 1 in (11 m); length 27 ft 6.75 in (8.40 m); height 10 ft 6 in (3.20 m); wing area 292.7 sq ft (27.20 m²)

Armament: two forward firing synchronized 0.31-in (7.92-mm) MG 17 machine-guns

4 WORLD WAR II

Democracies under Attack

Above: The first production Dutch Fokker G Ia long-range fighter (two 830-hp Bristol Mercury). On 10 May 1940 most G Is were destroyed by bombs, but the rest fought valiantly.

Left: Little suspecting the terror about to be unleashed, one of the first P.37 Elk bombers to reach the Polish air force is seen in 1938 with P.11c and P.24A fighters.

The late 1930s were a time of increasing international tension. Italy had crushed Abyssinia, and brutal wars were now being waged in China and Spain. Though these conflicts did not make headlines, the Soviet dictator Stalin was having tens of thousands of imagined opponents shot or sent to Siberian labour camps. Despite all this, the chief reason for tension was Germany, whose charismatic leader Hitler had begun to make territorial demands, backed up by what his No 2, Hermann Goering, proclaimed to be 'the largest and most powerful air force in the world'. By 1936 the previously locked doors of military funding in Britain and France began to open, and warplanes were ordered by the thousand. Realizing that it takes time to build factories, provide sources of raw material, and hire and train workers, both countries began placing large orders with companies in America. France ordered fighters from Curtiss and Grumman and fast bombers from Douglas and Martin. Britain ordered Hudson reconnaissance aircraft from Lockheed, Harvard trainers from North American, and a single Catalina flying boat for evaluation. These orders had a huge effect on the growth of these companies.

By August 1939 Hitler's Luftwaffe had 3,750 combat aircraft, all of modern and formidable types, backed by a monthly output of some 500 aircraft (working only a single-shift) and over 1,000 aircrew, mainly pilots. Most of the aircraft and many of the flying personnel had become experienced in Spain. Not least, almost the whole Luftwaffe was comprised of idealistic young men, unhindered by the hidebound traditional concepts and training of their opponents.

POLISH ATTACK

At 4.34 am on 1 September 1939 Luftwaffe Oberleutnant Bruno Dilley's section of three Ju 87B dive bombers destroyed the Dirschau bridge over the river Vistula, 11 minutes before Germany declared war on Poland. Two days later Britain and France declared war on Germany, but did nothing to help their ally. Most of the LW (Polish military aviation) was destroyed or otherwise put out of action in the first 48 hours, but remnants continued to be effective until 16 September.

Virtually all the LW fighter regiments were equipped with the distinctive but obsolete PZL P.11c. This high-wing monoplane was powered by a 645-hp Bristol Mercury engine made locally under licence. Fixed landing gear helped limit the speed to 242 mph (389 km/h), though most were fitted with four machine guns. Their harassed pilots did well to shoot down 126 Luftwaffe aircraft for the loss of 117 P.11cs in combat. By far the most important tactical bomber of the LW was the three-seat PZL P.23, powered by a locally made Bristol Pegasus engine. With a bomb load of up to 1,543 lb (700 kg) and speed of 198 mph (319 km/h), it was flown until mid-September. Alongside the P.23s were a handful of PZL P.37s, outstanding bombers powered by two 918-hp locally made Pegasus engines and with a bomb load of up to 5,688 lb (2,580 kg).

With Poland vanquished, nothing much happened for two months. France, and the large BEF (British Expeditionary Force) in France, had no intention of invading Germany, and merely waited. Then on 30 November 1939 the Soviet Union invaded Finland, ostensibly because the Finns refused to hand over part of their territory. Far from being overwhelmed, the Finnish LV (air force) fought back with a collection of British, Dutch, German, Italian and French aircraft.

On 9 April 1940 German forces invaded Norway, taking over Denmark in passing. Norway's handful of Gladiator biplanes were overwhelmed, but two days later British troops arrived, and Blackburn Skua dive bombers of the Fleet Air Arm sank a German cruiser. On 23 April the carrier HMS *Glorious* flew off 18 RAF Gladiators to operate from a frozen Norwegian lake. It was all futile.

On 10 May Hitler's forces struck against Holland, Belgium and France. While the campaign in the West went from bad to worse, it dawned on the British War Cabinet that their forces in Norway were in a hopeless position. On 7 June the last surviving Hurricanes flew onto the deck of *Glorious* to return to Britain. Sailing alone, the carrier was intercepted by German battlecruisers and sunk. This typified the whole Allied war to this point: courage cannot overcome pathetic planning and muddled direction.

War with the USSR

Against considerable difficulties, as well as many self-inflicted problems, the Soviet Union built up a huge air force. Stalin took a personal interest in all branches of armaments, and could be relied upon to order whichever aircraft was fastest. He also liked size, and the giant Tupolev TB-3 remained in production until 1937, 819 being built. By far the best and most advanced heavy bomber in the world in 1930, by 1937, even though its speed had been increased from 122 mph (196 km/h) to 186 mph (300 km/h), it was obsolescent.

These and other warplanes (pp. 46–47) equipped regiments right across the vast Soviet Union. Its enormous frontier adjoined states that were either only superficially friendly or definitely hostile. Along one stretch of over 621 miles (1,000 km) nomadic Mongolians, who hardly knew they were part of the Soviet Union, pastured their flocks without thinking that in 1931 Japan had seized Manchuria from the Chinese, renaming it Manchukuo, and now considered the frontier to be the Khalkin river. Any Mongolian would say the frontier was far to the East, on the high plateau of Nomonhan.

On 10 May 1939 Mongolians on the east bank of the Khalkin were driven back across the river by Manchukuo border troops. It was the spark that ignited a war, but a war that was not only undeclared but also almost unreported in the world's media. Within days the Japanese had committed 170,000 ground troops and the 2nd *Hikoshidan* (air division) with 35 squadrons. These were equipped with nearly 1,000 combat aircraft, the principal types being the Nakajima Ki-27 fighter, Mitsubishi Ki-21 and Fiat B.R.20 heavy bomber, Mitsubishi Ki-30 light tactical bomber and Mitsubishi Ki-15 reconnaissance aircraft. Against them the Soviet VVS initially ranged two IAPs (fighter regiments) equipped with the Polikarpov I-152 and I-16, and various *Eskadrili* (squadrons) equipped with R-5 and R-Z tactical biplanes and TB-3 heavy bombers.

INFLATED SCORES

Objective assessment of this conflict is difficult, because the aerial victory claims of the two sides are clearly fiction. For example, the

Japanese claimed that on 4 July 1939 Ki-27s destroyed '10 SB fast bombers, and 35 I-152s and I-16s, without loss'. What is beyond dispute is that many hundreds of aircraft were involved, and that some of the air battles (notably that of 22 June 1939) were by far the largest to take place since 1918. An oft-repeated story is that on 25 July the Japanese were startled to see their biplane opponents retract their landing

gear (it was the first day in action of the new I-153) and that this unnerved them. In fact, on balance the Ki-27 had the better of the air combats, though this may be because most of the chronicles have been written by Japanese.

After bitter fighting, in the course of which the Japanese were certainly defeated on the ground, the fighting came to an end on 16 September. The Japanese admitted the loss of 382 aircraft, of which 220 were Ki-27 fighters. They claimed the destruction of 1,260 Soviet aircraft, but the actual figure was probably closer to 400.

While the world knew virtually nothing about this remote war, it was well informed about two other Soviet wars. On 17 September 1939, in accord with an agreement reached with Hitler, Soviet forces invaded Poland from the East, hastening that country's final collapse.

The world's media branded Stalin an aggressor, as he obviously was, and it became even angrier when, with no declaration of war, Soviet armies invaded neighbouring Finland on 30 November 1940. The so-called Winter War was ostensibly over border territory, but was probably undertaken by Stalin as a test of his forces.

The conflict was so unequal there could be only one outcome, but the Soviet Union found

Above: In the final years of peace, large export orders were placed for the British Gloster Gladiator, an agile biplane fighter. Sweden gave up 30 (actually naval Sea Gladiators) to hard-pressed Finland, where they fought from January 1940.

SPECIFICATIONS

Polikarpov I-16 Type 24

Type: single-seat fighter

Powerplant: one Shvetsov M-62 radial air-cooled piston engine rated at 1,000 hp (746 kW) for take-off and 800 hp (597 kW) at 13,780 ft (4200 m)

Performance: maximum speed 273 mph (440 km/h) at sea level and 304 mph (489 km/h) at 9,840 ft (3000 m); climb to 16,405 ft (5000 m) in 5 minutes 48 seconds; service ceiling 31,070 ft (9470 m); range (clean) 373 miles (600 km) with external fuel tanks

Weights: empty 3,252 lb (1475 kg); maximum take-off 4,541 lb (2060 kg)

Dimensions: wing span 29 ft 1.5 in (8.88 m); length 19 ft 8 in (6.04 m); height 7 ft 9.75 in (2.41 m); wing area 160.06 sq ft (14.87 m²)

Armament: four 0.30-in (7.62-mm) ShKAS machine-guns (two synchronized in fuselage and two unsynchronized in wings) with 650 rounds per gun, or two fuselage-mounted ShKAS with 650 rpg and two wing-mounted 20-mm ShVAK cannon with 180 rpg; a single 0.5-in (12.7-mm) Berezin UB machine-gun with 300 rounds could be added to the fuselage mounted armament and with which the wing-mounted armament was usually deleted

it harder than it had expected. At the outset the IL (Finnish air force) had 145 aircraft, of which some 50 were modern machines fit for combat. Bristol had supplied 18 Blenheim light bombers and in early 1940 the RAF handed over 24 more. Orders were placed for such fighters as the Curtiss Hawk 75, Fiat G.50, Caudron C.714 and Morane-Saulnier M.S.406, but the only help that arrived in time was a Swedish volunteer squadron flying Gloster Gladiator biplanes. The chief IL fighter was the Fokker D.XXII, which despite having non-retractable landing gear reached 286 mph (460 km/h) on its 830-hp Bristol Mercury engine. The Finns built 38 under licence, and 29 were still on strength when they capitulated on 12 March 1940. In 1941 Finland joined the Axis powers (Germany and Italy).

Blitzkrieg

Above: Compared with the Heyford (p.54) the Fairey Battle was breathtakingly modern. In 1940 it proved to be totally vulnerable, easily intercepted and almost defenceless. At low level, its maximum speed was 210 mph (388 km/h).

Between the world wars military leaders studied the writings of strategists such as Britain's Capt. Liddell-Hart, who advocated a war of rapid movement. Britain's own generals could not imagine anything except static trench warfare, but Hitler's forces had other ideas, and planned *Blitzkrieg* (lightning warfare). The Polish campaign proved that the idea worked, using *Panzer* (armoured) forces on the ground closely supported by the Luftwaffe.

Key elements were the Messerschmitt Bf 109E and long-range Bf 110 fighters to control the sky and eliminate hostile aircraft, the Dornier Do 17, Heinkel He 111 and, from 1940, the Junkers Ju 88, to flatten cities, and the Junkers Ju 87 dive bomber to take out point targets such as bridges and forts with accurately placed bombs of 250 and 500 kg (551 and 1,102 lb). During the Polish campaign British and French leaders did nothing, though an invasion of Germany would have caused Hitler

problems. Once Poland was conquered, 60 German divisions were transferred to the West and the chance was gone.

The Allied commanders were locked in to the idea of the impregnability of France's Maginot Line, a 200-mile (322-km) stretch of forts and anti-tank obstacles along the eastern frontier. Hitler's *Fall Gelb* (Plan Yellow) ignored it, and instead involved major thrusts through the Netherlands, Luxembourg and Belgium, as well as through the forests of the Ardennes, which Allied generals had believed impregnable. With 174 divisions available, Hitler initially committed 75. Supporting them was an armada of 4,417 combat aircraft, of which 3,350 were committed, not including 475 transports (430 of them Ju 52/3ms) and 45 DFS 230 troop-carrying gliders.

The carefully planned campaign began before dawn on 10 May 1940. Airfields throughout the Low Countries were attacked by bombers and strafing fighters, while daring assaults were made on point targets. Most unexpected of all was the arrival of 11 gliders literally on top of the supposedly impregnable Eben Emael fortress at a key point on the river Maas (Meuse). At 13.15 on the following day the fortress surrendered; its commander shot himself and 1,200 defenders slouched out, at a total cost of six German casualties.

TERRIBLE LOSSES

On the 14th the Luftwaffe heavily bombed Rotterdam, and less than two hours later Holland surrendered. By this time the German spearheads had achieved all their initial objectives. Allied aircraft suffered from chaos at the command level, but valiantly tried to bomb vital bridges across the Maas and Albert Canal. On the first day 32 Fairey Battles of the RAF Advanced Air Striking Force attacked targets at Dippach, and lost 13. On the 12th the RAF's No 2 Group sent Blenheims against the Albert Canal bridges, losing 11, while in another attack AASF Battles lost 12. The crucial day was the 14th, when so many bombers of the *Armée de l'Air* and RAF/AASF were destroyed, in the air and on the ground, that the Allies were never again able to offer serious hindrance to the rapidly advancing Panzers. Though the German forces inevitably did suffer significant casualties, the Allies were so completely out-thought as well as out-fought that the end was no longer in doubt.

On the 13th Spitfires made a brief appearance over Holland, and from the 20th they assisted Hurricanes in trying to gain command of the air over the Panzers racing past Arras, making for the coast to split the Allies in two. On the 26th the Luftwaffe so demoralized the defenders that Calais surrendered, and on the same day the Admiralty authorized the start of Operation Dynamo, the evacuation of as many Allied troops as could escape from certain capture at Dunkerque. Amazingly, by 4 June an armada of little ships had evacuated 338,226 troops from the beaches. Most were British, but some were Belgian or French. Some French troops, uncertain where their loyalty lay, returned to France, and many later fought against the Allies. On 13 June French forces left Paris and eight days later over 400,000 French troops on the eastern front surrendered.

The Battle for France had cost the RAF 944 aircraft, including 386 Hurricanes and 67 Spitfires. As early as 15 May Sir Hugh Dowding, the Air Officer Commanding RAF Fighter Command, had pleaded with newly appointed Prime Minister Churchill that no more of his strength should be poured into the lost cause in France. Dowding could see that there would later be a Battle of Britain and that his command would need every fighter for the nation's greatest test since 1066.

Right: The Junkers Ju 87B *Stuka* dive bomber came to symbolize the *Blitzkrieg* concept. These are a later version, the Ju 87D, which found life harder.

Battle of Britain: The Attack

Civil War, the Luftwaffe had used flexible groups: the *Schwarm* (four fighters arranged like the fingertips), *Kette* (three) and *Rotte* (a pair), and soon the RAF learned to do the same.

By 8 August numerous engagements had resulted in the loss of 192 Luftwaffe aircraft, mostly fighters, and though about the same number of RAF fighters had been shot down Fighter Command was still a highly effective force. The British pilots, reinforced by outstanding escapees from European air forces, proved to be unexpectedly aggressive and capable, so that the numbers of fighters needed to escort bombers had to be revised sharply upward. An even more unexpected blow was that the *Zerstörer* (destroyer, Bf 110) long-range escorts were completely outclassed in combat with the Hurricane and Spitfire.

OUTMODED FORMATIONS

On 8 August the battle intensified, with far more bombers involved. Three major attacks were made on convoys, mainly by the Ju 87s. On 18 August StG.77 lost 16 of its Ju 87s in one

Above: The Dornier Do 17Z was one of the major types of tactical bomber used against Britain in 1940. Its crews liked it, but quickly found that it was easy meat for the RAF's fighters.

After the unprecedented conquest of the Low Countries and France, the German forces were exhausted. They needed time to rest and reorganize, and the Luftwaffe had to establish itself in all the best airfields from which operations could be mounted against the United Kingdom. It also had to put in place a vast supply organization for everything from fuel to bombs, because Hitler planned Operation *Seelöwe* (Sealion), the invasion. Landings were to be made in Sussex and Kent, and the shattered and (after Dunkerque) almost unarmed British Army driven back to a line Gloucester-St Albans-Maldon. By that point British resistance was judged to have collapsed.

The campaign was to start on *Adler Tag* (Eagle day) on 10 August 1940. It was calculated that RAF opposition in the South would be overcome in four days, and that in four weeks the RAF would effectively cease to exist. Accordingly, *Seelöwe* was planned for the second week in September.

During June *Fliegerkorps* VIII settled into airfields in Normandy, while *Fliegerkorps* II was established in the Pas de Calais. Other units were to operate from Belgian bases. By early July *Luftflotte* 2 (Kesselring) and 3 (Sperrle) deployed 2,600 aircraft, including 1,200 Do 17, He 111 and Ju 88 bombers, 280 Ju 87B dive bombers, 760 Bf 109E fighters, 220 Bf 110 long-range fighters and 140 reconnaissance aircraft. Another *Luftflotte*, No 5, forced the RAF to retain substantial fighter forces in Scotland and northern England.

On 10 July the Luftwaffe opened the campaign by attacking a convoy off the North Foreland. The objective was to close the Channel to British convoys, whilst testing the RAF. At the same time formations of Bf 109s began flying over southern England at high altitude to entice the RAF to come up and fight under a tactical disadvantage. At this time the RAF, which had not been able to learn much in the chaos of France, still put fighters up in rigid squadron V-formations. Ever since the Spanish

SPECIFICATIONS

Messerschmitt Bf 109E-7

Type: single-seat fighter

Powerplant: one 1,200-hp (895-kW) Daimler-Benz
DB 601N inverted V-12 liquid-cooled engine

Performance: maximum speed 359 mph (578 km/h)
at 12,300 ft (3749 m); initial climb rate 3,300 ft
(1006 m) per minute; service ceiling
36,500 ft (11125 m); range 680 miles (1094 km)

Weights: empty 4,400 lb (2014 kg); maximum take-off
6,100 lb (2767 kg)

Dimensions: wing span 32 ft 4 in (9.86 m);
length 28 ft 8 in (8.74 m); height 11 ft 2 in (3.40 m);
wing area 174 sq ft (16.16 m²)

Armament: two I Karia MG-FF 0.78-in (20-mm) cannon
in the wings, each with 60 rounds, and two 0.31-in
(7.92-mm) MG 17 machine-guns above the engine

action, and subsequently the once-feared *Stuka*
had to be withdrawn from British skies. *Adler
Tag* was postponed to 13 August, a day on
which the score was 46:13 in the RAF's favour.
On 15 August the Luftwaffe went all-out, flying
no fewer than 1,786 sorties in a determined
attempt to wreck RAF airfields. In the week to
19 August the RAF lost 121 Hurricanes and 54
Spitfires, with 94 pilots having been killed or
missing and 60 wounded, but against this 403
Luftwaffe aircraft were shot down and 127 were
seriously damaged.

Day after day, the mighty Luftwaffe formations filled the skies over southern England,
concentrating their attacks on the RAF airfields. Gradually the RAF was worn down.
Between 23 August and 6 September it lost
295 fighters, with 171 seriously damaged, but
the real crisis was in pilots, and especially in
experienced pilots. By early September most of

the crucial fighter stations had been seriously
damaged, and six of the seven key sector stations had been so heavily bombed that the
entire interception system was on the verge
of collapse. Then, from 7 September, the
Luftwaffe was switched to bombing London. It
gave Fighter Command the respite it needed,
and after a peak on 15 September the daylight
battles dwindled and finally ceased at the end
of October.

The Luftwaffe had shot down 1,140 RAF
fighters but lost 1,789 of its own aircraft. It had
failed to subdue the RAF, Britain was not
invaded, and from then onwards the German
aircraft that dared to venture over Britain in
daylight were usually small numbers of fighters
and fighter bombers such as Bf 109s, Fw 190s
and Me 410s. Indeed for a high number of sorties they achieved little and were regarded
mostly as a nuisance.

Battle of Britain: The Defence

In February 1935 the Air Ministry asked scientist Robert Watson Watt if there was such a thing as a death ray that could be aimed at enemy bombers. He answered in the negative, but said that it would be possible to invent a method of detecting the presence and even location of hostile aircraft by using radio waves. As a result, from 1936 British physicists and engineers created a totally new defence system in which tall towers emitted radio waves and received any reflections. Later called radar, it played a crucial role in 1940 in ensuring that enemy aircraft were always detected. Defending fighters never took off and searched aimlessly; instead they were guided accurately to intercept the enemy.

This amazing defence system was thus devised, just in time, by sheer chance. In the same way, the RAF's monoplane fighters, the Hawker Hurricane and Supermarine Spitfire, were developed only just in time and to a large degree also by chance. Hawker Aircraft worked on a monoplane version of the Fury, and it was only at the last moment that this was abandoned and replaced by an aircraft with the 1,000-hp Rolls-Royce Merlin engine, retractable landing gear and the unprecedented armament of eight machine guns. It was by chance that the company's Board decided at their own risk to tool up and make 1,000 Hurricanes before any had been ordered!

Supermarine flew a fighter to Specification F.7/30, but it could not exceed 228 mph (367 km/h). On their own initiative they started afresh, and in March 1936 flew the first Spitfire, which was smaller, better streamlined and had a Merlin engine, and thus reached 350 mph (563 km/h). Unfortunately, it was not easy to make (man-hours per airframe were double that needed for the rival Bf 109), and it suffered from the same deficiencies as the Hurricane, such as absence of cannon armament, inability to make negative-g manoeuvres without the engine stopping, and the fact that all the first batches had a crude fixed-pitch propeller. It also had other weaknesses, notably poor lateral control which at high speeds reduced rate of roll close to zero, but it was a great basis for improvement.

BUILD QUALITY

Another weakness of the procurement system was that nobody had thought to order a long-range twin-engined fighter, nor a fighter able to operate at night. The radar designers, however, did miracles in creating a set called AI (Airborne Interception) that could fit into an aircraft. First flown in an Anson in August 1937, AI even got into action in a Blenheim in the summer of 1940: on the night of 22 July AI operator Sgt Leyland guided F/O Ashfield's Blenheim astern of a Do 17 which they then shot down.

From September 1940 the Luftwaffe increasingly raided southern England by night, and by October the 'Night Blitz' was on in earnest. At first the defenders were utterly ineffectual. On 15 November the Air Minister told the Prime Minister 'Last night... 300 [actually 481] German aircraft converged on a known target

Below: Entering service after the Battle of Britain, the Bristol Beaufighter filled a vital gap in providing defence at night. The photograph shows an early Mk IC of 253 Sqn., without radar.

[Coventry]... 100 fighters were airborne... yet the only casualty is claimed neither by the fighters nor by the guns'.

Fortunately chance again helped the RAF to shoot down enemies in the night sky. From the Beaufort torpedo bomber Bristol were able quickly to develop the Beaufighter. Powered by two 1,600-hp Bristol Hercules engines, it had the flight performance needed despite being burdened by a pilot, an observer, a radar set, and the devastating armament of four cannon and six machine guns.

At last the RAF was beginning to get the equipment it needed to defend Britain by night as well as by day. The immediate task was to train pilots and, especially skilled radar observers, to work as a deadly team able to hunt down any enemy on the darkest night. From 1942 the 'Beau' was augmented and progressively replaced by night-fighter versions of the de Havilland Mosquito. Originally designed as a bomber so fast that it needed no defensive armament, this amazing all-wood aircraft later became as versatile as the Luftwaffe's Ju 88, able to do virtually anything. Powered by two Merlins, most Mosquitos could fly for long distances at over 400 mph (644 km/h).

SPECIFICATIONS

Supermarine Spitfire Mk IA

Type: single-seat fighter

Powerplant: one 1,030-hp (768-kW) Rolls-Royce Merlin IIA V-12 liquid-cooled piston engine

Performance: maximum speed 364 mph (586 km/h) at 18,500 ft (5639 m); climb to 20,000 ft (6096 m) in 9 minutes 24 seconds; service ceiling 31,500 ft (9601 m); normal range 395 miles (636 km)

Weights: empty 4,341 lb (1969 kg); maximum take-off 5,800 lb (2631 kg)

Dimensions: wing span 36 ft 10 in (11.23 m); length 29 ft 11 in (9.10 m); height 11 ft 5 in (3.48 m); wing area 242 sq ft (22.48 m²)

Armament: eight wing-mounted 0.303-in (7.7-mm) Browning machine-guns with 500 rounds per gun

The War at Sea

Above: A type which had no counterpart in Britain or the USA was Italy's Cant Z.506B. Named *Airone* (Heron), its three 750-hp engines gave a speed of 217 mph (350 km/h), even with a bomb or torpedo load.

From the start, World War II involved every kind of maritime operation. The United Kingdom was and remains totally dependent on shipping, and in World War I suffered severely from the depredations of German U-boats (submarines). Amazingly, between the wars almost nothing was done to improve defence against U-boats, so that in 1939 the technology was what had existed in 1918. In contrast, Germany had developed mines triggered by changes in the Earth's magnetic field caused by a ship, as well as new forms of torpedo.

Worse, whereas in 1939 Hitler's *Kriegsmarine* had 22 Type VII U-boats, during the war their total was to rise to 721. On the first day of the war one sank the liner *Athenia* and later in 1939 Type VIIs sank the carrier *Courageous* and the battleship *Royal Oak*. In 1941 U-boats sank 4.3 million tons of shipping, followed by 6.2 million in 1942. By April 1943 sinkings were at the level of 600,000 tons each month, and the situation was critical.

By this time Allied aircraft were equipped with improved ASV (air to surface vessel) radars, new sonobuoys, intensely powerful Leigh lights to illuminate targets at night, and more lethal depth charges. They were proving so dangerous that the U-boats, newly fitted with multiple AA guns, stayed on the surface to fight. They lost, and on 24 May 1943 Admiral Doenitz recalled his U-boat packs, which were never again a serious threat.

In September 1939 the RAF's biplane flying boats were fast being replaced by the mighty Sunderland (p.55). In Coastal Command this vital aircraft was at first partnered by the Avro Anson, which was soon relegated to communications and crew-training (which it did well, no fewer than 11,020 being built) and the Armstrong Whitworth Whitley, a pensioned-off heavy bomber which pioneered the use of radar at sea. From 1942 specially developed versions of Vickers Wellington became numerically the most important RAF maritime reconnaissance and ASV aircraft.

CLOSING THE GAP

For the oceanic task, the *Sunderland* was, from the summer of 1941, ably partnered by two aircraft made by Consolidated. Both powered by 1,200-hp Pratt & Whitney Twin Wasp engines, they had the range to close the mid-Atlantic gap where no aircraft could previously reach. One was the Catalina. The other was the four-engined Liberator landplane, an early version of which was equipped by RAF Coastal Command not only with radar but also with four 20-mm (0.78-in) cannon firing ahead.

The idea that long-range fighters might play a maritime role had not occurred to the peacetime RAF, but from 1942 the Beaufighter and later the Mosquito equipped many squadrons of Coastal Command. The Beaufighter Mk X could carry a torpedo, in which role it was much more lethal than the slower Beaufort which had preceded it. Mosquitoes ranged far up the coast of Norway strafing and bombing, and the Mk XVIII even attacked ships (including U-boats) with a 57-mm (1.57-in) gun.

The Luftwaffe's maritime operations were essentially offensive. Over the Bay of Biscay important types were the outstanding Ju 88, which served as a bomber, torpedo bomber and long-range fighter, and the Arado Ar 196 twin-float seaplane which, though used mainly for coastal reconnaissance, was armed with two 20-mm (0.78-in) cannon and bombs. For operations far into the Atlantic the chief type was the Focke-Wulf Fw 200C Condor. At first a scourge of convoys, this big aircraft, originally designed as an airliner, suffered from a weak structure and was prone to breaking its back in a heavy landing! Over the North Sea reconnaissance and minelaying were the tasks of the Dornier Do 18 and Blohm und Voss 138 flying boats and the Heinkel He 115 seaplane.

In August 1943 the Luftwaffe went into action with two of the first types of guided missile to be used in warfare. Do 217E-5 bombers based at Cognac in western France scored their first success by sinking the sloop HMS *Egret* with the Hs 293, a long-range rocket-propelled bomb rigged as a miniature aircraft with guidance commands transmitted from an operator in the aircraft through trailing wires. In the Mediterranean long-span Do 217K-2s took off to stop the Italian fleet from being handed over to the Allies. They used the FX-1400, a 5,511-lb (2,500-kg) armour-piercing bomb with radio guidance operating tail controls. The battleship *Roma* was sent to the bottom and the *Italia* was crippled.

The chief maritime types of Italy's own *Regia Aeronautica* have already been mentioned on pp.48–49. Japanese types appear in following pages.

Right: Another large float seaplane, the Heinkel He 115 was powered by two 960-hp BMW engines and carried out a wide variety of overwater missions. Two, sold to Norway, escaped to Britain in 1940.

Barbarossa

Left: Variously painted white and red, these MiG-3 fighters were one of many Soviet types completely unknown in Western countries in June 1941, yet 3,170 had been delivered in one year. Their speed of 398 mph (640 km/h) exceeded that of any fighter in any Western air force at that time.

This was the code name of Hitler's invasion of the Soviet Union in June 1941. By this time he had made Germany master of all Continental Europe. Even before the Battle of Britain Operation Barbarossa was being planned in detail, but first substantial forces had to be diverted to rectify the situation in the Balkans and North Africa (p. 80). These units were therefore not available for the assault in the East.

Despite this, the forces that invaded the USSR at 3 am on 22 June were the largest ever assembled. They included 117 German armoured and infantry divisions, backed in the southern part of the 1,200-mile (1,931-km) front by the Hungarian Army Corps and 14 Romanian divisions. Four of the five *Luftflotten* (air fleets) were used, initially with 2,770 combat aircraft but later with more. Many of Hitler's generals were apprehensive, but Hitler said, 'England is beaten and the USSR will collapse in six weeks'.

Despite ample warning, the assault appeared to catch the Russians by surprise. Fleets of aircraft were lined up on the western airfields, so that on the first day 1,489 were destroyed on the ground, as well as 322 in air combat, for the loss of a mere 32 Luftwaffe aircraft. On the ground the Panzers simply kept encircling enemy forces and then annihilating them. In the two biggest encirclements, at Uman and Kiev, 665,000 Soviet troops were killed or captured. By the end of June *Luftflotte* 1 in the north claimed the destruction of 1,211 aircraft in the air and 487 on the ground, while Army Group North had encircled Leningrad. Claims on the Central Front amounted to 1,570 aircraft destroyed, while *Luftflotte* 4 in the South claimed 1,300.

RUSSIAN QUALITY

On the other hand the Soviet aircraft were not quite the rubbish that had been predicted. The MiG-3 was faster than any Luftwaffe fighter, the all-wood LaGG-3 was respected, and the agile Yak-1 was possibly the best of all. The twin-engined Petlyakov Pe-2 tactical bomber was a real shock to the Germans, combining as it did almost the speed of the British Mosquito with a heavy (3,527-lb, 1,600-kg) bomb load. Perhaps the most feared of all was the Ilyushin Il-2, dubbed the *Stormovik* (assaulter). It looked like a rather large fighter, but its purpose was to destroy tanks, with heavy cannon and spin-stabilized rockets. Seemingly vulnerable, it was in fact heavily armoured against ground fire.

Such aircraft were desperately needed, but despite incessant planning the Soviet aircraft industry was still almost entirely either in the Moscow area or in the Western part of the country. The rapidity of the German advance was horrifying. By late November the Panzers were 19 miles (30.5 km) from Moscow. From late September the Soviet design staffs and production factories had had to be evacuated to the East, in most cases beyond the Ural mountains

into Siberia, initially by rail and then on track-ways of mud or ice. In almost every case they found either no suitable habitation or a half-finished one, yet by the end of the year output was back to its previous level and rising fast.

Thus, while the German figures of Soviet aircraft losses – 15,877 destroyed or captured by 20 November – referred almost entirely to types that were obsolete, the aircraft coming off the newly built production lines were as good as those of the Luftwaffe and in many cases better. The tricky LaGG was developed into the La-5, powered by the 1,630-hp ASh-82FN radial, while the Yak-1 gave way to the Yak-7 and Yak-9, which were not only excellent but also made in vast numbers.

Both the VVS (air force) and AV-MF (naval aviation) also deployed excellent tactical bombers, notably the Ilyushin DB-3F and

derivative Il-4, which in naval use carried torpedoes. The only thing the Russians lacked was a large strategic bomber force. The once formidable force of TB-3s were by 1941 retired or converted into transports, in which role they operated intensively throughout the long battlefront. The successor, the Pe-8, was an impressive machine, larger than such counterparts as the Lancaster and B-17, but only 149 were built (with four types of engine, the AM-35A vee-12, the ASh-82 radial and the M-40 and ACh-30B diesels). On 19 May 1942 Pe-8 No 66 arrived at a remote Scottish airfield, Tealing near Dundee. On board was Foreign Minister Molotov, who flew in a D.H.95 to meetings in London. He then returned to Tealing, and the Pe-8 took him on to Washington. It was the first Soviet aircraft to arrive in the West since 1929, and it caused amazement.

Above: Likewise, when this Pe-8 arrived in Scotland in May 1942 it was completely unknown. Even five months later a British aviation journal said it was 'the ANT-14' weighing '50,000 lb'. Its ANT number was 42, and its weight 35 tonnes (77,160 lb).

Pearl Harbor

Above: Powered like all B-17s by Wright R-1820 Cyclones with turbosuperchargers, the B-17C was the fastest version of this famous bomber, with a speed of 323 mph (520 km/h) at 25,000 ft (7620 m). Later versions were burdened by much heavier armament to enable close formations to fight their way to heavily defended targets in daylight.

At 7.02 am on Sunday 7 December 1941 the US Army's newly installed SCR-720 radar at Kahuka Point, Hawaii, spotted approaching aircraft. The operators thought 'Ah, it's those B-17s we're expecting'. It was instead 135 Aichi D3A1 dive bombers armed with heavy armour-piercing bombs, 144 Nakajima B5N2 torpedo bombers armed with heavy bombs or with large torpedoes set to run in shallow water, and 135 escorting Mitsubishi A6M2 fighters. Achieving total surprise, the assault was devastating. Almost all the US aircraft on the five military airfields were destroyed, but the real objective was the Pacific Fleet moored in Pearl Harbor. It was effectively knocked out, the only failure from the Japanese viewpoint being that the vital carriers *Saratoga*, *Lexington* and *Enterprise* were elsewhere.

This crushing blow was timed to coincide with the landing of invasion forces at Hong Kong, Kota Bharu in Malaya, Guam, Wake and the Gilbert Islands and, two days later, the Philippines. The Japanese successes were without precedent in warfare. On 6 December an RAF Hudson spotted a Japanese fleet sailing to Malaya. The Royal Navy sent out the 35,000-ton battleship *Prince of Wales*, the 32,000-ton battlecruiser *Repulse* and four attendant destroyers. They did not know the radius of action of

the Mitsubishi G4M (or, indeed, of its existence). Operating from Saigon, G4Ms and G3Ms of the 22nd Flotilla quickly sank both capital ships, effectively ending the Royal Navy's presence in the theatre.

SINGAPORE FALLS

On 15 February 1942 the 'impregnable' fortress of Singapore surrendered, to Japanese invaders who came from the land, not the sea. At a cost of 92 aircraft the Imperial Army and Navy had destroyed 390 British aircraft, and at the cost of 2,900 casualties the Imperial Army had killed well over 9,000 British Empire troops and taken 130,000 prisoner, a high proportion of whom were to die in captivity. On 9 April the last outposts in the Philippines surrendered and another 78,000 men became captives.

In four months the Imperial Army and Navy had conquered about one-quarter of the planet. The incredible plan to create a Greater East Asia Co-Prosperity Sphere seemed to have worked. Japanese forces were at the very gates of Australia, which lay almost defenceless to the south. With huge economic gains, including rubber and the much-needed petroleum of the former Dutch East Indies, the plan now was to make the Co-Prosperity Sphere so impregnable that even the mighty USA would talk peace terms.

Just as Hitler's attack on the USSR suddenly gave Germany (and, a surprising time later, the rest of the world) details about the previously unknown Soviet aircraft, so did the amazing campaign by Japan reveal the previously unknown aircraft which enabled it to happen. The one uniform feature was that, apart from the Army Kawasaki Ki-61 fighter (which had basically the same engine as the Messerschmitt Bf 109), all Japanese aircraft were powered by air-cooled radial engines. Outwardly the Japanese aircraft appeared supremely undistinguished, but they were ideal for their purpose.

In contrast, they were opposed by a motley collection of aircraft, almost all of which had been designed for other theatres. Those in the Hawaiian islands included a handful of B-17D Fortress heavy bombers, Curtiss P-36 and P-40

Left: Flying an A6M2, the Japanese ace Lt. Saburo Sakai (64 victories) was photographed on his 12th mission. With only 925 hp, the lightweight A6M2 nevertheless carried two 20-mm (0.78-in) cannon and two machine-guns.

Below: The surprise assault on 7 December 1941 destroyed aircraft as well as warships. Possible survivors seen here included a PBY Catalina and OS2U Kingfisher and SOC Seagull float seaplanes.

fighters and a few Navy PBY flying boats. Most were caught on the ground, but four pilots managed to take off in P-40s. One, Lt George Welch (later a famed test pilot), shot down four of the enemy, three other pilots also scoring. This at least showed that the Japanese pilots were not supernatural.

Even though they had advance warning, the US forces in the Philippines suffered devastating blows from the sky from 8 December onwards. On that day G3M and G4M bombers destroyed 108 US aircraft, which were still parked in neat rows. Casualties included 18 of 35 early-model B-17s, 56 of the 72 Curtiss P-40s and most of the obsolescent Seversky P-35s. Few of the survivors lasted more than a further two days. On the 10th a single B-17 managed to drop three 600-lb (272-kg) bombs on the heavy cruiser *Asigara*, but on returning to Clark Field the Fortress was shot down by Japanese fighters, even though the nearest Japanese airfield was 640 miles (1,030 km) away. Carrying a drop tank, the A6M dubbed 'Zero' by the Allies was to keep appearing in places where Japanese aircraft had not been expected and in 1942 it destroyed almost every aircraft it encountered. A popular song in the USA was 'Johnny got a zero' (a pun on getting a zero mark in class), by implication underlining the Japanese fighter's superiority.

The Rising Sun

Above: By 1944 Japanese aircraft factories, like those in Germany, were desperately trying to increase production despite shortage of materials and incessant bombing. Here workers at Nakajima's Ota plant are churning out Ki-44 fighters. Unlike the A6M in 1942, they would meet superior opposition.

The Imperial Japanese Army and Navy had embryonic flying units from 1913, but at the Armistice in November 1918 there was still virtually no indigenous aircraft industry. To rectify the absence of Japanese aircraft, established designers were therefore hired from Western companies, especially from Britain, where many were available. By 1930 Japan was self-sufficient in aircraft, though the outside world knew as little about them as it did of the aircraft of the USSR.

A little detail emerged when fighting began in Manchuria in 1931, quickly spreading to China. War on a larger scale flared up in China in July 1937, when it should have become clear that Japanese aircraft were formidable. Some, such as the Kawasaki Ki-10 biplane fighter, Kawasaki Ki-32 monoplane tactical bomber and Mitsubishi Ki-1 heavy bomber, had V-12 water-cooled engines, but most had air-cooled radials. By World War II radial engines were almost universal.

In the late 1930s the chief fighters were the Army Nakajima Ki-27 and the Navy Mitsubishi A5M. Both had modern stressed-skin structures, engines of 650–750 hp and fixed landing gear, and they made up for weak armament (usually two machine guns) by extraordinary manoeuvrability. The chief bombers were both Mitsubishi designs, the Army Ki-21 and Navy G3M. Remarkably, although their power, dimensions and weights were very similar, their designs were utterly different. A notable feature of the G3M was its exceptional radius of action, which in December 1941 was to astonish the luckless crews of HMS *Prince of Wales* and *Repulse*.

UNPRECEDENTED OUTPUT

Until 1937 Japanese factories had never produced 1,600 aircraft in one year, but by Pearl Harbor the figure had reached 5,000. Then output rose meteorically, to peak in 1944 at over 28,000. By this time the front-line aircraft were formidable. Radial engines in the 2,000-hp class enabled high flight performance to be matched with heavy armament, armour and self-sealing tanks, which in 1941 had generally been lacking.

By 1942 Army units were receiving the chunky little Nakajima Ki-44 *Shoki* (Demon), which had a small wing and was not well suited to rough front-line bases, but combined adequate performance with various gun installations with calibres of 30, 37 and even 40 mm (1.18, 1.45 and 1.57 in). However, the best Army fighter in wide service was the Nakajima Ki-84 *Hayate* (Gale), which had two 20-mm (0.78-in) cannon in the fuselage and either two 20-mm or 30-mm (0.78-in or 1.18-in) in the wings, as well as the ability to carry two 551-lb (250-kg) bombs. A captured example matched in 1946 against US fighters at 20,000 ft (6,100 m) proved to be not only more agile but also faster than all, even the P-51D.

The Navy kept the A6M 'Zero' in production to the end, but did have small numbers of better fighters, such as the Nakajima N1K. Powered by engines of up to 2,200 hp, this was derived from a fighter seaplane! It had no shortcomings, and combined excellent manoeuvrability with heavy armament. The Mitsubishi J2M *Raiden* (Thunderbolt) was the opposite of the same company's A6M in having an engine of 1,825 hp and heavy cannon armament but a small wing. There were too few to be important, and the outstanding A7M *Reppu* (Hurricane) never got into service.

Both services had a wealth of excellent twin-engined fighters and reconnaissance aircraft, some of which had oblique upward-firing armament and even radar for intercepting bombers at night. The Navy also had many types of seaplane, some of which – such as the Nakajima A6M-2N, a version of the 'Zero' – were fighters. Nakajima followed the B5N torpedo bomber of Pearl Harbor fame with the much more powerful B6N, while the successor to the Aichi D3A dive bomber was the Yokosuka D4Y *Suisei* (Comet), which carried a 1,102-lb (500kg) bomb internally.

In 1941 the standard long-range oceanic flying boat was the Kawanishi H6K, which had four engines in the 1,000-hp class mounted on a wing carried on struts above the shallow hull. It was succeeded by the same company's H8K, widely regarded as the best oceanic reconnaissance flying boat of World War II. Its four 1,825-hp engines were mounted on a wing attached at the top of a very deep hull. Despite a heavy load of bombs, torpedoes or depth charges, and up to five 20-mm (0.78-in) cannon and five machine guns, it could reach 290 mph (467 km/h).

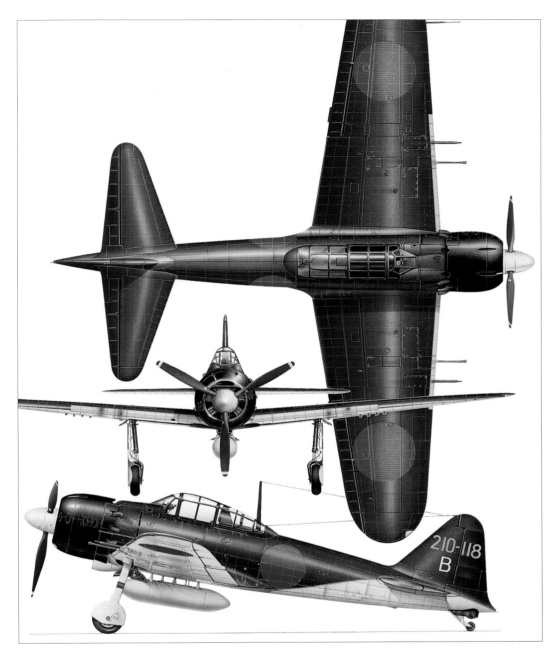

SPECIFICATIONS

Mitsubishi A6M5c Reisen

Type: single-seat carrier-based fighter/fighter-bomber

Powerplant: one 1,130-hp (843-kW) Nakajima NK1F Sakae 21 radial piston engine

Performance: maximum speed 351 mph (565 km/h); climb to 19,685 ft (6000 m) in 7 minutes; service ceiling 38,520 ft (11,740 m); maximum range 1,194 miles (1922 km)

Weights: empty 4,136 lb (1876 kg); maximum take-off 6,025 lb (2733 kg)

Dimensions: wing span 36 ft 1 in (11 m); length 29 ft 11.25 in (9.12 m); height 11 ft 6 in (3.50 m); wing area 229.27 sq ft (21.30 m²)

Armament: one 0.52-in (13.2-mm) Type 3 heavy machine-gun in the fuselage decking (breech in the cockpit), two 0.78-in (20-mm) Type 99 cannon in the wings and two 0.52-in (13.2-mm) Type 3 guns in the wings outboard of the cannon, plus two 132-lb (60-kg) bombs under the wings (suicide mission, one 551-lb (250-kg) bomb

The Royal Navy

Above: With a maximum speed of 139 mph (224 km/h) and a single machine-gun in the rear cockpit, the Fairey Swordfish was an outstanding example of a totally obsolete aircraft, which, because it was tough, reliable and flown by courageous crews, achieved enormous success years beyond its 'sell-by date'. Indeed, a Swordfish serving with the RAF attacked a U-boat three hours before the German surrender.

In World War I many of the greatest advances were made by the Royal Naval Air Service, including the first strategic bombing raid and the first victory by an aeroplane over a Zeppelin. The RNAS was responsible for the Handley Page heavy bombers, even though it was also charged with the air defence of Britain and for all aerial operations over the sea. Yet on 1 April 1918 it disappeared, merged into the RAF. At that time it had 2,949 operational aeroplanes and 103 airships.

The Admiralty smarted, and by degrees restored the situation. By 1923 it had been agreed that all observers and up to 70 per cent of the pilots of naval-type aircraft should be naval officers, and of course aircraft carriers were RN-manned. At last in May 1939 the Fleet Air Arm emerged, with Royal Naval Air Stations and its own aircraft, though large over-water aircraft remained with RAF Coastal Command. The FAA did operate shore-based aircraft, but its primary task was to fly from carriers and from the catapults of warships.

In general, ship-based aircraft tended to be inferior in performance to those able to use airfields. They had to have a lot of extra equipment, and their structures were heavier in order to have folding wings and to resist the stresses of being shot off catapults and arrested by cables stretched across the deck. Moreover, as each fresh design had been planned by the RAF the naval aircraft took second place, and in September 1939 the FAA was equipped almost totally with out of date fabric-covered biplanes.

There was just one modern machine, the Blackburn Skua dive bomber. Powered by a 905-hp Bristol Perseus sleeve-valve engine, one shot down a Do 18 flying boat to claim Britain's first aerial victory of the war. In 1940 Skuas sank the German cruiser *Königsberg*. Yet by 1941 the Skua was obsolete, while a slow fabric-covered biplane remained in production until 1944, 2,391 being delivered. Though its 750-hp Bristol Pegasus engine seldom drove it faster than 100 mph (161 km/h), the Fairey Swordfish, popularly called the 'Stringbag', decimated the Italian Fleet at Taranto in November 1940, crippled the mighty *Bismarck* (enabling the Fleet to catch her), scored the first success with rockets by sinking a U-boat 750 miles (1207 km) west of Ireland and, in appalling Arctic weather, sank four U-boats in a single voyage by one escort carrier.

TYPE VARIETY

Fairey also produced the Albacore, a modernized Swordfish, the Seafox for warship catapults, the Barracuda torpedo and dive bomber, and the Fulmar and Firefly carrier-based fighters, which were burdened by having to carry a navigator. Of the single-seat fighters, the Gloster Sea Gladiator, a traditional biplane, fought valiantly against much more powerful enemy aircraft over Norway and Malta, while the situation was alleviated by the quick production of the Hawker Sea Hurricane and Supermarine

Above: Another product of Fairey Aviation was the Fulmar, a fighter in the same class as the Hurricane, with eight machine-guns and a Merlin engine; but the need to carry a navigator was a factor limiting speed to 247 mph (397 km/h). Far more formidable were the US-supplied Grumman Martlets (later named Wildcat) seen in the rear. In the background HMS *Valiant* practises with her 15-in guns.

Seafire. The former was a stop-gap which did not even have folding wings, but it did valuable service catapulted from merchant ships to shoot down the dreaded Fw 200C Condors, the pilot subsequently ditching or parachuting near an Allied ship. In contrast, the Seafire passed through many marks (development stages), each better than the last, until the Seafire FR.47 of 1948 had 2½ times the power of the first version, armament of four 20-mm (0.78-in) cannon and, despite being twice as heavy, was 120 mph (193 km/h) faster.

However, in the crucial period prior to 1943 the Fleet Air Arm was saved by a chunky fighter imported from the United States. First flown in 1937, the Grumman G-36 (US Navy F4F) was ordered by France, deliveries being switched to Britain after France fell. Powered by a Twin Wasp or Cyclone of 1,200 hp, and named Martlet (later changed to the US name of Wildcat), this tough and manoeuvrable aircraft

filled a crucial role in many theatres. From 1943, FAA squadrons were also equipped with Grumman's more powerful Hellcat fighter and Avenger torpedo bomber, both generally superior to any British counterpart. A further 19 FAA squadrons operated the formidable Vought Corsair (US Navy designation F4U), mainly against the Japanese in the final 18 months of the conflict.

American factories also supplied the FAA with such aircraft as the Martin Maryland reconnaissance bomber, Beech Expeditor and Traveller communications transports, NAA Harvard pilot trainer, and Stinson Reliant navigator (observer) trainer and the unsatisfactory Curtiss Seamew trainer for TAGs (telegraphist/air gunners). British types included the Supermarine Walrus and Sea Otter multi-role amphibians, Miles Martinet and Monitor target tugs and de Havilland Queen Bee radio-controlled target aircraft.

Aircrew Unlimited

Though little money was available, by 1936 a few people in the British Air Staff and even in the Government thought perhaps the RAF ought to be expanded. The situation was difficult, because anyone who said 'Look at the growth of Hitler's Luftwaffe' was instantly branded as 'a warmonger'. However, as the years went by the money voted for aircraft was many times multiplied, but the first thing to be done was to think about future aircrew.

In July 1936 the RAF Volunteer Reserve was formed. It provided for civilians to be trained as pilots at each weekend at flying clubs all over the country. Despite the modest numbers involved, they were vital: in the Battle of Britain nearly half the pilots were sergeants who had been weekend flyers in the VR. Indeed, the vast intake during World War II, the author included, were all members of the RAFVR, not the 'regular' RAF.

In the final year of peace the Air Ministry became seriously worried about the supply of aircrew. Increasingly it became obvious that a huge plan had to be set up for training to take place in parts of the British Empire far from Britain, where the weather was better, the skies were less crowded and training could not be disrupted by the enemy. A British businessman, Lord Riverdale, was put in charge, but for months his brash manner resulted in the Empire Air Training Scheme failing to be launched. Not until the war had started did anything happen, and then it was because of an approach to Britain by Southern Rhodesia, whose white population was a mere 45,000. As a result, on 24 May 1940 No 25 Elementary Flying Training School at Belvedere, outside the capital, Salisbury, actually began training. Soon the Rhodesian Air Training Group was in full swing, with ten additional newly built airfields intensively operating Tiger Moths, Cornells, Harvards, Oxfords, Ansons, Battles and other types.

Eventually the vast Empire plan overcame many hurdles of self-interest and the question of who would pay, and the main agreement was signed in December 1939. The biggest participant was Canada, where an initial 67 schools were to be set up, 20 airfields expanded and 60 new ones constructed. Communities across the Dominion lobbied to have one of the new training stations. The scheme also embraced schools in Australia and New Zealand. A different Joint Air Training Plan brought in South Africa, and other schools were opened in India and Kenya.

CROWDED SKIES

Of course, training continued at a vastly accelerated level in Britain, but there were many problems. Among these were the frequent onset of severe weather, the fact that the sky was crowded, and navigating across the dense mass of towns, railways and roads was very difficult. Moreover, from August 1940 the sky over Britain was itself perilous. On the 16th of that month two Ju 88s circled the busy airfield of Brize Norton in daylight. Then they dropped their bombs, destroying 46 aircraft in hangars and damaging another seven, and then destroyed 11 Hurricane fighters at a Maintenance Unit across the airfield. A few days later, on a dark night, another Ju 88 bombed and strafed Kidlington. Many Oxford trainers were destroyed, and two in the circuit (one flown by a pilot on his first night solo) were shot down. Small wonder that all the staff and equipment of many training schools were shipped to Canada.

From early 1941, long before Pearl Harbor, the USA had assisted in RAF training. First it helped to provide six British Flying Training Schools. Then, in April 1941 Gen. H. H. 'Hap'

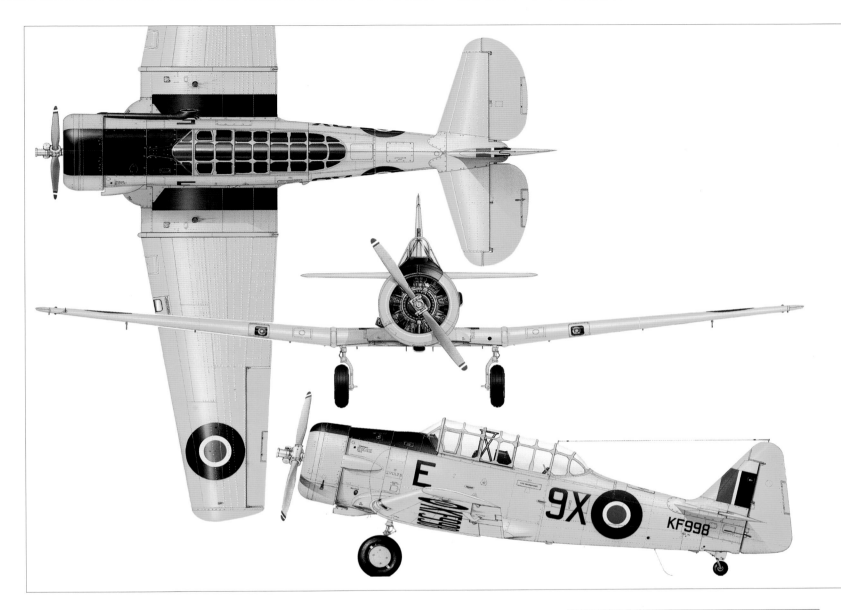

Left: In 1940, pilot training in England was intensive but dangerous. These Tiger Moths could encounter the enemy at any moment. Note the D.H.95 Hertfordshire transport in the background.

Arnold, Chief of Staff of the US Army Air Corps, set up a scheme to train RAF pilots under the Lend-Lease Act, while Admiral John H. Towers of the US Navy set up a similar scheme to train pilots for the Fleet Air Arm and RAF flying-boat squadrons.

Considering only schools in what had in 1942 been renamed the Commonwealth Air Training Plan, by 1943 their total number had peaked at 333. By 30 September 1944 the supply of aircrew exceeded the demand. By that date output totalled 75,152 pilots, 40,452 navigators, 15,148 bomb-aimers and 37,910 WOP/AGs (wireless operator/air gunner). Of this grand total of 168,662 no fewer than 116,417 had graduated in Canada, 23,262 in Australia, 3,891 in New Zealand, 16,857 in South Africa and 8,235 in Southern Rhodesia.

SPECIFICATIONS

North American Harvard Mk IIB

Type: two-seat advanced trainer

Powerplant: one 550-hp (410-kW) Pratt & Whitney R-1340-49 Wasp radial piston engine

Performance: maximum speed 205 mph (330 km/h); service ceiling 23,000 ft (7010 m); range 750 miles (1207 km)

Weights: empty 4,158 lb (1886 kg); maximum take-off 5,250 lb (2381 kg)

Dimensions: wing span 42 ft 10 in (13.06 m); length 29 ft (8.84 m); height 11 ft 8 in (3.56 m); wing area 253 sq ft (23.50 m²)

Armament: none fitted to Mk IIB, some Harvard/Texan variants could be fitted with two 0.5-in (12.7-mm) machine-guns for armament training/light attack duties

The Mediterranean

Benito Mussolini, the *Duce* of Italy, declared war on the Allies in June 1940. He had ideas as inflated as his own stature, and called the Mediterranean *Mare nostrum* (our sea). He also had a huge *Regia Aeronautica* (pp. 48–49), but its achievements were not on the same scale.

In late September 1940 Hitler sent his troops to occupy Romania. Mussolini was not told. Piqued at being ignored, a month later, after various threats to Greece, he sent his own troops into that country from Albania, which he had previously occupied. Instead of being a pushover, Greece not only fought back but by 22 November had taken thousands of prisoners and ejected the last Italian troops from Greek soil. Hitler was furious. His ally's inept invasion had put the RAF into Greece. He had to turn aside from planning for Barbarossa (pp 70–71) and send 24 divisions to drive the Allies from Greece and Crete and then establish the *Afrika Korps* in Libya.

By January 1941 *Fliegerkorps* X was established in Sicily, and it put Malta under siege, both it and British ships suffering severely from the air, and defending aircraft being almost all destroyed in the air or on the ground. Then in March came a respite, as Luftwaffe units were moved to support operations in the Balkans. On Palm Sunday, 6 April, the Luftwaffe began a *Terrorangriff* on the city of Belgrade which killed over 17,000 civilians. Crack Panzer divisions eliminated opposition, and on the 17th Yugoslavia surrendered. The Germans had suffered 151 men killed, and took 254,000 prisoner.

Other armoured forces pushed down into Greece, which capitulated on 26 April. Within a year of Dunkerque the British Army and RAF suffered a further humiliating evacuation, losing 12,000 troops and all their heavy equipment. The RAF claimed 231 German aircraft shot down (the true figure was fewer) but lost 209 of its own aircraft, most destroyed or abandoned on their airfields.

ASSAULT ON CRETE

The island of Crete came next. Some 155 miles (250 km) south of Athens, it had to be invaded from the sky, in an airborne operation bigger than any previously attempted. About 22,750 troops were assigned, 750 landing by DFS 230 assault glider, 10,000 by parachute, 5,000 by Ju 52/3m and 7,000 by sea. The assault began on 20 May. It took 11 days of bitter fighting to wipe out or eject the British and Commonwealth troops.

This time German casualties amounted to 1,990 killed, 327 drowned at sea and 1,995 missing. Against this was the virtual elimination of British and Commonwealth air and land forces from the whole of south-east Europe. In passing, the Luftwaffe had sunk three British cruisers and six destroyers, and put out of action three battleships, a carrier, six cruisers and seven destroyers. The campaign also restored the Luftwaffe's belief in its invincibility, which had been badly shaken over England.

Left: Though agile, the Macchi C.200 *Saetta* (Lightning) was armed with just two 12.7-mm (0.5-in) machine-guns and could barely exceed 300 mph (482 km/h). Macchi, Breda and Ambrosini delivered 1,153 before production switched to more powerful derivatives.

Above: Powered by 1,200-hp Twin Wasp engines, the Martin Maryland was ordered by France and diverted to the RAF. Malta-based 431 Flight began flying reconnaissance missions in October 1940, and many Maryland units served in North Africa. They were soon replaced by the more powerful Martin Baltimore.

While this campaign was in progress combat units of the Luftwaffe were being moved to Iraq through Syria. Held by the Vichy French, which opposed the Allies, Syria was invaded on 7 June by British and Free French forces, which accepted the French surrender on the 12th. While the armies fought inconclusively in the North African deserts of Libya and Cyrenaica, the Allies set up a strategic supply route from ports in West Africa, such as Accra and Takoradi, for supplying the entire Middle East and India. On 5 May 1942 British forces landed in Madagascar, but did not succeed in overcoming all Vichy French resistance on that island until 5 November.

On that very day Vichy French Admiral Darlan flew to Algiers to see his sick son. Darlan had been nominated by Marshal Pétain to succeed him as head of the Vichy French state. Strongly pro-German, his presence in Algiers was unwelcome, because on 8 November the biggest amphibious landing up to that time, Operation Torch, was putting Allied troops ashore in Casablanca, Oran and Algiers. Vichy French forces reacted furiously. French fighters and bombers strafed the Allied beaches, several US Army Douglas C-47s were shot down, Curtiss Hawk 75s supplied by the US to defend France fought with US Navy F4F Wildcats from the USS *Ranger*, while (until it was put out of action) the giant battleship *Jean Bart* fired on the Allies at Casablanca. Darlan ordered resistance to cease on 11 November.

The Pacific Theatre

In the first three months of 1942 Japanese forces invaded and occupied one quarter of the planet. No campaign on such a scale, and at such a speed, had ever happened before. The Allies were demoralized, losing not only vast areas of territory but also people and equipment on a huge scale.

Within a month of Pearl Harbor the Imperial Army and Navy had occupied the whole of south-east Asia, including supposedly impregnable Singapore, and begun taking over the Dutch East Indies covering an area the size of Europe. By February 1942 the unthinkable was happening: Australia was being bombed. Some of the attacks, mainly on Darwin, were by small carrier-based aircraft, but the heaviest loads were dropped by Nakajima Ki-49s of the Army and Mitsubishi G4Ms of the Navy.

By spring 1942 greater familiarity with the Japanese aircraft gradually overcame the enormous initial shock, and in many cases showed that they were no better than the often second-rate aircraft of the Allies which opposed them. For example, while the Army Ki-43 and Navy A6M fighters were incredibly agile, they were lightly constructed, and the former was also lightly armed, with only two machine guns. The otherwise formidable G4M had neither armour nor self-sealing fuel tanks, and was quickly dubbed 'The honourable one-shot lighter'.

THE FIGHT BACK

From Pearl Harbor onwards the Allies faced a serious difficulty in that everyone was faced by Japanese aircraft, of far greater diversity and quality than had been suspected, whose identity was unknown. It took until July 1942 for a junior intelligence officer, Capt Frank T. McCoy Jr, to start inventing a system of code names. In general he allotted male names to fighters and float seaplanes and girls' names to bombers and flying boats. He assigned 75 names in the first month. To this day there are countless survivors of the Pacific war who know what you mean if you say Frank or Betty, but have never bothered to learn that

these were actually the Nakajima Ki-84 and Mitsubishi G4M.

On 21 April 1942 the famous flyer Jimmy Doolittle, then a lieutenant-colonel, bravely led a force of 16 Army B-25 bombers off the heaving deck of the carrier *Hornet* and set course for Tokyo. It was a one-way trip, one B-25 landing at sea, one in Siberia and the rest in China, but it lifted Allied morale. Across the Pacific in Seattle Boeing was assembling the prototype of an incredibly advanced bomber, the B-29 Superfortress. Powered by four 2,200-hp turbocharged engines, it had pressurized crew compartments and five gun turrets controlled from remote sighting stations. First flown on 21 September 1942, the B-29 became the subject of a vast nationwide manufacturing programme, with assembly lines at Boeing, Bell and Martin. The gleaming B-29s built up the 21st Air Force, dedicated to bombing the heartland of Japan and Manchuria.

On 8 May 1942 Japanese and US fleets met in the Coral Sea. For the first time a furious sea battle took place fought entirely by aircraft.

Above: Grumman designed the TBF Avenger torperdo bomber in 1940–41, and together with Eastern Aircraft (former car plants) 9,836 were soon delivered. They played a huge role in the Pacific war, and went on in modified versions long after 1945.

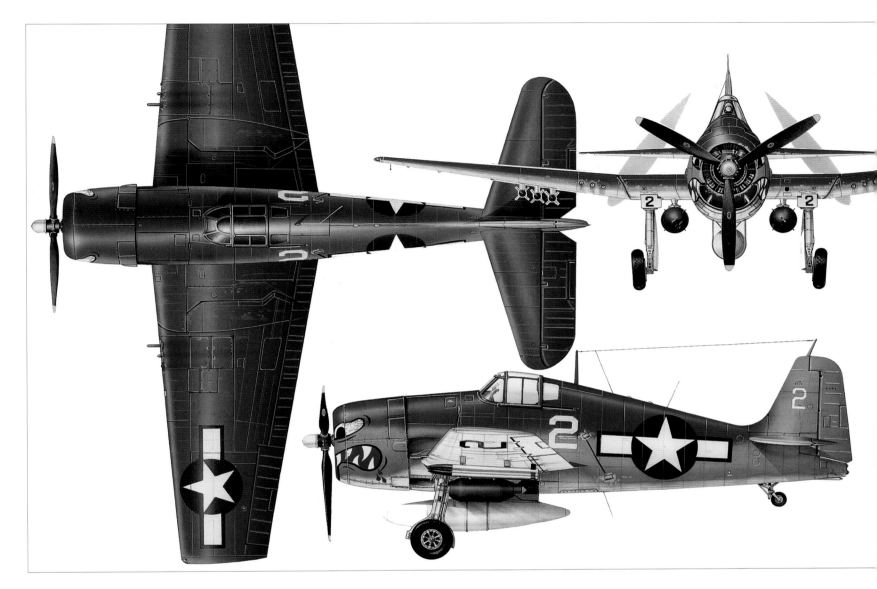

The opposing fleets never saw each other. It was a tactical victory for the Allies, though losses were roughly even. However, a month later an even bigger battle took place near the island of Midway. Torpedo Squadron 8, comprising 15 obsolete Douglas TBD Devastators, was wiped out before a single torpedo could be launched. In contrast, in the space of five minutes Douglas SBD Dauntless dive bombers destroyed half the Japanese carrier force. The Imperial Navy was never again to have superiority in the Pacific.

A long-term result of the Pacific war was that Australia gradually ceased to look to 'the old country' (the UK) and instead turned to the USA. Its aircraft industry did build the Bristol Beaufort and later the formidable Beaufighter, plus a locally designed 'last ditch' fighter called the Boomerang. However, Australia was really saved from invasion by

US aircraft, including fighters such as the Curtiss P-40 Kittyhawk and long-range Lockheed P-38, and in particular by bombers – the North American B-25, Douglas A-20 and B-24 Liberator. After the

war Australia, like the USA, had no time for 'colonial' policies, and did nothing to help the Dutch retake the East Indies. After bitter fighting this vast stretch of islands became Indonesia.

SPECIFICATIONS

Grumman F6F Hellcat

Type: single-seat carrier-based fighter/bomber

Powerplant: one R–2800 Double Wasp Pratt & Whitney engine, 1641-kW (2,200-hp)

Performance: maximum speed 621 km/h (386 mph) at (3,410 ft) per minute; service ceiling 11369 m (37,300 ft); range on internal fuel 1674 km (1,040 miles)

Weights: empty 4152 to 4191 kg (9,153 to 9,239 lb); maximum take-off 6991 kg (15,413 lb)

Dimensions: wing span 13.08 m (42 ft 10 in) or (folded 4.93 m (16 ft 2 in); length 10.23 m (33 ft 7 in); height 3.99 m (13 ft 1 in); wing area 31.03 m2 (334.00 sq ft)

Armament: six wing-mounted 0.50-in (12.7-mm) Browning machine-guns each with 400 rounds, plus plus provision for two or three bombs up to maximum total of 907 kg (2,000 lb) and six 5-in (127-mm) HVAR rockets

The Eastern Front

Left: Smaller than most Allied fighters, the Yak-9D was a long-range version of one of the chief types of Soviet fighter. A total of 16,769 were built, most powered by a 1,180-hp M-105PF engine with a cannon firing through the propeller hub.

Below: The Focke-Wulf Fw 190 was a brilliant design which suffered from none of the Bf 109's shortcomings. Almost all versions were heavily armed. This Fw 190A-4 was carrying an SC250 (551-lb) bomb, and also had wing bomb racks.

Hitler had always seen 'expansion to the East' as the way of getting *Lebensraum* (living space) for the German people. He scorned the supposed military might of the Soviet Union. 'You have only to kick the door', he said, 'and the whole rotten edifice will cave in'. Even the Luftwaffe agreed with his estimate that Operation Barbarossa would be over in six to eight weeks.

At first it looked as if this judgement was correct. As noted on p.70, the frontier was crossed on 22 June 1941, and giant pincer movements collected prisoners by the hundred thousand. For example, on 5 August 331,000 were taken around Smolensk, and in the third week of September 665,000 were killed or captured around Kiev. Moreover, the VVS (Soviet air force) appeared to have been largely destroyed, and the rapidly advancing Panzer divisions had by late 1941 overrun almost the whole of the Soviet aircraft industry, which was located almost entirely in the European part of the USSR.

It was the largest battle in human history. At the start the Germans committed 3.2 million of their 3.8 million men under arms, and soon had 148 divisions engaged over a front of 1,490 miles (2400 km). But it was not quite a walk-over. The T-34 tank was an unpleasant surprise, as was the Il-2 *Stormovik* anti-tank aircraft with armour-piercing cannon. Once the front began to stabilize, another surprise was the tenacity of the Soviet soldiers and, as a particularly bitter winter set in, German troops suffered and the swift advance ground to a halt.

RUSSIAN REVIVAL

By this time the great factories of Britain and increasingly, the USA, were pouring out war material and the trickle sent to the beleaguered USSR became a flood: Hurricanes, Spitfires, Dakotas, Bostons, Mitchells, Kittyhawks and,

especially, Airacobras and Kingcobras. Even so, Lend-Lease supplies were miniscule compared to Soviet production. By 1942 a vast new complex of Soviet factories had been constructed far to the East, most of them even beyond the Ural mountains, and here production got under way on all the latest Soviet warplanes.

Apart from thousands of *Stormoviks* the most numerous were the various Yak fighters. Like other Soviet fighters, these were made mainly of wood and, though relatively small, they had large engines. Though lightly armed, they had good performance and outstanding manoeuvrability, so that once their pilots had become proficient (if they lasted that long) they could achieve parity with the Luftwaffe. Moreover, while a flood of new pilots came from Soviet training schools, German losses could not be replaced at the same rate, and a particularly serious trend was that – accelerated from late 1942 by massive daylight raids over Germany by the US 8th AF – the Luftwaffe progressively lost its previously unbeatable *experte* pilots who had given it its initial superiority.

In the winter 1942-43 the siege of Stalingrad on the Volga marked the turning point of the War. It annihilated not only the 6th Army Group but also most of the Luftwaffe's transport aircraft. From then on, the still enormous German forces were pushed backwards. At first it was a ding–dong conflict, which in July 1943 reached its climax in battles between thousands of tanks around Kursk. When what the Germans called Operation *Zitadelle* (citadel) was over, it was the Soviet armies that moved forward. The cream of the Panzer armies had been destroyed and from that time on the Soviet forces had an increasing superiority.

By September 1943 the front had rolled West past Smolensk, taking in Kiev and the Ukraine by November. Thanks to the newly built factories the VVS regiments received 16,769 Yak-9s and over 15,000 Lavochkin La-5s and La-7s, while the 11,427 Petlyakov Pe-2 fast tactical bombers were being supplemented by Tupolev's outstanding Tu-2. Deliveries of Ilyushin's Il-4 bomber reached 5,256, while the *Stormovik* was made in larger numbers than any other warplane (36,163). By October 1944 it was being supplemented by the faster and even better protected Il-10.

From the disasters of 1941 the Soviet VVS, air-defence PVO, long-range ADD and naval AV-MF emerged by 1944 as masters of the Eastern skies. Not only the aircraft but the standard of flying personnel had greatly improved, and eight Soviet fighter pilots had each achieved over 50 confirmed victories. The pendulum could hardly have swung more completely.

Above: Seen here in its Il-2M3 form, with a gun for rear defence, the Il-2 *Stormovik* was made in larger numbers than any other single type of aircraft (36,163 in four years). This was despite severe difficulty in forming the vital armour plate around the engine and cockpit. Most had the 1,750-hp AM-38F engine, giving a speed of about 270 mph (435 km/h).

Airlift I

Until 1940 most air forces made little use of aeroplanes as pure transport vehicles. An exception was Britain's Royal Air Force, which saved money by inventing a class called bomber-transports. These were large and sedate biplanes which could either drop bombs or carry troops. One such, the Vickers Victoria, has already been described.

Also covered earlier were the impressive TB-3 bombers of the USSR, which ended their days carrying parachute troops and air-landed armies. Most air forces ignored such new ideas, but the reborn German Luftwaffe took them

on board and developed them further. One innovation was the use of assault gliders. The Soviet Union played with 'trains' of small gliders, typically six all towed on one rope by a tug aircraft, but the Luftwaffe bought gliders large enough to be useful.

First came the DFS 230, and though this only carried eight troops, it proved decisive in the fighting in the Low Countries in May 1940 and in Crete in May 1941. It was followed by the Gotha Go 242, distinguished by a tail carried on twin booms in order to enable the cabin to be opened by a full-width rear door.

Above: Airspeed Horsas of the RAF litter a field near Arnhem on 17 September 1944, when 320 were used to bring the 1st Airborne Division. A further 296 were sent on the following day. The two larger gliders are tank-carrying Hamilcars.

The Go 242 carried 21 troops or small vehicles, and led to the Go 244 powered by two engines of 700 or 750 hp.

By far the most important Luftwaffe transport was the Ju 52/3m, of which over 4,800 were delivered, many from the French Amiot factory at Colombes. It was followed by the more powerful Ju 252 and by the Ju 352, made of non-strategic steel and wood. Small numbers were made of the four-engined Fw 200C and Ju 290, but a really bold development was the huge Me 321 *Gigant* glider, with a span of 181

ft 5⅜ in (55 m). This could carry 130 troops or 48,500 lb (22 tonnes) of cargo, but towing it posed problems. After dangerous experiments with the *Troika-schlepp*, comprising three Bf 110 fighters in formation, it was decided to use the He 111Z, formed by joining two He 111 bombers side-by-side with a fifth engine on the centreline. By 1942 Messerschmitt had derived the more practical Me 323, powered by six 1,200-hp engines supplied from France.

Britain was not slow in copying the German use of assault gliders. By November 1940 the

Above: Having discarded the idea of a gigantic glider, which was difficult to use more than once, the Luftwaffe was glad to operate 198 Me 323s, each with six French-supplied engines. These were among the largest aircraft of World War II.

General Aircraft Hotspur was on test, a wooden eight-seater later used in large numbers for training. By far the most important RAF glider was the Airspeed Horsa, also made of wood, which had a tubular fuselage seating up to 25 troops. It could also carry Jeeps and similar loads, accessed by hinging open the two-seat nose cockpit or removing the tail. Horsa production totalled 3,656. Equally successful was the huge General Aircraft Hamilcar. Like the Horsa, this was made of wood and had a sideways-opening nose. Two pilots occupied tandem cockpits above the cavernous hold, which

could carry 17,500 lb (7,938 kg) of cargo, including a Tetrarch or Locust light tank.

AMERICAN TRANSPORTS

The most numerous of all the Allied gliders was the CG-4A, called Haig by the USAAF and Hadrian by the RAF. This was designed by Waco, but no fewer than 13,906 were built by 16 contractors. Made of welded steel tubing with fabric covering, the CG-4A seated a crew of two in a nose which hinged upwards to permit Jeeps or other bulky cargo to emerge. As a troop carrier the maximum load was 13. Waco also produced 427 CG-15As, and smaller numbers of the 42-seat CG-13A, but these were too late to see action.

Though the RAF operated a motley collection of British transports, such as the York, Albemarle, Warwick, Buckingham, Wellington, Whitley and versions of the four-engined Stirling and Halifax, the standard transport of the Allies was the Douglas DC-3. Powered by 1,200-hp Pratt & Whitney Twin Wasp engines, this usually seated 28 troops and could be equipped to tow gliders. The USAAF called it the C-47 Skytrain or C-53 Skytrooper, while British forces called it the Dakota. Production totalled 10,926.

First flown in February 1942, the four-engined Douglas DC-4 was initially produced for the USAAF as the C-54 Skymaster and for the Navy as the R5D, in most cases seating 50 troops. Wartime contracts covered 1,163 aircraft, most of which served until about 1960. Large numbers were also delivered of the Consolidated C-87 and Navy RY-3, both transport versions of the B-24 bomber, some being used to carry fuel to China. Within the United States Army and Navy versions of the 18-seat Lockheed Lodestar served in large numbers, many being used to train glider-tug pilots.

Significant numbers of marine aircraft also operated in the transport role, notably including the Short Sunderland and C-class flying boat, and the American Consolidated Catalina and Martin PBM Mariner. Later versions of the Mariner could carry 40 passengers or 9,000 lb (4,082 kg) of cargo (see overleaf).

US Navy and Marines

Pearl Harbor found the US Navy and Marine Corps overstretched in both the Atlantic and (in what the C-in-C, Adm. Ernest J. King, decided was No 1 priority) the Pacific. German U-boats operated within sight of the brightly lit US east coast, sinking 307,059 tons of shipping in January 1942, the rate increasing to a horrifying 752,000 tons in May/June 1942. By this time the ships were marshalled in convoys, and Navy patrol squadrons were rapidly increasing in strength with deliveries of PB4Y Liberators, Lockheed Venturas, Consolidated Catalinas, Martin Mariners and blimps (small airships).

Despite desperate efforts, including the use of US Navy and RAF long-range Liberators to close what had been a mid-Atlantic gap where land-based aircraft could not previously reach, 'wolf packs' of U-boats took a heavy toll of Allied shipping throughout the North Atlantic until the spring of 1943. Production of U-Boats, especially of the Type VIIC, had greatly exceeded losses, while sinkings of Allied ships far outstripped the rate of new construction. Gradually the situation was reversed, and massive production of escorts, aircraft and CVEs (small escort carriers) sank U-boats at an increasing rate until in the first three weeks of May 1943 the total reached 41. On the 24th of that month the U-boats were ordered back to port, or to the supposedly less dangerous South Atlantic.

The CVEs played a crucial role. With a displacement of 13,000–14,000 tons, by mid-1944 US yards had built 51 on the basis of merchant hulls and a further 50 built as carriers from the keel up. Each typically accommodated 20 aircraft, such as a squadron of Grumman FM-2 Wildcat fighters and one of Grumman TBM Avenger torpedo bombers.

CARRIERS SUPREME

The giant Fleet Carriers (CVs) operated mainly in the Pacific. On 7 December 1941 it was sheer chance that the pre-war *Ranger*, *Lexington*, *Saratoga* and *Enterprise* were not caught in Pearl Harbor. In 1940 the Navy had ordered an unprecedented 11 CVs of the 27,000-ton *Essex* class, each accommodating 80 aircraft, and a further 13 were ordered in 1942. Of these, ten were in commission by late 1944, with the rest joining fast. Together with Navy submarines, they almost wiped out the Japanese fleets.

The F4F and TBF bore the brunt of action in 1942, together with the Douglas SBD Dauntless dive bomber, which sank more Japanese tonnage than any other US weapon. In 1940 Chance Vought had flown the prototype XF4U Corsair, powered by a 2,000-hp Double Wasp engine, which, despite its size and carrier equipment, was the first fighter ever to exceed 400 mph (644 km/h). After prolonged development, this

distinctive fighter-bomber entered service with the Marines at Bougainville in February 1943, proving itself a great ground-attack aircraft and the master of all Japanese opponents. On 1 June 1943 it entered service with British FAA squadrons, later going aboard RN escort carriers, but the US Navy did not operate it from carriers until April 1944. Production continued after the war.

Grumman followed the F4F/FM-2 with the F6F Hellcat. Unlike the F4U, this was developed swiftly, and no fewer than 12,275 were delivered in 1943–45. By August 1943 the F6F was operating from Navy carriers, and by VJ-Day (p.99) these pugnacious fighters had claimed 5,156 Japanese aircraft destroyed in the air, almost three-quarters of the Navy/Marines total. Like some F4U versions, the F6F-3N and –3E were fitted with radar, with the dish antenna in a pod on the starboard (right) wing. These were the first naval night fighters.

To replace the SBD the Navy bought the Curtiss SB2C Helldiver. On paper it was far superior, the SB2C having a 1,900-hp engine and a 2,000-lb (907-kg) bombload, half carried internally. Development was difficult and even after it entered service most pilots disliked the aircraft, saying the designation stood for 'son of a bitch 2nd class', but from its combat debut over Rabaul in November 1943 the 7,200 Helldivers fought

Right: Navy seaplane tenders had no difficulty in hoisting the Martin PBM-3 Mariner, a load of up to 30 tons. These fine machines carried their bombs and torpedoes in the nacelles behind the 1,900-hp Cyclone 14 engines. The large box above the cockpit housed radar.

in every major action in the Pacific. The Army bought 900, most of which were transferred to the Marines.

In 1941, when most fighters had an engine of 1,000 hp, the Navy ordered the Grumman F7F Tigercat, which had two Double Wasps of 2,400 hp each! Though equipped for carrier operation, most F7Fs operated from Marine airfields. Some had the devastating armament of four 20-mm (0.78-in) and four 12.7-mm (0.5-in) guns, rockets, 1,000-lb (454-kg) bombs or a torpedo, while others had radar for night fighting. At the other end of the scale came the agile Grumman F8F Bearcat, with a single Double Wasp and just four 12.7-mm (0.5-in) guns.

SPECIFICATIONS

Douglas SBD-3 Dauntless

Type: two-seat carrier-based scout bomber and dive-bomber

Powerplant: one 1,000-hp (746-kW) Wright R-1820-52 Cyclone air-cooled radial piston engine

Performance: maximum speed 256 mph (412 km/h) at 16,000 ft (4875 m); initial climb rate 1,080 ft (329 m) per minute; service ceiling 27,260 ft (8310 m); maximum range 1,305 miles (2205 km)

Weights: empty 5,652 lb (2564 kg); maximum take-off 10,360 lb (4699 kg)

Dimensions: wing span 41 ft 6.5 in (12.66 m); length 32 ft 1.25 in (9.79 m); height 13 ft 7 in (4.14 m); wing area 325 sq ft (30.20 m²)

Armament: two fixed forward-firing synchronized 0.5-in (12.7-mm) machine-guns in the nose and two rearward firing belt-fed 0.30-in (7.62-mm) machine-guns in the rear crewman's position, plus up to 1,600 lb (726 kg) of bombs under the fuselage and 650 lb (295 kg) of bombs under the wings

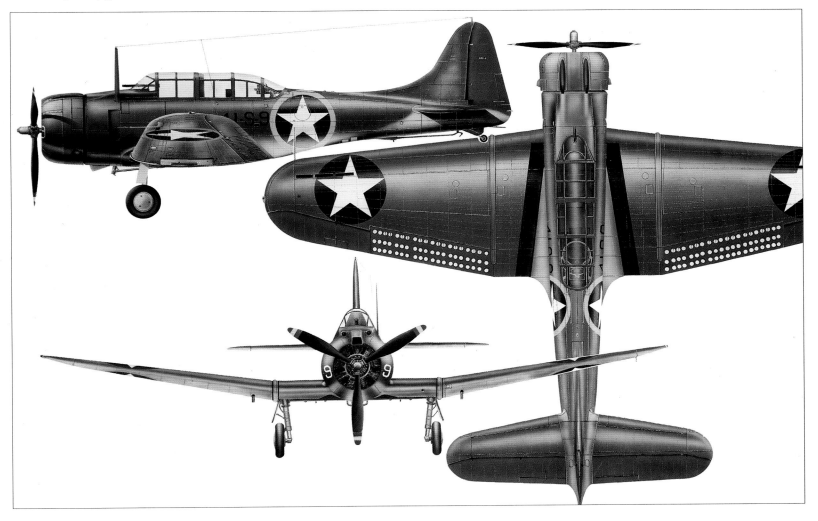

RAF Bomber Command

Several of the RAF's early leaders were convinced that, though to win a war an enemy country must be occupied, the victory could be brought about solely by strategic bombing. Once the menace of Nazi Germany had reluctantly been accepted, after 1936 more money was spent on Bomber Command than on any other single branch of the armed forces.

On 3 September 1939 this command went to war with what appeared to be formidable aircraft. The fabric-covered biplanes, such as the Heyford and Hind, had only recently been replaced by stressed-skin monoplanes capable of speeds from 220 to 280 mph (354–451 km/h). In ascending order of size came the Fairey Battle (1,030-hp Merlin), Bristol Blenheim (two 920-hp Mercury), Hampden (two 1,000-hp Pegasus), Wellington (two 1,000-hp Pegasus) and Whitley (two 1,145-hp Merlin). The last two were defended by guns in power-driven turrets at nose and tail.

The Air Staff appeared to have given little thought to imagining what might happen in a real war. They learned the hard way. On 18 December 1939 a formation of 24 Wellingtons, then considered the RAF's most formidable bomber, made a pointless 'reconnaissance in force' off the German coast. They were intercepted by Bf 109s and 110s, and within a few minutes ten had been shot down, and almost all the rest badly damaged. Bomber Command was forced to learn to operate by night.

At first, night raids were a farce. On 19 March 1940, 50 bombers took off to attack the seaplane base on Sylt, a distinctive island in the North Sea. On return, nine crews said they could not find the island, while 41 said they had bombed the target, but subsequent reconnaissance showed that not one bomb had even hit the island at all. One bomber captain frankly admitted 'We were lost as soon as we left the airfield'.

FIRST OF THE HEAVIES

By 1937 the RAF was ordering far more formidable four-engined bombers. The greatest was expected to be the Short Stirling, powered

by 1,650-hp Bristol Hercules sleeve-valve engines. Entering service from August 1940, it was a great aircraft marred by the fact that its span was restricted to 99 ft (30.18 m) in order to enter RAF hangars and this meant that it found it difficult to climb higher than 16,000 ft (4,877 m). This made the Stirling vulnerable, despite its outstanding manoeuvrability for so large an aircraft.

Above: Most impressive of all the RAF bombers, the Short Stirling was loved by its crews, who (if they survived) found the Lancaster harsh and austere by comparison. This Stirling is awaiting a train of incendiaries.

Opposite top: Unlike most Lancasters the Mk II had Bristol Hercules sleeve-valve radial engines. Note the long exhaust pipes which prevented flames being visible to enemy night fighters. Camouflaged green/grey on top. The sides and underside of all RAF heavies were painted a non-reflected black.

Above: To the astonishment of the Air Staff, who scorned the idea of an unarmed bomber, the outstanding performance of the twin-Merlin de Havilland Mosquito enabled it to survive with no defensive gun turrets. Made of wood, it was developed to carry a 4,000-lb (1,814-kg) bomb, and many of the 7,781 built were radar-equipped night fighters, or long-range reconnaissance aircraft. There were versions with heavy cannon, and a naval variant with a torpedo.

Two more 'heavies' entered service in November 1940. The Handley Page Halifax was powered by four Rolls-Royce Merlin engines and, unlike the Stirling, could carry the large bombs of 4,000, 8,000 and 12,000 lb (1,814, 3,629 and 5,443 kg) which were used from 1942. Though adequate from the start, the Halifax kept being improved, and its square-tipped wing of 98 ft 10 in (30.14 m) span was replaced by a round-tipped one of 104 ft (31.7 m), with four Hercules engines, a redesigned tail, and better defences with a single hand-aimed gun in the nose but Boulton Paul four-gun turrets in the dorsal and tail positions. Including ocean-patrol and transport versions 6,176 Halifaxes were delivered.

The other newcomer was the Avro Manchester. To the Air Ministry's surprise this proved to be quicker and cheaper to build, easier to maintain and in almost every way superior to the other heavy bombers. Its weakness was that it had two 1,845-hp Rolls-Royce Vulture engines, which were unreliable. Avro quickly redesigned the wing, extending the span from 90 ft (27.43 m) to 102 ft (31.1 m) and fitting four Merlin engines. The result was a heavy bomber so good

the RAF wished to cancel the others. Eventually Lancasters carried the 22,000-lb (9,979-kg) Grand Slam 'earthquake' bomb, and the 'Upkeep' spinning mines used against the German dams. Lancaster production totalled 7,377.

Thus, Bomber Command grew to be a mighty armada, but this would have meant nothing without the ability to find targets. The answer lay in electronics. By March 1942 every 'heavy' was equipped with Gee, a receiver which picked up synchronized signals from four stations in south-east England. Shortly afterwards an élite Pathfinder Force was created, with especially skilled crews, to mark targets with distinctive pyrotechnics. Pathfinders had Oboe, a UK-based aid which was so accurate that a target could be marked on a cloudy night with accuracy measured in metres.

Not least, most 'heavies' had H_2S, a mapping radar which painted a picture of the terrain below. This occupied the place which in some bombers had been a downward-firing turret. Many hundreds of bombers were shot down by Luftwaffe night fighters with upward-firing cannon before the RAF realized that being defenceless underneath was suicidal.

The US Army 8th Air Force

Above: Created to the order of the British, the North American Mustang was eventually adopted by the USAAF, as the P-51 fighter and A-36 attack bomber. The Merlin-engined P-51D seen here proved to be a better long-range escort to bombers than any of the special long-range rivals. With a speed of 437 mph (703 km/h) and six 0.5-in guns it simply swept the opposition from the sky.

Though the US Navy looked mainly towards Japan, the Commanding General of the Army Air Force, Henry H. 'Hap' Arnold, thought the first task was to defeat Germany. In January 1942 the 8th Air Force was activated, with a mission to proceed to England and there build up a force of 60 combat groups with 3,500 aircraft – larger than the front-line strength of the RAF at that time. The primary purpose of the 8th was to operate heavy bombers on precision-attack missions against strategic targets throughout German-occupied Europe.

Most of the groups were to be equipped with the Boeing B-17 Fortress, the remainder operating the Consolidated B-24 Liberator. Both were powered by four 1,200-hp engines, the B-17 having the Wright R-1820 Cyclone and the B-24 the Pratt & Whitney R-1830 Twin Wasp.

Doctrine for their deployment had been worked out in the 1930s. Though unpressurized, the bombers would have turbosuper-charged engines in order to fly high, up to

25,000 ft (7620 m). They would attack in day-light. They would be heavily defended by mul-tiple guns of 0.5-in (12.7-mm) calibre (much longer-ranged and more destructive than the puny rifle-calibre guns used by RAF bombers) and would fly in formation to protect each other. Not least, they would use the newly per-fected Norden bombsight in order to hit indi-vidual buildings from five miles up.

Arrival of 'The Mighty Eighth' in England was a culture shock. Among other things, most of the white-starred bombers had a name and possibly artwork painted on the nose. On 17 September 1942 the first mission was mounted, by 12 B-17Es of the 97th Bomb Group, led by Col Frank Armstrong in *Butcher Shop*. The lead aircraft of the second flight, *Yankee Doodle*, car-ried the 8th's Commanding General, Ira C. Eaker. It was a textbook mission, and all 12 air-craft put bombs accurately on the marshalling yards at Rouen-Sotteville, just inland from the Channel coast.

Gradually the 8th built up strength. Soon it was penetrating Germany, encountering fierce opposition from every kind of Luftwaffe fighter. On occasion the losses were severe, such as the two attacks on the ball-bearing factories of Schweinfurt, beyond the range of escorting fighters. The second one, on 14 October 1943, involved a total of 288 B-17s of which 60 were shot down, 5 crashed on return, 12 were writ-ten off because of their degree of damage, and 121 others needed repairs. On the other hand, three vital factories had been heavily hit and 288 German fighters were claimed (a figure later amended to 188).

MORE GUNS, LESS PAINT

This was a low point. From then onwards, things got better. One major factor was that the defensive armament of the bombers was improved. The mass-produced B-17G, for example, eventually had 13 heavy Brownings pointing in all directions. As the invading armadas, trailing contrails, could be seen from afar there was no point in painting the bombers in the previous olive-drab colour, and this saved weight, drag and cost. Boeing built 4,035 of this

model, while Vega and Douglas added a further 2,250 and 2,395 respectively to bring the grand total of all B-17 versions to 12,731. Including spares, the grand total of all B-24 versions was 19,203 – the greatest of any US warplane – equipping 45 groups all over the world, but it was in a minority in the 8th AF.

An even greater reason for reduced bomber casualties was fighter escort. From the outset, the 8th's bombers were escorted, by Spitfires, Lockheed P-38 Lightnings and, especially, Republic P-47 Thunderbolts, but on the longest missions these had to turn back well short of the target. It all changed from December 1943 with the advent of the long-ranged North American P-51B Mustang, powered by a Packard-built Merlin. This was at last able to accompany the bombers on the longest missions. Range of the P-51D was even greater – all the way to Russia on occasion.

Even without escorts, the 0.5-in (12.7-mm) guns of the bombers had shot down so many Luftwaffe fighters and in doing so had killed so many of the experienced pilots, that opposition became progressively weaker. In the great battles over Germany in 1944 the defending fighters became desperate. Big Bf 110G and Ju 88G night fighters were pressed into use in the daytime, often with the same tired crews. The Bf 109s and Fw 190s backed up their cannon with large rockets fired at the bombers from underwing tubes, while others tried to scatter bomblets on the formations from above.

While they were doing this they were almost bound to find a P-51 on their tail. Hitler's No 2, and leader of the once-proud Luftwaffe, was Reichsmarschall Herman Goering. He said 'When I saw those Mustangs over Berlin I knew that the war was lost'.

Above: The majority of the 12,731 Boeing Fortress bombers were unpainted B-17Gs, which like earlier versions were powered by 1,200-hp Wright R-1820 Cyclone engines with turbosuperchargers to maintain power at high altitude. They bristled with 0.5-in (12.7-mm) guns.

Defence of the Reich

Partly because its leader was Goering, and partly because the Nazi party was building a 'Third Reich' untrammelled by tradition, the Luftwaffe was Germany's pre-eminent armed force. This contrasted with Britain, where the RAF was very much an also-ran in the social pecking-order and had had to fight for its very existence.

It was therefore taken for granted that the aircraft painted with black crosses and swastikas would sweep all before them, and their failure to defeat the RAF in the Battle of Britain was a profound shock. Worse was to come. The Nazi leaders failed to plan ahead and the principal aircraft with which it began the war were still in production at the end. Increasingly, shortages of fuel curtailed flying training and even kept front-line aircraft on the ground. Overall, the tasks asssigned to the Luftwaffe on the huge Eastern front, in the Mediterranean theatre and in the north-west against the UK, were increasingly incapable of fulfilment.

As originally organized in 1935, the Luftwaffe was to comprise mighty air fleets sweeping away opposition over enemy heartlands, to make life easier for the Panzers on the ground. The idea of having to defend the airspace over Germany was hardly considered; indeed, Goering proclaimed 'No enemy aircraft will ever cross the German frontier!'. At the same time, an enormous air-defence organization was put in place, with the newly invented radar and thousands of the best *flak* (anti-aircraft guns) in the world, in calibres of 20, 37, 88 and 105 mm (0.78, 1.47, 3.46 and 4.13 in).

Having been scorned as unsuitable (p.57), the Messerschmitt Bf 109 became virtually the standard German fighter. By 1942 the Bf 109G, popularly called the *Gustav*, and powered by a DB 605 engine of up to 2,000 hp, was available in large and increasing numbers. Despite heavy bombing, the numerous Bf 109 factories increased production until deliveries in 1944 alone amounted to about 14,000. The basic aircraft remained flawed in various respects, but continued to combine adequate performance and manoeuvrability with outstanding firepower from superb guns to keep it in the front line.

FORMIDABLE FOCKE-WULF

This massive Bf 109 production was despite the emergence just before the war of a fundamentally better aircraft, the Focke-Wulf Fw 190. Powered by the BMW 801 radial engine of (typically) 1,700 hp, this had no limitations whatsoever. By 1943 the 190, which like the 109 was smaller than most British or American fighters, was being burdened by an incredible variety of weapons for use against aircraft, ground targets and even large ships. One version carried a torpedo, and another a bomb of 3,968 lb (1,800 kg).

By 1942 great efforts were being made to increase the performance of the Fw 190 at high altitude. The eventual results were the Fw 190D-9, powered by the Junkers Jumo 213A liquid-cooled inverted-V-12 engine of 2,240 hp and the derived family of Focke-Wulf Ta 152 fighters with either the Jumo 213 or a DB 603. These represented a pinnacle of piston-engined fighter development, but they were too late.

Increasingly, all available fighters were brought back from the battlefronts to stem the tide of RAF and USAAF aircraft attacking the Reich itself. Among the 'last-ditch' weapons tested were the SG 113A, SG 116 and SG 117. The 113A had six 77-mm (3.03-in) barrels which fired sabot-type armour-piercing projectiles almost vertically downwards, triggered automatically by flying over the target. The 116 was similar but used six barrels from the MK 103 heavy gun, while the 117 comprised seven MK 108 gun barrels firing ahead, each with a single projectile.

The increasingly damaging raids by RAF Bomber Command took place at night. Though many 109s and 190s were used at night, the chief night fighters were the

Left: In spring 1945 Germany was a mass of bomb craters, dotted with wrecked aircraft. Here one of the last of some 35,000 Messerschmitt Bf 109s stands forlornly on its nose. It is probably a 109K, with Galland hood and wooden tail.

Messerschmitt Bf 110G and the Junkers Ju 88C and 88G. The Bf 110 had originally been intended as a *Zerstörer* (destroyer) for use by day, but fared badly in the Battle of Britain. As a radar-equipped night fighter both it and the Ju 88 were formidable, especially when fitted with so-called *Schräge Musik* (Jazz) cannon firing upwards into the unprotected bellies of the RAF bombers.

In April 1936, seven years after Frank Whittle (p.100), a German, H.P. von Ohain, invented a turbojet engine. Unlike Whittle, he received instant support. Aircraft manufacturer Ernst Heinkel at once began developing the engine, and the result was the first flight of a jet aircraft, the He 178, on 27 August 1939. By 1942 over 6,000 people were working on German turbojets and on jet and rocket aircraft, as explained overleaf.

SPECIFICATIONS

Focke-Wulf Fw 190D-9

Type: single-seat fighter

Powerplant: one Junkers Jumo 213A-1 12-cylinder inverted-V piston engine developing 2242 hp (1670 kW) at sea level with MW 50 methanol boosting

Performance: maximum speed 426 mph (686 km/h) at 21,654 ft (6600 m), 357 mph (575 km/h) at sea level; climb to 6560 ft (2000 m) in 2.1 minutes; maximum range on internal fuel 520 miles (837 km)

Weights: empty 7694 lb (3490 kg); maximum take-off 10,670 lb (4840 kg)

Dimensions: wing span 34 ft 5 in (10.50 m); length 33 ft 5 in (10.19 m); height 11 ft 0.25 in (3.36 m); wing area 197 sq ft (18.30 m²)

Armament: two wing-mounted 0.78-in (20-mm) MG 151 cannon with 250 rounds per gun, two 0.5-in (12.7-mm) MG 131 machine-guns with 475 rounds per gun above the engine; ETC 504 fuselage rack for one 1102-lb (500-kg) SC 500 bomb

Twilight of the Gods

Above: Powered by Jumo 004B turbojets, the Messerschmitt Me 262 was an outstanding design, in most respects dramatically superior to the rival Gloster Meteor. This was especially the case in terms of aerodynamics, fuel capacity and armament.

Various factors combined to promote the development in Nazi Germany of terrifying new weapons. One was the maniacal vision and drive of the *Führer* (leader), Adolf Hitler. Another was the absence of stultifying tradition and the fact that the resurgent armed forces were built up not to police an empire but to conquer Germany's neighbours. Another was the Versailles Treaty of 1919, which by prohibiting German development of heavy artillery prompted what became the A4 (the so-called V2), the first long-range rocket.

Another radical development was the jet engine. Unlike his English predecessor, von Ohain's proposed turbojet was instantly taken up by German industry. Despite petty jealousies and other problems, by 1941 the development of gas-turbine aero engines – turboprops and turbofans as well as turbojets – had become a mighty effort, involving 50 times the number of people working on such engines in Britain. The pioneer firm, Heinkel, teamed with the Hirth engine company but never got a turbojet into production. Neither did Daimler-Benz, and the leaders emerged as Junkers and BMW.

Both worked on slim turbojets with multistage axial compressors. Frantic development

brought them to the point where in 1944 they could be put into production in vast underground plants worked mainly by thousands of prisoners held in concentration camps. Between March 1944 and the German defeat in May 1945 about 6,000 Jumo 004B turbojets were delivered. Rated at 1,984 lb (900 kg) thrust at sea level, this engine powered many prototypes, as well as two important aircraft which reached the Luftwaffe. The rival BMW 003A was fractionally smaller, and rated at 1,764 lb (800 kg). Compared with contemporary British engines these turbojets were similar in power, in some ways more advanced in design and significantly quicker and cheaper to make, but they were heavier and had nothing remotely like the long life and reliability of the British engines.

OUTSTANDING JET

By far the most important German jet aircraft was the Messerschmitt Me 262. Powered by two Jumo 004B engines slung under the thin wings (which for reasons of longitudinal balance were slightly swept back), this fighter had outstanding performance, sweet flying qualities (much better than the Bf 109) and the devastating armament of four 30-mm (1.18-in) MK 108 cannon. It was first delivered to a test unit (EKdo 262) in April 1944, but did not reach a true front-line unit (*Kommando Nowotny*) until 3 October. Britain's Meteor reached a regular unit (No 616 Sqn) on 12 July. The difference was that, while Britain built a mere handful of wartime Meteors, Me 262 deliveries reached 1,433, some being radar-equipped two-seat night fighters. Hitler's demand that it should be used as a bomber made little difference to the timing or numbers, but did give the Allies problems trying to defend vital targets, such as the Remagen bridge over the Rhine. However, by the time 262s were available in numbers the Luftwaffe was crippled by bombed airfields and shortage of fuel. The other 004B-engined aircraft was the Arado Ar 234B. Designed as a high-flying bomber, it served mainly in an unarmed reconnaissance role but it could carry up to 3,307 lb (1,500 kg) of bombs externally. A developed version had two MG 151/20 cannon firing *to the rear*.

The BMW 003A likewise was produced on a huge scale, but the only production application was the Heinkel He 162. Officially named *Salamander* but popularly called the *Volksjäger* (people's fighter), this was a 'last-ditch' effort designed and built with incredible rapidity. The requirement was issued on 8 September 1944, the first example flew on 6 December and the first was delivered on 20 January 1945, by which time factories were planning to build 4,000 per month to be flown by hastily trained Hitler Youth. Amazingly, by late April over 300 had been produced, with over 800 more on assembly lines.

One other 'jet-propelled' type got into service. In 1937 the Helmut Walter Werke was developing rocket engines fed with *T-stoff* (concentrated hydrogen peroxide) and *C-stoff* (a mix of hydrazine and alcohol). A year later Alex Lippisch began designing a tailless rocket aircraft, and the eventual result was the first flight of the Me 163B *Komet* in August 1943. Armed, like early versions of He 162, with two 30-mm (1.8-in) guns, this tailless machine was designed to take off from a trolley, climb steeply with unprecedented speed to intercept Allied bombers and finally glide back to land on a skid. Though almost impossible for the Allies to counter, the *Komet* killed as many of its own pilots as it did of the enemy, either in explosions or by being dissolved alive by leaking propellants.

Left: More like a missile than a fighter, the all-wood Bachem Ba 349 was fired almost vertically up a ramp to intercept Allied bombers. Its rocket engine gave it a speed of 621 mph (1,000 km/h). After firing the battery of 24 or 33 rockets from the nose, the pilot was to bale out, the valuable rocket engine also being recovered by parachute.

Above: More conventional was the Dornier Do 335 *Pfeil* (Arrow). Produced in various versions, including a radar-equipped night fighter, its unusual feature was that inside the fuselage were two 1,900-hp DB603 engines, driving propellers at both the nose and the tail. Maximum speed of the fastest version was 474 mph (763 km/h).

Sunset

The conquests of Japan in the first half of 1942 covered a geographical area greater than that of any previous campaign in history. The Allies, of which by far the most important in the Pacific theatre were the United States and Australia, were now faced with the task of retaking one island after another, until an invasion could be mounted against the islands of Japan itself. The prospect was daunting.

In a totally different kind of war, Indian, British, Ghurka and various other troops were engaged in a bitter struggle in the jungles of Burma, while large armies in China were supplied by air by C-47s, C-46s and C-87s flying over 'The Hump' of the Himalayas. The main cargo was fuel and by 1944 a huge effort had been mounted to bomb Japan. The only aircraft able to do this was the Boeing B-29 Superfortress. First flown on 21 September 1942, it combined more new technology than any other aircraft. It was powered by four 2,200-hp Wright R-3350 engines, each with two large turbosuperchargers and driving a four-blade propeller of 16 ft 7 in (5.06 m) diameter. The tubular fuselage housed the crew of 10–14 in pressurized compartments. The gunners sighted through transparent domes and operated controls which aimed a 20-mm (0.78-in) cannon and 12 0.78-mm (0.5-in) guns in remote powered barbettes and a tail turret. The wings bore the unprecedented loading of 77.6 lb/sq ft (35 kg/0.30 m^2) – more than double that of a B-17 – and had skins thicker than any previously used. A proportion were fitted with H2X, APQ-7 or APQ-13 radar. The intention was that the B-29 should fly at over 30,000 ft (9,144 m) to targets 2,000 miles (3200 km) away.

Over 700,000 coolies toiled to build a complex of large Chinese bases, mainly around Chengtu. From here operations against Japan began on 15 June 1944, and built up steadily. Meanwhile, in a series of bloody assaults, Allied forces retook the Philippines, Marianas and other islands. On 25 October 1944 a Task Force off Leyte in the Philippines was attacked by A6M5 fighters which, each carrying a 551-lb

(250-kg) armour-piercing bomb, dived on the ships almost vertically and crashed into them. It was the start of a terrifying campaign of *kamikaze* (suicide) attacks, which destroyed many Allied ships.

SUPERFORT BASES

By early 1945 the rapidly growing Allied forces were engaged in a bitter and costly struggle to take the islands of Iwo Jima and Okinawa, the last before Japan. At Okinawa the Allies lost 763 aircraft and 48,025 troops, but the cost to the Japanese was far greater. Meanwhile, the B-29 raids, now only from bases in the Marianas, laid waste one Japanese city after another. One raid alone, with incendiary bombs against Tokyo, killed 83,793 people, more than any other single bombing raid in history.

Frantic efforts were made to defend Japan. Even the obsolete Ki-27 (p.74) was resurrected as a fighter and as a bomb-carrying *kamikaze*

aircraft. In contrast, the much-bombed factories produced prototypes of the Mitsubishi Ki-83 fighter with two 2,200-hp engines, the Ki-109 with a 75-mm gun, and the A7M with a 2,250-hp turbocharged engine, the Yokosuka R2Y with a six-blade propeller driven by a twin-engine unit of 3,400 hp, the Kyushu J7W with a six-blade pusher propeller behind the tail driven by a 2,130-hp engine, and the Nakajima *Kikka* (Orange blossom) twin-jet inspired by the German Me 262.

The Nakajima company even designed a simplified aircraft specifically for *kamikaze* attacks. The Ki-115 *Tsurugi* (Sabre) was a small fighter-like machine powered by a 1,150-hp engine. It had an open cockpit, there was no need for defensive armament, the landing gear was made of steel tube with no shock absorbers and was jettisoned after take off and, as the Ki-115 was not going to make a normal landing, the wing was quite small. This never got into

Left: One of many kinds of outstanding Japanese fighter in production in 1945 was the Kawanishi N1K2-J, called 'George' by the Allies (its real name was *Shiden*, violet lightning). A 2,000-hp engine gave a speed of about 365 mph (587 km/h) and in the wings were four 20-mm (0.78-in) guns.

action, but a potentially much more formidable *kamikaze* aircraft did.

The Yokosuka MXY-7 *Ohka* (Cherry Blossom) comprised a tubular fuselage with a tiny wing and twin-fin tail. In the nose was a warhead weighing from 1,323 lb (600 kg) to 2,646 lb (1,200 kg). At the back was the enclosed cockpit and in the tail were three rocket engines. Between September 1944 and March 1945 755 of these manned missiles were built. Carried by Mitsubishi G4M2 bombers near to Allied ships, the MXY-7 was released to dive on its target at 575 mph (925 km/h). Other versions had turbojet engines for longer range and some were fired from submarines. It was all to no avail.

A Uranium-235 atom bomb was dropped on Hiroshima on 6 August 1945 and a Plutonium-239 bomb exploded over Nagasaki three days later. On 15 August the Japanese Emperor Hirohito surrendered. The greatest of all wars was at last over.

SPECIFICATIONS

Boeing B-29A Superfortress

Type: long-range strategic bomber/reconnaissance aircraft

Powerplant: four 2,200-hp (1641-kW) Wright R-3350-Cyclone 18 turbocharged piston engines

Performance: maximum speed 358 mph (576 km/h); cruising speed 230 mph (370 km/h); service ceiling 31,850 ft (9710 m); range 3250 miles (5230 km)

Weights: empty 70,140 lb (31,815 kg); maximum take-off 124,000 lb (56,245 kg)

Dimensions: wing span 141 ft 3 in (43.05 m); length 99 ft (30.18 m); height 29 ft 7 in (9.02 m); wing area 1736 sq ft (161.27 m²)

Armament: four remote-controlled power-operated turrets each housing two or four 0.5-in (12.7-mm) machine-guns, and one tail turret containing three 0.5-in (12.7-mm) machine-guns or two 0.5-in (12.7-mm) machine-guns and one 0.78-in (20-mm) cannon, plus a bombload of up to 9072 kg (20,000 lb)

5 THE JET AGE

New Propulsion

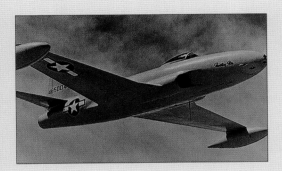

Above: The 13th production Lockheed P-80A Shooting Star. Later redesignated F-80, this was the first American jet fighter to enter service, in 1946.

Left: The last RAF aircraft flown by the author was a de Havilland Vampire F.1, similar to these of 247 sqn, which was the first to receive these distinctive aircraft. The parent firm had no spare capacity, and all the first batches were made by English Electric.

Many sea creatures use jet propulsion. Even the man-made kind goes back 2,000 years. Before 1200 the Chinese were making rockets, and rocket-propelled manned aircraft have flown since June 1928. In 1933 F.A. Tsander's OR-2, a rocket engine running on liquid oxygen and kerosene, began testing at the GIRD (group for studying reaction engines) in Moscow. Subsequently a wealth of rocket aircraft flew in the Soviet Union, and the BI-1 fighter designed by Berezniak and Isayev, even got into limited production in 1941.

The German Me 163 was followed by projected improved versions, and German teams also worked on ramjets. These were originally just carefully profiled tubes. Air entered at the forward-facing inlet, was slowed in the expanding interior, mixed with fuel and ignited and violently accelerated out of the nozzle at the rear. The greatest ramjet worker was France's René Leduc, who created aircraft whose ramjet duct actually formed the fuselage. His later versions were almost supersonic fighters, but work was abandoned in 1958.

In 1944 the US Army Air Force and NACA (National Advisory Committee for Aeronautics) decided to order a piloted aircraft to fly faster than sound. The result was the Bell XS-1, which achieved this objective on 14 October 1947, and led to improved X-1 versions which exceeded Mach 2 (twice the speed of sound). In a rival programme the Navy also exceeded Mach 2 with the Douglas D-558-II Skyrocket. The knowledge and confidence gained by 1959 led to the North American X-15, which in the 1960s reached Mach 6.71 (4,534 mph, 7,297 km/h) and an altitude of 354,200 ft (107,960 m).

ROCKETS VERSUS JET ENGINES

Rockets have often been used to boost the speed or altitude of aircraft for brief periods, or to assist them to take off, but since 1945 not one rocket aircraft has got into military service. On the other hand, what are loosely called 'jet engines' have totally transformed aviation, starting with fighters and progressing to large civil airliners.

Frank Whittle, the inventor, failed for seven years to get anyone to show interest. He was told

officially that he was wasting his time, but in 1936 he and some friends scraped together just enough money to make an engine. After slight damage to his prototype in March 1937, Whittle at last completed a test run, on 12 April 1937. Instead of this being the start of high-priority development of British turbojets, Whittle still had to fight every inch of the way.

Though an aeroplane was ordered to fly Whittle's engine – the Gloster E.28/39 flew on 15 May 1941 – nothing would have happened quickly had not the commanding general of the US Army Air Force heard about Whittle's engine. To say the situation changed is an understatement. The US General Electric Co. was told to make Whittle's engine, and soon hundreds were pouring off the production lines. By the end of the war there were 13 British jet aircraft of three types, while in the USA there were nearly 100 examples of six types. In Germany there were over 2,500 of 13 types.

It is thus all the stranger that the first jet aircraft to enter regular front-line service was the British Gloster Meteor I, with No 616 Squadron RAF, on 12 July 1944. On 4 August one of the squadron's aircraft downed a V1 flying bomb in the first jet-v-jet engagement (the Meteor's four 20-mm (0.78-in) guns failed to fire, and F/O Dean courageously tipped the bomb over with his wingtip). The pioneer US jet, the Bell P-59 Airacomet, had flown in October 1942, but this was used for training and research.

Powered by a de Havilland version of Whittle's engine, the prototype D.H. Vampire flew in September 1943. This neat aircraft carried its tail on twin booms in order to give the single engine a short jetpipe. Three months later de Havilland generously took the engine out of their second Vampire so that it could be sent to Lockheed in California. Here it powered the XP-80 Shooting Star on 8 January 1944.

The existence of Allied jets was disclosed on that day. Stalin angrily asked his own designers why they had not produced such aircraft (though Arkhip M. Lyulka had been working on turbojet engines since 1936). The first, using German engines, were the MiG-9 and Yak-15, first flown on the same day, 24 April 1946.

Aircraft Construction

The German Junkers company was a pioneer of all-metal construction, using Duralumin, a range of strong and light alloys of aluminium, copper and other elements. Until 1935 Junkers skinned his aircraft in corrugated sheet, for inherent rigidity and resistance to damage, but eventually it was accepted that smooth skins reduced aerodynamic drag and enabled aircraft to fly faster. For the same reason, like other manufacturers, Junkers replaced rivets with projecting heads by so-called flush rivets in countersunk holes, to maintain a smooth external surface.

The most famous corrugated-skin Junkers aircraft, the Ju 52/3m, was the forerunner of the Ju 252 with a smooth skin. In turn, by 1943 this gave way to the Ju 352, which at first glance looked similar but was a totally redesigned aircraft. To conserve strategic materials (ones in short supply), this had a wing made of wood. The nose was similar to that of the 252, but immediately behind the cockpit it was joined to a main cabin made of welded steel tubing, with the rounded section preserved by wooden formers on which fabric skin was stretched. Many other German aircraft were redesigned to reduce consumption of light alloys. For example, later versions of the Bf 109 fighter had the tail section made of wood.

One of the most versatile aircraft ever built, the de Havilland Mosquito, was made entirely of wood. Powered by two Merlin engines, it was conceived in 1939 as a bomber or reconnaissance aircraft with such a high performance that it did not need defensive armament. The Air Ministry thought such a concept ridiculous and by this time de Havilland had experience of Duralumin stressed-skin construction, but they stuck to their beliefs and eventually 7,781 Mosquitos were delivered for almost every military and civil task. Much of the structure was a sandwich of low-density balsa between inner and outer skins of spruce plywood. Similar construction was successfully used for the nacelles of Vampires and Venoms flying at over 650 mph (1,050 km/h).

WOOD AND ALLOYS

In the Soviet Union progress was in the reverse direction. Though *Kolchug* (Dural) was used from 1923 in Tupolev aircraft, the high-speed

Left: Between the World Wars Britain's RAF had little interest in advancing technology. This Wapiti, a type still in use in 1939, had an airframe virtually identical with the 1917-designed D.H.4, but with wooden parts redesigned in aluminium. Likewise, the Jupiter engine had been designed in 1917, and most of the weapons date from even earlier.

Above: The fuselage of the all-wood de Havilland Mosquito was made in left and right halves. This is the front end of a fighter version. Note the enormous cutout for the wing, which was made in one piece. Under the wing would be constructed the bomb bay, ahead of which in, this aircraft, would be four cannon.

fighters of Yakovlev and Lavochkin originally had complex structures made almost entirely of advanced forms of wood, with multiple layers of veneer formed to three-dimensional shape and bonded with special adhesives. By 1943, as light alloys became more plentiful (partly because of supplies from the USA) the proportion of such metals in the structure increased, until in the jet era wood had almost ceased to be used.

Occasionally aircraft have had unusual structures. The most numerous British twin-engined bomber, the Vickers Wellington, featured geodetic construction. This was a kind of light-alloy basketwork made from thousands of small tubes, brackets and connectors, with an overall covering of fabric. It proved capable of surviving incredible battle damage. A few aircraft have also had airframes made from magnesium alloy or stainless steel.

By 1945 giant machine tools were coming into use to cut away parts of large forgings or heavy plate to sculpture complex shapes. The next stage was so-called integral construction, in which large and heavily stressed panels were first produced as massive forged slabs. About 90 per cent of the metal was then machined

away to leave a skin of modest thickness reinforced by an interior array of ribs and stringers which in earlier aircraft would have been made separately and attached by riveting or adhesive bonding.

Integral construction, today machined under computer control, can save weight and cost, and give a perfectly smooth exterior. On the other hand, if a small crack were to appear and then gradually grow by fatigue, it could eventually break the entire part. Modern airframes are designed to arrest cracks, to make it impossible for a crack to be hidden from view and to bear flight loads until the part can be repaired.

Use of airborne radar forced radomes and coverings over other antennas to be made from dielectric (insulating) materials, notably resin-bonded glassfibre. In turn this led to various kinds of composite construction, of which by far the most important today are based on fibres of carbon or graphite. Sometimes the fibres are bonded into sheets or plies of various thicknesses, which in turn are assembled into dies and bonded to form the structure. Alternatively the structure can be fabricated rather like a spider making a web, by winding a filament on to a mandrel or other former of the correct shape.

The Berlin Airlift

Above: A famous photograph showing young Berliners watching traffic at Gatow. This arrival is a Douglas C-54M Skymaster, one of 319 C-54s committed to 'Vittles'.

The Soviet Union suffered far more than any other country at the hands of Nazi Germany, and also did more than any other to defeat the invader. After the war, Germany was divided into zones, each policed by one of the Allies. In the north-east was the former capital, Berlin. Though devastated, this city was still home to over 2,100,000 people. It was itself divided into different Allied Sectors and despite being deep in the heart of the Soviet Zone, the Western Allies were able to use road and rail routes to supply their garrisons.

Stalin was determined that Germany would never again be a menace, and he distrusted the other Allies. He decided to drive them out of Berlin, and ordered his troops to harass their traffic. US General Lucius D. Clay said he would push trains through by force, but President Truman said, 'Fire only if you are fired upon'. Allied aircraft flying on lawful business along designated corridors to Berlin were 'buzzed' by aggressive Soviet fighters. On 5 April 1948 a Yak-3 sliced the wing off a Viking of British European Airways. Moscow said their innocent fighter had been 'brutally rammed by the Viking'!

By mid-June canal traffic had ceased, few trains could run and just a single road was left (with a hand-operated ferry across the Elbe). On 18 June 1948 replacement of the inflated Reichsmark by the Deutschmark was seized upon by the Russians as the excuse for a blockade. This stopped the 13,500 tons that had previously been supplied each day.

There was no way such a tonnage could be flown in, but there was no alternative to an airlift. The USAF called this Operation Vittles, and the RAF Plainfare (a pun). The planned start date was 26 June, but four days earlier 25 USAF C-47s began flying in cargo from Rhein-Main and Wiesbaden. On 28 June the RAF began operations with Dakotas from Wunstorf. Aircraft on the airlift were required to fly to Berlin along one of three corridors, one from Frankfurt in the US zone and two, from Hanover and Hamburg, in the British zone. Each was 20 miles (32 km) wide and extended up to a height of 10,000 ft (3,048 m).

VITTLES AND PLAINFARE

Radio beacons were installed on the ground, while frantic preparations were made to improve airfields, relocate the squadrons previously based there, and install all-weather navigation aids, enhanced control towers and maintenance facilities, emergency lighting and accommodation (initially tents) for greatly increased numbers of personnel. Progressively better arrangements were made for handling every kind of cargo, and also whenever possible to evacuate Berliners, mostly women and children, on the return flights.

The main American airfield in Berlin was Tempelhof, the original city airport. This had three parallel runways, and could sustain a movement (flight) every 90 seconds. Aircraft flew in along the corridor from Frankfurt but returned via the middle corridor to Hanover, then turning south. Soon the C-47s were

joined and eventually replaced by 200 more capable C-54 (DC-4) Skymasters. To enable them to carry their full 18,000 lb (8,165 kg) of coal sacks or fuel drums, 50 C-54s were moved to Fassburg in the British sector. The RAF also brought in four-engined aircraft, at first 40 Avro Yorks and two squadrons of Short Sunderlands which linked Hamburg Finkenwerder with Berlin's Havel See. Their corrosion-proof Alclad hulls enabled them to carry salt. When their bases froze, the vitally needed salt was brought in containers slung externally under the RAF's new Handley Page Hastings, which carried the same payload as the C-54. Later in the airlift new types included the Fairchild C-82 and the huge Douglas C-74 Globemaster.

Gradually the monthly total built up. Threat of RAF/USAF fighter escort kept the Soviet Yaks and Lavochkins from being too dangerously aggressive, but inevitably in so intense an operation there were casualties. From 4 August civil transports joined in, most of them being British-registered converted bombers such as the Halton, Lancastrian and Liberator, with a few Tudors. Further big contributions were made by the US Navy, and by the air forces of Australia, South Africa and New Zealand.

Despite bad weather, the highest monthly total of 171,960 tons was achieved in January 1949, while the peak day was 16 April with an amazing 12,940 tons in 1,344 sorties. After 318 days the Russians backed down, and removed the barricades at midnight on 11–12 May. To build up reserves the Berlin airlift continued, tapering off to stop on 30 September 1949. The total tonnage was 2,325,808.7, carried in 277,685 sorties. A Russian told the author 'We never thought we would be the ones to back down'.

Above: Virtually a Lancaster with a new fuselage and third fin, the Avro York was an effective lash-up which did at least give the RAF a British airlifter. It was joined by the Hastings, likewise a traditional tailwheel design.

Strategic Air Command

Left: The addition of two pairs of General Electric J47 turbojets under the outer wings gave later B-36 bombers more speed and altitude. As one passed high overhead, it was strange to hear the jet roar supimposed on the reverberating snarl of the six giant pusher propellers.

hough a part of the US Air Force, Strategic Air Command was in many respects the most powerful armed force the world had ever seen. Its motto was 'Peace is our profession', and its primary duty was to show the world proof of so terrifying an arsenal of nuclear weapons that nobody would dare start a major war and certainly not attack the USA.

In 1935, when the B-17 was designed, the only role the USA could imagine for heavy bombers was to repel a hostile fleet. Within the 1,000-mile (1,600-km) radius of action of such aircraft there was no country posing a threat. But by 1941 the huge Convair B-36 was being designed to hit targets in Europe from the USA, and by 1945 there were nuclear weapons. This transformed the global scene. From being an ally, the Soviet Union turned itself into a hostile giant which could be relied upon soon to have strategic bombers and nuclear weapons. Accordingly, SAC was created on 21 March 1946.

In its early years SAC's main instrument was the wartime B-29 and its more powerful successor the B-50. While newer fission bombs were developed, work went ahead on the cataclysmic fusion (thermonuclear) weapon. Popularly called the H-bomb, this was shown to work on 1 March 1954. Henceforth the yield of bombs was to be measured in MT (megatons, millions of tons of TNT equivalent) and by 1958 the B28 bomb with yields up to 1.45 MT was operational in the weapon bays of B-47s and B-52s.

FLIGHT REFUELLING

Other new technologies were also transforming SAC's capabilities. The British had demonstrated a practical all-weather method of refuelling aircraft in flight. This was adopted by SAC, but was replaced by a Boeing-devised method in which a crew-member looking down and to the rear from the tail of the tanker fires an extensible tube, called a boom, into a fuel-tight socket on the receiver aircraft. This extended SAC's global reach.

In 1951 SAC received its first Boeing B-47. This beautiful six-jet bomber relied heavily on air-refuelling, so Boeing partnered it with 592 KC-97G tankers. The B-47 soon far outnumbered SAC's other bombers, and 2,032 were built. By 1954 all piston-engined bombers had gone, except for over 300 of the monster B-36s, whose speed and altitude were boosted by adding two pairs of turbojets under the outer wings. By 1956 Boeing was working frantically, delivering not only B-47s but also the first of 744 monster eight-jet B-52s, partnered by 732 KC-135A jet tankers (from which stemmed the 707 jetliner). Boeing also built many other C-135 versions for special kinds of multisensor reconnaissance.

In 1960 the Convair B-58 Hustler entered service, able to cruise at over Mach 2, but this tailless delta aircraft served for only ten years. Its drawbacks were inadequate range and high

Above: Like the B-29 before it, the B-47 Stratojet made a giant leap forward in technology. It set totally new standards in aerodynamics, wing loading, skin thickness, fuel capacity and takeoff and landing speed. It also made severe demands on its pilots. Its engines were again J47s, of which 36,500 were delivered.

cost, and the same contractor's replacement, the swing-wing FB-111A was also too small to fly strategic missions. The even more costly North American B-70 Valkyrie never entered service at all, and the same contractor's B-1 was cancelled in 1977. In 1981 this decision was reversed, and 100 B-1B Rapier bombers were delivered to SAC squadrons.

Unlike the original B-1 the B-1B was from the outset designed to penetrate hostile airspace at low level. At great cost and with much difficulty, the venerable B-52 was also modified to attack at low level, and its effectiveness was enhanced futher by a wealth of electronic countermeasures and by equipping it to launch the AGM-69 SRAM (short-range attack missile) and the AGM-86B ALCM (air-launched cruise missile).

From the outset, SAC was interested in missiles. It briefly operated a winged cruise missile, the Northrop Snark, but the Navaho long-range supersonic cruise missile was cancelled. Wingless ICBMs (intercontinental ballistic missiles), arching over distances to over 6,300 miles (10,140 km) at 15,000 mph (24,000 km/h), could deploy 'the deterrent' far more effectively. SAC deployed the Atlas ICBM from 1959. Later versions of Atlas, and the two-stage 103-ft (31.4-m) Titan, were installed in vast underground complexes called silos, where they could not be destroyed by the enemy. They still had to be filled with liquid fuel, and the ideal deterrent weapon was found in Boeing's Minuteman. Already filled with solid propellant, 1,000 of these awesome missiles were carefully lowered into silos, and brought to instant readiness. First came Minuteman I and II, followed by Minuteman III with three W62 warheads each. Last of all came the Peacekeeper missiles, each with ten warheads. Today merged into USAF Air Combat Command, the force is no longer on alert status, and its numbers are gradually being reduced.

Shocks from the Soviets

In the immediate postwar era the Western Allies were still largely ignorant of Soviet aviation. Previously unknown Soviet aircraft burst on the world stage by taking part in flypasts over Moscow. However, Western cameramen took such poor quality photographs of them that Western analysts had a very difficult time trying to decide their role, their capability and from which design bureau they had come. The USAF invented names for these planes, as had been done with wartime Japanese aircraft.

In fact, when the first Soviet turbojet fighters were eventually revealed to the world in the Air Force Day flypast of 18 August 1946 not a single word or photograph appeared in the Western press! The aircraft were the single-engined Yak-15 and twin-engined MiG-9. They remained unknown until on 17 May 1947 the British magazine *Aeroplane Spotter* published very poor illustrations of the MiG-9, calling it a 'Lavochkin research aircraft'. The three heavy cannon in the nose were said to be 'pitot tubes, one being a yaw meter'.

Further revelations were made on Soviet Aviation Day, 3 August 1947. During the war three B-29s had made forced landings in the Soviet Far East. Now an obvious derivative aircraft, with an enlarged passenger fuselage, took part in the flypast, while three red-starred aircraft resembling the B-29 also took part; because of an air-traffic error they flew in the wrong direction and had to dive to 200 ft (65 m) to avoid the rest! Other aircraft in the parade included a twin-jet fighter, a twin-jet bomber and a four-jet bomber, which years later were identified as the Su-9, Tu-12 and Il-22 respectively.

Nearly a year later the *Aeroplane Spotter* published the first illustrations of the Tu-12 and Il-22 to appear in the West, but they were drawings prepared after getting verbal descriptions! The newspaper's final issue, dated 10 July 1948, hinted at the Su-9 by saying that the USSR had demonstrated a 'twin-jet... resembling the Me 262... believed to be in squadron service' (it was not).

JETS TO ORDER

In March 1946 Soviet fighter designers were called to the Kremlin and told to design a highly manoeuvrable fighter able to reach at least Mach 0.9. To power it, Vladimir Klimov's engine design bureau tried to copy the most powerful turbojet then known to exist, the British Rolls-Royce Nene. Soviet agents hoped to obtain details of the Nene by the end of 1946, but two Russians suggested to Stalin 'Why not ask the British to sell us a Nene?' Stalin growled 'What fool will sell us his secrets?' The answer was 'A British fool'. In September 1946 the deal was signed, and the Soviet team returned to Moscow accompanied by ten Nenes in crates. No Nenes were delivered for British military aircraft for a further four years!

The immediate result was that the Tu-12 (see above) flew on 27 July 1947, the much better Il-28 flew on 8 July 1948, and between

Below: To the astonishment of Western observers, the Soviet Union produced a huge bomber with swept wings and propellers! It was made possible by Tupolev's design bureau, Kuznetsov's 15,000-hp NK-12MV engine and the 18ft 4in (5.6-m) AV-60M eight-blade contraprop. This example is a Tu-95MS-6.

these dates, on 30 December 1947, Viktor Yuganov flew the S-01, the first MiG-15. This swept-wing fighter simply demolished the competition and (not including over 800 constructed in China) 15,285 were delivered. One took part in the 1948 Aviation Day flypast, but apparently without being noticed by Western observers. Thus, when it was encountered over North Korea in November 1950 it was an unpleasant shock. The RAF did not receive its first Hunter until June 1954, but this British counterpart could not fire its guns and was subject to other limitations.

On May Day 1954 the flypast included a formation of nine swept-wing bombers. Though they had only two engines, buried in the wing roots, they were as big as the British four-engined V-bombers, which existed only as prototypes. An even bigger shock was that behind them came a single swept-wing

bomber with four engines. Formatting with it were four MiG-17 fighters (the next generation beyond the MiG-15). Scaling the big bomber against the fighters gave a span of about 164 ft (50 m). Given the NATO name 'Bison', it was actually the Myasishchev M-4, and production M-4 and 3M bombers were even larger. The smaller bomber, called 'Badger', was the Tu-16, 1,515 of which were delivered.

In July 1955 the Aviation Day parade included an equally large bomber with a swept wing and tail, yet powered by turboprop engines. Stunned Western observers called it 'Bear'. Little did they think that the Tu-95 and Tu-142 would be produced for 40 years, over 500 being delivered in many versions. Without using flight refuelling, these great aircraft can fly for up to 30 hours carrying many tons of weapons or sensors.

SPECIFICATIONS

Myasishchev 3MS-2

Type: long-range bomber/maritime reconnaissance aircraft

Powerplant: four Soyuz (Mikulin) RD-3M-500A turbojets each rated at 20,944 lb st (93.20 kN)

Performance: estimated maximum level speed at 36,090 ft (11000 m) 620 mph (998 km/h); service ceiling 44,950 ft (13700 m); range 7,705 miles (12400 km)

Dimensions: wing span 174 ft 4 in (53.14 m); length 169 ft 7½ in (51.70 m); estimated height 46 ft 3 in (14.10 m); wing area 3,767 sq ft (350.00 m²)

Weights: empty 166,975 lb (75740 kg); normal take-off 423,280 lb (192000 kg)

Armament: maximum bomb load of 52,910 lb (24000 kg)

War in Korea

Above: Grumman F6F Panthers of Navy squadron VF-112 ranged aboard USS *Philippine Sea*. The Panther was the first Navy jet ever to go into action, on 3 July 1950. Some had Allison J33 engines and others the Pratt & Whitney J42 (British RR Nene made under licence).

On 25 June 1950 the first jet bomber form USAF Strategic Air Command, a B-47A, made its maiden flight. At the same time troops of Communist North Korea swarmed over latitude 38°N and invaded South Korea. Over the next three years the war was to ebb and flow and encompass even part of SAC's bomber force, called to temporary duty to add weight to the bomber offensive against the North although, Presidents Truman and Eisenhower rejected calls for SAC to drop nuclear weapons on China.

The first air engagements were on 27 June when the F-82 Twin Mustang, a long-range fighter with two stretched F-51 fuselages sharing the same wing, shot down five Yak-7s attacking transports evacuating civilians from Seoul, the South Korean capital. On the same day American jets had their baptism of fire when Lockheed F-80 Shooting Stars shot down two Il-10 *Stormoviks* which were attacking targets at Kimpo.

On the following day a USAF RF-80A made the first jet reconnaissance mission, taking off from Japan, while Douglas B-26 Invaders attacked Pyongyang airfield in the first bombing mission. First flown in 1942, the B-26 (a designation used previously for the Martin Marauder) was to prove valuable in Korea and later in the Vietnam war. Before 28 June was over B-29s had started a campaign which left North Korean targets in ruins. They dropped both conventional bombs and precision-guided weapons, such as the 12,000-lb (5,443-kg) VB-13 Tarzon.

Naval aircraft joined in on 3 July when AD-4 Skyraiders, F4U Corsairs and F9F Panther jets from USS *Valley Forge* and Fireflies from HMS *Triumph* raided Pyongyang. By the end of July the enemy air force had been effectively eliminated, but the North Korean armies had overrun the whole of South Korea except for the Pusan peninsula in the extreme south. Here the invaders besieged the United Nations forces.

The stubborn defence bought time, as UN troops came from all over the globe.

HELICOPTERS AN ASSET

Early in the conflict helicopters began to prove useful. On 4 September an F-80 pilot, downed on his 95th mission, was rescued from behind the battlefront. This soon became commonplace. On 1 December the first Bell H-13Ds began bringing casualties to MASH (Mobile Army Surgical Hospital) units close behind the front line. By the end of the war the 2nd Helicopter Detachment alone had brought in over 17,700 casualties.

On 17 September the Pusan bridgehead was strong enough to start pushing the invaders back. Assisted by a giant amphibious landing at Inchon, the North Koreans were forced back to the 38th parallel on 1 October. The entire conflict might have been resolved at this point, but instead it escalated enormously. The People's Republic of China said they would enter the War if UN forces crossed the 38th parallel.

Supreme Commander MacArthur told US President Truman he did not believe they would, 'and, anyway, they have no air force'. By this time Soviet factories had delivered over 1,200 MiG-15 fighters, and Stalin agreed to supply a substantial number to China, along with a handful of experienced Russians as instructors.

While battles raged on the ground, sunlight reflected off the polished wings of the swept-wing jets, causing a shock to UN pilots. The first engagement came on 7 November, when a MiG was downed by a USAF F-80C. Apart from Meteor/V1 engagements in World War II, this was the first jet-v-jet combat. The growing conflict tilted in favour of the UN after the arrival of North American F-86 Sabres, which flew their first mission on 17 December 1950. Huge Chinese armies once more pushed back the UN forces. With their bases overrun, the F-86s had to operate from Japan. The low point was the summer of 1952 when airfields around Antung housed over 300 MiGs, while only 89 F-86As were ranged against them.

Eventually greatly increased F-86A and F-86E supplies again turned the tables. The UN offered $50,000 for a MiG pilot to defect, but got no takers until after the war when a pilot defected with his aircraft. By then the experienced Russians had been withdrawn. They were unimpressed by the F-86, and Evgeny Pepelyaev (19 victories over the F-86) said 'The fifty-calibre rattled on the MiG like peas; we could take damage far better than the F-86'. After their departure it was almost a 'turkey shoot' against the inexperienced Chinese. The USAF originally claimed an overall 14:1 kill ratio, but the actual figure was just over 3:1.

At this time the only British swept-wing jets were prototypes. Meteor 8s served in Korea with No. 77 Sqn., Royal Australian Air Force. It is a fair reflection on the aircraft (not on the men) that they claimed three MiG-15s but lost 32 of their own pilots. After the Armistice of 27 July 1953 all No. 77s were hastily re-equipped with Australian-made Sabres.

Right: This MiG-15 of the Korean People's Army Air Force was flown to Kimpo by a defector shortly after the Armistice of 27 July 1953. Armed with devastating guns, and in many other respects superior to any Allied fighter, what it lacked was good pilots. It is seen here on flight test at Wright Field, Ohio.

Transonic Flight

At a conference in 1935 two German aerodynamicists, Busemann and Betz, predicted that aircraft could go faster if their wings were angled backwards. Nobody outside Germany listened, so that when the Allies discovered such 'swept wing' aircraft in 1945 it was another great shock. The new technology was instantly put to use in the USA and Soviet Union and by 1950 the MiG-15, F-86 Sabre and the giant six-jet B-47 were all in service. Britain's Hunter took a further four years to enter service.

In fact Britain had flown a swept-wing research aircraft on 15 May 1946, entirely because of the drive of de Havilland Aircraft. The D.H.108 explored not only transonic flight (at Mach numbers near the speed of sound) but also the stability and control of aircraft with no horizontal tail. In the USA John K. Northrop had from 1929 pursued his goal of a flying wing, and he eventually created aircraft that had no body or tail. These culminated in the giant XB-35 and eight-jet YB-49 strategic bombers. By chance their span of 172 ft (52.4 m) was the same as that of today's Northrop Grumman B-2 (pp.178–179).

In the post-war era a major problem encountered by jet designers was pitch-up (an uncommanded violent nose-up rotation). One cause was that pulling out from dives at high Mach numbers could cause flow to break away from the outer wings. Designers tried adding rows of vanes above the wing, set at an angle to the airflow. Another idea was to extend the leading edge of the outer wing forwards, 'drooped' slightly down and with an abrupt inboard end called a dogtooth.

CURING PITCH-UP

Another cause of pitch-up and other forms of control loss was ineffectiveness of the tailplane. In 1952 it was found that, if the tailplane was mounted as low as possible, the pitch-up caused by stall of the outer wings could be automatically countered by loss of the usual download on the tail. The first aircraft to use this were the first supersonic fighters, the MiG-19 (which originally had a T-tail, the tailplane on top of

the fin), F-100 Super Sabre and F8U (later F-8) Crusader. In defiance of government experts, the English Electric Lightning also had a low tailplane. The F-104 Starfighter stayed with a T-tail, and had to have an automatic stick-shaker and stick-pusher to avoid violent pitch-up.

In 1944 the Junkers designers tried to avoid pitch-up by using an FSW (forward-swept wing). First tested on the Ju 287, it was continued on the

Type 140 bombers designed by OKB-1 in the Soviet Union. With light alloys it is difficult to make a safe FSW, but the situation changed with the advent of strong and stiff composite materials based on carbon fibre. The first really effective FSW was tested on the Grumman X-29.

Assuming that stability and control problems are solved, the most basic requirement of a transonic aircraft is a thin wing. The t/c

Left: One of the most amazing sights in the sky, the first XB-35 on test on 25 June 1956. Despite its astonishing shape it flew beautifully, the only serious trouble coming from the propellers.

(thickness/chord) ratio of 1940 fighters was typically 18 per cent. Such a thick wing would experience an enormous increase in drag as the speed of sound is approached. Simply making a wing thinner means that it has to be much heavier in order to retain strength. The F-104 had a tiny wing with a t/c ratio of only 3.36 per cent, so it had to be almost solid metal. An alternative answer is to increase the chord, and from 1942 many designers were attracted by the delta (triangular) shape, omitting a horizontal tail. Britain used a fairly thick delta wing in the 650 mph (1,046 km/h) Vulcan bomber, but deltas with a t/c ratio of around 3.5 per cent enabled aircraft to reach Mach 2. Examples are the Convair F-102, F-106 and B-58 and the French Mirage III and Mirage 2000. Soviet designers combined thin delta wings with tailplanes in such aircraft as the MiG-21 and Su-9.

Together with English Electric, the MiG and Sukhoi designers were also successful in solving the aeroelastic problems of wings swept at 60°. In contrast, the 45° wing of the F-100 caused North American such difficulty they had to

move the ailerons inboard, which meant that flaps had to be omitted. With the Crusader, Vought boldly adopted variable incidence. Its wing was mounted on pivots so that, as the pilot landed on a carrier, he had a good view ahead from a horizontal fuselage.

Specifications

Convair F-102 Delta Dagger

Type: single-seat interceptor

Powerplant: one Pratt & Whitney J57-P-23 turbojet rated at 52 KN (11,700 lb st) dry and 77 KN (17,200 lb st) with afterburning

Performance: maximum speed, clean at 12190 m (40,000 ft) 1328 km/h (825 mph); initial climb rate 5304 m (17,400 ft) per minute; service ceiling 16460 m (54,000 ft; tactical radius with two 871-litre (230-US gal) drop tanks and full armament 805 km/h (500 miles); maximum range 2173 km (1,350 miles)

Weights: normal loaded, clean 12565 kg (27,700 lb); maximum take-off 14288 kg (31,500 lb)

Dimensions: wing span 11.62 m (38 ft 1.5 in); length 20.84 m (68 ft 4.5 in); height 6.46 m (21 ft 2.5 in); wing area 61.45 m2 (661.5 sq ft)

Armament: three AIM-4C Falcon infra-red homing air-to-air missiles and one AIM-26A Nuclear Falcon, or three AIM-4A/4E beam-riding and three AIM-4C/4F infra-red homing air-to-ar missiles; up to 24 unguided 70-mm (2.75-in) folding-fin aerial roackets were originally carried but these were eventually deleted

Supersonic Flight

Above: Britain stupidly cancelled its M.52 supersonic aircraft three days after hearing of the first flight of the American XS-1 (later redesignated X-1). The Bell aircraft recognized that swept-back wings and tail were not necessary.

I n 1943, in a rare moment of farsighted planning, Britain's Ministry of Supply ordered Miles Aircraft to build an aircraft to explore flight at speeds faster than sound. The resulting M.52 was making good progress when on 28 January 1946 the Director-General of Scientific Research, Ben Lockspeiser, told Miles the M.52 was cancelled. Later, newly knighted Sir Ben announced 'The impression that supersonic aircraft are just around the corner is quite erroneous...' and his Ministry said the M.52 was 'a piece of dead research'.

Years later Lockspeiser told the author the real reason for the cancellation was that the M.52 did not have swept wings. Neither did the American Bell XS-1 (later X-1) which first flew three days before the M.52 was cancelled. That the two events were connected is obvious. Powered by a rocket engine burning alcohol and liquid oxygen, the X-1 was flown to Mach 1.06 by Charles E. 'Chuck' Yeager on 6 August 1947. Later the same aircraft reached Mach 1.45 (about 957 mph, 1,540 km/h). The US Navy's Douglas D-558-II Skyrocket was the first aircraft to exceed Mach 2, but the USAF was first beyond Mach 3, reaching 3.196 (2,094 mph, 3,370 km/h) in September 1956.

In anticipation of manned flight at such speeds Republic Aviation won a contract in 1951 for the XF-103, a missile-armed interceptor. It was to be powered by a Wright J67 turbojet with afterburner (based on the British Bristol Olympus), which in supersonic flight could be converted into a ramjet. At full power this was to accelerate the steel/titanium XF-103 to Mach 3.7 (2,446 mph, 3,936 km/h). By 1957, while Britain was proclaiming all fighters and bombers to be obsolete (p.150), the USAF was faced with unprecedented expenditure on ICBMs (p.107). Trying to balance the budget, the XF-103 was cancelled.

COMBAT AT MACH 3?

At Mach 3 (2,000 mph, 3,220 km/h) a manned fighter must travel in a nearly straight line. Even at the marginally supersonic speed of an F-100 the best radius of turn is several miles, and the idea of dogfighting at transonic speeds has always been fiction. On the other hand, aircraft that do not need to make rapid changes in direction can indeed fly at high Mach numbers, and some people had the vision to imagine this. In 1938 Eugen Sänger and Irene Bredt proposed a rocket-engined bomber able to take off normally and fly in semi-orbit half-way round the world at 13,422 mph (21,600 km/h). Some people who worked on this 'Antipodal bomber' later worked on the Bell BoMi (Bomber Missile) of 1951–55, which likewise was designed to 'skip' along the upper reaches of the atmosphere.

Famed US Navy designer Ed Heinemann of Douglas was thwarted in his wish to follow the D-558-II by the D-558-III to investigate Mach 9 (almost 6,000 mph, 9,656 km/h). Instead the USAF and NACA (National Advisory Committee for Aeronautics) funded the North American X-15. At first powered by two rocket engines based on those fitted to the X-1 and D-558-II, the X-15s (three were built) were later fitted with a single LR99 burning ammonia and liquid oxygen to give a thrust at high altitude of 57,850 lb (26,241 kg), considerably more than the weight of the aircraft. The X-15s reached 354,200 ft (107,960 m) in 1963 and Mach 6.70 (4,520 mph, 7,274 km/h) in 1967.

Such research certainly assisted the design of the fastest military aircraft. The North American XB-70 Valkyrie was a huge four-seat bomber made almost entirely of a special steel,

and designed to fly intercontinental distances at just over Mach 3 (2,000 mph, 3,220 km/h). Powered by six General Electric J93 engines of 27,200 lb (12,338 kg) thrust each, it was almost 200 ft (60 m) long and weighed 250 tons. One survives in the Air Force Museum in Ohio. A Soviet counterpart was the slightly smaller Ilyushin T-4.

In the Soviet Union Mikoyan created the MiG-25 interceptor and reconnaissance aircraft. Powered by two R-15BD-300 after-burning turbojets of 24,700 lb (11,200 kg) each, these welded-steel aircraft could cruise at Mach 2.82 (1,864 mph, 3,000 km/h). Excluding prototypes, 1,186 were built in 35 versions, far outnumbering all other 3,000 km/h aircraft. The only aircraft with similar performance were the Lockheed YF-12A and SR-71 family of 'Blackbirds'. Powered by two 32,500-lb (14,742-kg) Pratt & Whitney J58 variable-cycle (turbojet/turboramjet) engines, the SR-71 served for 30 years as an un-interceptable reconnaissance aircraft, flying at over Mach 3 at 100,000 ft (30 km).

Above: Sooty jets thunder from the J93 engines of the fantastic XB-70 as they are tested at Edwards AFB. Its shadows shows its dramatic shape. Flying at high speed, its outer wings were pivoted sharply downwards.

Right: First flown in September 1964, the MiG-25 is the fastest aircraft ever to have entered service, with a speed of Mach 2.83 (1,864 mph, 3000 km/h). This example is one of 65 MiG-25PD interceptors supplied to Libya. It is carrying an R-40RD, and R-40TD and four R-60 missiles.

All-weather Fighters

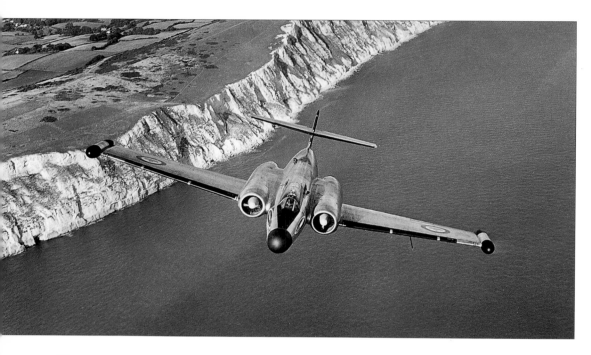

Left: As the 'white cliffs' show, this Avro Canada CF-100 Mk 4B visited Britain for the 1955 Farnborough airshow. Primary armament comprised 30-tube tip pods each with 29 Mighty Mouse rockets loaded.

Nothing drives technology forward faster than a war. The converse is also true: after 1918 most air forces did little or nothing to improve their capability at night. Navigation was possible because in peacetime the lights of towns could be seen, but finding other aircraft at night was both difficult and dangerous.

The answer lay in the development of smaller radars. The breakthrough was made in England: the magnetron valve enabled high-power microwaves to be generated with wavelengths of only a few centimetres. This enabled radars, which were originally as big as a house, to be carried in aircraft. In 1940 radars flew in large twin-engined fighters. By 1942 radars were flying in single-engined fighters, such as the F6F, F4U and Firefly.

After the war the first generation of jet night fighters were little more than the wartime radars and guns installed in jet aircraft. By 1956 the RAF was receiving the Gloster Javelin, the Soviet PVO received the Yak-25, the USAF got the Northrop F-89 Scorpion, the Royal Canadian Air Force received over 500 Avro Canada CF-100s and the US Navy used the Douglas F3D Skyknight (one of Heinemann's

brilliant designs which did what the others did in an aircraft that was 40 per cent lighter and had half the power).

At first all these had cannon armament, but soon they were equipped with either AAMs (p.122) or with spin-stabilized rockets. Called Mighty Mouse, the FFAR (folding-fin aircraft rocket) had a calibre of 2.75 in (70 mm), and a single hit could bring down most aircraft. Though unguided, it was fired automatically by a computer-controlled guidance system which attempted to steer the interceptor to approach its target from the side, where it looked bigger than from astern (from above or below would have been even better, but that was difficult). The FFARs were then fired in a salvo. The Lockheed F-94C Starfire could launch 24 from compartments in the nose, and a further 24 from containers on the wings. Northrop's F-89D could obliterate the enemy with a salvo of 104.

MISSILES BEHIND DOORS

By 1956 the latest interceptors were being armed with AAMs. The first supersonic interceptor was the Convair F-102. The prototypes of this tailless delta aircraft failed to exceed

Mach 1, but after the fuselage was lengthened and reshaped supersonic flight was easily achieved with the original J57 engine. Another new feature of the F-102 was that its primary armament of six missiles was carried internally. The power-operated doors over the missile bay each housed 12 FFARs. The derived F-106, with the more powerful J75, exceeded Mach 2, and served the USAF for over 30 years.

Less than half as fast, the RAF's Javelin was modified to carry four Firestreak AAMs, but these were on external pylons, as were the two Firestreaks (later replaced by the better Red Top) carried by the supersonic Lightning. By far the most advanced interceptor was the Avro Canada Arrow. The prototypes were powered by two Pratt & Whitney J75 afterburning turbojets, each of 26,500 lb (12,000 kg) thrust (the same engine as the single-engined F-106), while production Arrows had the brilliant Orenda Iroquois. The Arrow was designed to fly at Mach 2.5 for hundreds of miles carrying up to seven large Sparrow 2 AAMs plus up to eight short-range Falcons, most of the weapons being in an internal bay 'larger than the bomb bay of a B-17'. In 1959 the Arrow was foolishly

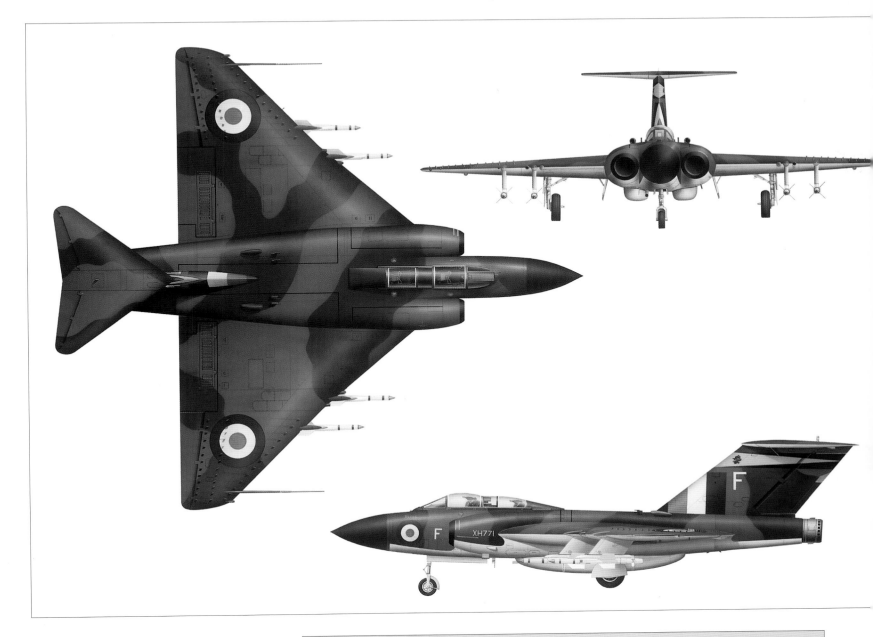

cancelled by politicians who took their cue from Britain in thinking fighters obsolete.

By 1958 the AAM had so mesmerized the customers that such interceptors as the British Lightning, American F-4 Phantom II and Soviet Su-9 went into production with no guns. This made it absolutely essential to have a radar with enough power and discrimination to see aircraft in any weather and from any aspect, at a range of at least 50 miles (80 km) and if possible from double this distance, and with computer processing to pick out which if any were hostile. It was then desirable to prioritize the hostiles in order of the threat they posed.

There was nothing wrong with this reasoning, except that in the Vietnam war it became obvious that omitting a gun had been a mistake.

SPECIFICATIONS

Gloster Javelin FAW. 9

Type: two-seat all-weather interceptor

Powerplant: two Armstrong Siddeley Sapphire Sa.7R turbojets, each rated at 12,300 lb (5579 kg) thrust with afterburning

Performance: maximum speed (clean) 702 mph (1,130 km/h) at sea level; climb to 50,000 ft (15,240 m) in 9 minutes 15 seconds; service ceiling 52,000 ft (15,849 m)

Weights: normal take-off (clean) 38,100 lb (17,272 kg); maximum overload take-off 43,165 lb (19,578 kg)

Dimensions: wing span 52 ft (15.85 m); length 56 ft 9 in (17.30 m); height 16 ft (4.88 m); wing area 927 sq ft (86.12 m²)

Armament: four fixed 1.18-in (30-mm) Aden cannon, plus four de Havilland Firestreak IR-guided air-to-air missiles

When the RAF added missiles to the Javelin they kept two of the guns, but with the Lightning they began with guns, left them off the F.3 version and then in the F.6 made it possible to put them back into a ventral pack. As for the Royal Navy, they took the guns out of the D.H.110 to produce the Sea Vixen and never put any back.

Guns

Above: The VW gives an idea of the size of the GAU-8/A and its magazine housing 1,350 rounds, each as big as a wine bottle. This is the largest of a family of rotating-multi-barrel guns made by General Electric.

E ven in World War I a few aircraft used guns of greater than so-called 'rifle calibre', which for the UK was 0.303 in, for France 7.7 mm, for Germany 7.92 mm and for the USA 0.300 in (all very similar). In 1918 the American Browning was being fitted to aircraft in both rifle calibre and in the far more powerful 0.5 in (12.7 mm) calibre. Amazingly, Britain did so little to develop new guns that the Browning was the RAF's standard machine gun throughout World War II!

A few French aircraft were armed with large Hotchkiss cannon (the name for guns firing explosive shells). Germany produced many types of aircraft gun, and so did companies in Italy, Denmark, Czechoslovakia and the Soviet Union. In 1932 Marc Birkigt developed an excellent Hispano-Suiza cannon in 20-mm (0.78 in) calibre, and this was adopted by the RAF. At first fed by a 60-round drum, it later (delayed a year by foolish British armament experts) was fed by a belt from a magazine of any desired capacity.

In World War II the Western Allies managed with the venerable Browning and Hispano, plus a handful of 'tank-busting' Hurricanes armed

with 40-mm (1.57-in). The USA used small numbers of larger guns up to 75 mm (2.59 in). By far the best guns were those of Germany and the Soviet Union, all of modern design. The most important German guns were the MG 151/20, which fired electrically fuzed ammunition, and a variety of guns of 30-mm (1.18-in) calibre. The mass-produced Soviet guns were the ShKAS, which fired at almost double the rate of other rifle-calibre weapons at 1,800 rds/min, the 12.7-mm (0.50-in) Beresin, the 20-mm (0.78-in) ShVAK, the 23-mm (0.90-in) VYa (twice as powerful as the ShVAK) and the devastating NS-37.

REVOLVER CANNON

At the end of the war the Germans were urgently developing the MG 213C, a 30-mm (1.18-in) gun which fed its electrically fired ammunition into a five-chamber revolving drum. By dividing the action into five parts rate of fire was increased, whilst reducing velocities and stresses. This gun was so much better than anything else that it was copied immediately. The British developed the Aden and the French the DEFA, both in 30-mm (1.18-in) calibre,

Above: One of GE's 20-mm six-barrel guns is the GAU-4, seen here firing in an SUU-23A pod attached under a Phantom of the RAF. Early Phantoms were delivered without an internal gun.

while the USA produced the 20-mm (0.78-in) Pontiac M39.

By 1951 General Electric's armament team at Burlington, Vermont, had gone one better with Project Vulcan. At first this was developed for the USAF in 20-mm (0.78-in) calibre with the revolving breech rotor feeding rounds into six spinning barrels. This 'Gatling gun' has been produced in large numbers as the M61 for almost every US fighter since 1955, while the T171 version was the sting in the tail of the B-52H and B-58. Since 1965 the same basic action has been used in a prolific range of guns with calibres from 5.56 to 30 mm (0.21 to 1.18 in). The smaller calibres have selectable rates of fire up to 10,000 rds/min (167 per second), while the monster GAU-8/A Avenger fitted to the A-10A attack aircraft can fire over a ton of tank-killing 30-mm (1.18-in) ammunition at 2,100 or 4,200 rds/min. Different GE revolver guns are driven by electric, hydraulic or pneumatic power, or by the ammunition itself.

True to form, the Soviet Union continued to be second to none in aircraft guns. Among major weapons are: the GSh-23 of 1961, with two barrels firing high-power 23-mm (0.90-in) ammunition at 3,600 rds/min; the 9A624 (YakB) of 1968 for helicopters with four barrels firing 12.7-mm (0.50-in) at 5,000 rds/min; the GSh-6-23 of 1973 with six barrels firing 23-mm (0.90-in) at 6,000 or 8,000 rds/min; and the GSh-30/I of 1979, the most powerful single-barrel aircraft gun in the world, firing 30-mm (1.18-in) high-velocity ammunition at 1,800 rds/min. The 30/I weighs only 108 lb (49 kg), compared with 265 lb (120 kg) for the M61, and each round has seven times the destructive power of the 20-mm (0.78-in).

Switzerland also developed a powerful single-barrel 30-mm gun, the Oerlikon KCA, used in the Swedish Viggen. Germany's famed Mauser company developed the BK27, a single-barrel gun in 27-mm (1.06-in) calibre, and this is used in the Tornado and Saab Gripen. France's GIAT produces a variety of powerful guns in 20- and 30-mm (0.78- and 1.18-in) calibre.

The only country with a poor track record is Britain. Despite having so small a front-line air force, it uses ammunition in 5.56, 7.7, 20, 27 and 30-mm (0.21, 0.30, 0.78, 1.06 and 1.18-in) calibres. As if this was not enough, it would. have added a further calibre, 25-mm (0.98-in), in a modified Aden firing percussion-fuzed ammunition, but after 20 years of toil this entire programme collapsed in 1998. The only gun specified for Eurofighter is the German BK27. The whole scene is a shambles, because 27-mm (1.06-in) is just 3-mm (0.11-in) too small to use NATO's vast stocks of 30-mm (1.18-in) ammunition and 2-mm (0.07-in) too large to use the 25-mm (0.98-in) calibre standardized by NATO. The only 25-mm gun at the Millennium was GE's GAU-12/U, used only by the Marine Corps Harrier.

Above: The Russians have for many years excelled in aircraft armament. This Sukhoi Su-25 close-support aircraft has a choice of 24 types of weapon, as well as its internal gun, a twin-barreled AO-17A, seen under the heavily armoured nose.

Bombs

As explained earlier, the first bombs were either modified artillery shells or local lash-ups. By 1914 properly designed bombs existed, with fins to stabilize their fall, but the largest (carried by German Navy airships) still only weighed 110 lb (50 kg). By the November 1918 Armistice one British bomber, the Handley Page V/1500, could carry 30 bombs of 250 lb (113 kg) or two monster bombs each of 3,300 lb (1,497 kg).

Between the world wars most of the developments were made in the Soviet Union and, after 1933, Germany. Early in World War II the proportion of GP (general-purpose) bombs that failed to detonate was often as high as 20 per cent. The German Luftwaffe soon had bombs of 3,968 lb (1,800 kg), but RAF Bomber Command thought on an even larger scale. By late 1941 the 4,000-lb (1,814-kg) LC (light-case) 'Blockbuster' was in use and by 1942 pairs or triples of these were dropped bolted together.

By 1943 German U-boat pens were being protected by a reinforced-concrete roof 23 ft (7 m) thick. One way of piercing this was the Disney, a 4,500-lb (2,041-kg) bomb with a slim armour-piercing case, dropped from 20,000 ft (6,096 m). At 5,000 ft (1,524 m) a rocket in the tail accelerated the bomb to 2,400 ft (732 m/sec). Even more effective were the armour-piercing weapons devised by Barnes Wallis at Vickers-Armstrongs. These were streamlined to free-fall faster than sound, whilst being spun by tailfins. The Tallboy weighed 12,000 lb (5,443 kg), and a single hit destroyed Germany's greatest warship, the *Tirpitz*. The Grand Slam weighed 22,000 lb (9,979 kg), and one dropped nearby caused an earthquake (as it was designed to) that destroyed the rail viaduct at Bielefeld.

BOUNCING BOMB

Another Wallis creation was the unique Upkeep. Specifically designed to destroy large concrete dams (in wartime protected by giant arrays of anti-torpedo nets), this bomb was a steel drum carried with its axis across the bomb bay of a modified Lancaster. Nearing the target, it was rotated at 500 rpm in what seemed the wrong direction. Carefully released at a height of 60 ft (18.3 m), it skipped in a precisely predicted way across the water until it gently hit the dam and sank, still slowly spinning, in contact with it. At a depth of 30 ft (9.14 m) the filling of 6,600 lb (4,173 kg) of RDX was detonated.

Every air force used various types of anti-personnel fragmentation bomblet, and at least one form of incendiary bomb. At first Thermite (powdered aluminium mixed with iron oxide [rust] powder) was common, but in World War II the usual material was magnesium. The RAF and the US 8th and 9th Air Forces used the British magnesium bomb, which looked like a piece of hexagon (six-sided) bar, so designed because hundreds could be packed together with no wasted space.

Warfare was transformed by the development, by an international team mostly working at Los Alamos, USA, of the first NW (nuclear weapons). To make such devices a huge production plant was constructed at Oak Ridge, Tennessee, to produce Uranium-235 while an even larger factory was built at Hanford, Washington, to create Plutonium-239 (which does not occur in nature). That a violent chain

Below: Fat Man was the first Pu-239 weapon, dropped on Nagasaki. This is a dummy, displayed at the Los Alamos Scientific Laboratory where all the earliest NW were developed. Today a similar yield bomb would be a fraction of this size and weight.

Above: Modern bombs come in many forms. Here an RAF Tornado makes a high-speed pass whilst dispensing 30 runway-cratering bomblets and 215 area-denial submunitions from twin JP233 containers.

reaction of fissile material could be initiated, but without destroying the Solar System, was demonstrated on 16 July 1945 in the first man-made nuclear explosion.

That device was detonated on top of a remote tower in the New Mexico desert. The first bomb was dropped on 6 August 1945 on the Japanese city of Hiroshima from a B-29 named *Enola Gay* after the mother of the aircraft commander, Col. Paul Tibbets, CO of the USAAF's 509th Composite Group. The bomb, called *Little Boy*, contained a mass of U-235 in one end of a gun-like barrel. At a height of 1,900 ft (579 m) above the target a second mass of U-235 was fired down the barrel to

make the combined mass supercritical. The bomb weighed 9,040 lb (4,100 kg), and had a yield equivalent to 12.7 kilotonnes of 2,4,6-trinitrotoluene (TNT).

The second bomb was dropped on Nagasaki on 9 August from a B-29 named *Bock's Car*, flown on this mission not by Bock but by Maj. Charles W Sweeny. Called *Fat Man*, it was a totally different kind of bomb in which a central mass of Pu-239 was made supercritical by a shell of uranium surrounded by two layers of high explosive. It weighed 10,000 lb (4,536 kg) and had a yield of 22.35 kilotonnes. It was the basis from which many later nuclear weapons were derived.

Guided Missiles

The first guided missiles to enter service were naval torpedoes. Those dropped by aircraft were initially little different from standard patterns, but they grew additional aerodynamic fins and occasionally a small retarding parachute. Today most air-launched torpedoes are quite small (eg, 12.75-in, 324-mm, diameter) helicopter weapons driven at up to 53 kt (98 km/h) by an electric motor or high-energy chemical system and carrying a shaped-charge warhead.

A shaped charge is one hollowed out at the front, often with a conical liner. When detonated, it projects a jet forwards with such speed that it can punch through (for example) 6 ft (1.8 m) of concrete or 30 in (0.76 m) of the best armour. Such warheads are universally fitted to anti-tank missiles, which were among the first species to be developed. Early types were guided by a human operator whose commands were sent along thin wires unreeled from the missile. Today many types of guided air-to-armour missile are in use, essentially all launched from helicopters. A few have wire guidance, but most have some kind of homing system or ride a laser beam. To defeat modern armour some have two warheads in tandem, the second firing its jet through the hole made by the first.

The first guided AAM (air-to-air missile) was the German X-4 of 1944, with wire guidance. Next, in 1956, came the USAF Hughes Falcon. The first version had SARH (semi-active radar homing) in which the target is 'illuminated' by the fighter's radar and the missile steers towards the reflections. A second version had IR (infra-red) homing, the missile steering towards the heat radiated from the target's engine(s). Falcons were short-ranged (up to 7 miles, 11.3 km), but over 59,000 were delivered by 1966.

SIDEWINDER

From 1949 the US Navy developed a simple IR-homing weapon, the AIM-9 Sidewinder, which looked like a length of 5-in (127-mm) pipe. Over the years it has been improved, some even having SARH guidance, and by 1999 deliveries exceeded 171,000. At the other end of the scale are AAMs with active radar guidance.

The Sparrow II, intended for the Arrow (pp.116–117), never entered service, but the AIM-54 Phoenix, with a range of over 124 miles (200 km), has been carried by the US Navy F-14 Tomcat for over 25 years.

By far the greatest range of AAMs in the world are those of the former Soviet Union. While the USAF and its Allies make do with Sidewinders and Sparrow derivatives, Russian interceptors have an eye-watering range of options. The Vympel company alone market over 22 different AAMs, including the awesome R-40 family and the prolific R-27 family which, though having modest launch weights in the region of 770 lb (350 kg), have a powerful 86-lb (39-kg) warhead and an effective range of 75-106 miles (120–170 km). Vympel have followed with several later AAMs, one (the R-77 family) having unique lattice-type rear control surfaces.

The two pioneer ASMs (air-to-surface missiles) were used operationally by the Luftwaffe in the summer of 1943. The Henschel Hs 293, initially carried by the Do 217E-5, was a miniature aeroplane based on the SC500 1,102-lb (500-kg) bomb, with an underslung rocket motor, tail flares and 18-channel radio command

Below: In true British style, Avro spent ten years developing the inertially guided Blue Steel cruies missile, only to see it swiftly junked in favour of a succession of other weapons. The ground crew were protected against the highly reactive HTP rocket fuel.

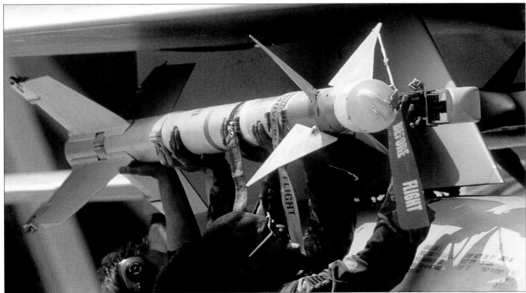

guidance. On 27 August 1943 one sank HMS *Egret*. FX 1400 was a free-fall bomb with spoiler-type tail controls commanded by a radio link from the carrier Do 217K-2. On 10 September 1943 this powerful 3,461-lb (1,570-kg) weapon was used against the Italian fleet as it sailed to join the Allies. One FX 1400 sank the battleship *Roma*, and another crippled the *Italia*.

By the end of the War there were many American ASMs, and in the early post-War period SAC fielded the AGM-28 Hound Dog, with a J52 turbojet and W28 thermonuclear warhead, while in the 1960s the RAF had a rocket-driven ASM called Blue Steel. Later weapons include the AGM-69A SRAM (short-range [up to 105 miles, 169 km] attack missile) and turbojet-engined AGM-86B ALCM (air-launched cruise missile) with a range up to 1,550 miles (2,500 km). The surviving ALCMs are having their W80 warheads replaced by conventional (non-nuclear) types.

Almost every air force has stocks of tactical ASMs. The US services have for many years had several species of rocket-propelled Maverick with different warheads, Paveway LGBs (laser-guided bombs) in 500, 1,000 and 2,000-lb (227, 454 and 1,102-kg) families, Shrike and HARM anti-radar missiles, and various forms of turbojet-engined AGM-84 Harpoon, which also exist in versions launched from ships and submarines.

Above: Originally designed 50 years ago, Sidewinder is the most widely used AAM in the world. Including Soviet and Chinese copies the total made approaches half a million.

Top: The most powerful fighter available in 2000, the Sukhoi Su-35 (Su-27M) can carry 11 different types of guided missile, nine more than equivalent British or American aircraft. Maximum weapon load is 8000 kg (17,635 lb).

Airlift II

Left: In such a fast-moving technology as aviation it seems amazing that the C-130 should remain in production for half a century. This C-130J looks almost identical to the original prototype, but in fact almost every part has been modified to increase capability. After an incredibly troubled start, this new version should find many customers.

As noted on p.87, in World War II Britain used as transports an unsuitable collection mostly based on failed bombers, having agreed that the USA should provide the transport aircraft. The result was that, by the Korean war, the RAF had the Avro York, Handley Page Hastings and Vickers Valetta, all tailwheel aircraft with side doors to a high sloping floor. In contrast, the USAF had the Douglas C-74 and C-124 Globemaster, the Boeing C-97 Stratofreighter and the Fairchild C-119 Boxcar, which were in a different class altogether.

In 1951 the USAF Tactical Air Command issued a requirement for a new transport. The result was the Lockheed C-130 Hercules, flown on 23 August 1954. This assembled the obvious features of a modern long-life airframe, a level floor at truck-bed height, powerful turboprop engines for economical cruising at high altitude, reverse-pitch propellers for powerful braking on short airstrips, a pressurized interior equipped for cargo, troop seats, litters (stretchers) or other loads, an APU (auxiliary power unit) to make the aircraft independent of ground support, retractable landing gear with low-pressure tyres suitable for unpaved front-line airstrips, a modern flight deck with all-round vision and comprehensive avionics including radar, and a rear ramp door for loading vehicles and other bulky loads which could be opened in flight if necessary.

In order to manufacture the C-130 Lockheed switched the programme from California to a vast plant at Marietta, Georgia. Early versions had T56-7 engines rated at 3,755 shp, but the C-130H introduced the T56-15 rated at 4,591 shp. This version continued to be built until 1998, at which point the total delivered was 2,156, for 61 countries. Since

Above: With NK-12MV turboprops similar to those of the Tu-95, but with even larger (20 ft 4 in, 6.2-m) propellers, the An-22 is essentially a bigger C-130 with four times the power. This picture shows the prototype, which lifted a 100-ton payload to 25,748 ft (7848 m).

then the C-130J has taken over, with the more economical 4,591-shp AE2100 engine driving a high-efficiency propeller with six curved blades supplied by Dowty in Britain. No other aircraft in history has come off the same assembly line for 45 years, and deliveries could well continue for at least a further ten.

BRITISH APPROACH

The production C-130 appeared in 1955, and in the same year a British factory produced the Beverley, for the RAF. This was much larger (wing area 67 per cent greater) but had piston engines of only 2,850 hp, burning increasingly rare high-octane petrol. It had fixed landing gear, neither radar nor pressurization, cruised at less than half the speed, had barely one-third of the range, and had rear doors that could not be opened in flight but which with difficulty could be disconnected and left behind.

The only serious shortcoming of the C-130 was a rather constricted cross-section of 123 in (3.13 m) wide and 110.7 in (2.8 m) high. To save time and cost the same cross-section was repeated for Lockheed's C-141 StarLifter, which had swept wings and tail and four TF33 turbofan engines. In the space of four years (1964–67) the Marietta plant built 285, which gave outstanding service throughout the Vietnam war, taking supplies west across the Pacific and bringing back casualties. From 1980–82 Marietta rebuilt 270 into the C-141B, with the fuselage stretched from 145 ft (44.2 m) to 168 ft 3 in (51.29 m) to enable heavier (but not more bulky) loads to be carried.

In 1954 the USAF signed a contract with Douglas at Long Beach for an airlifter with a larger cross-section, and this flew in 1956 as the C-133A Cargomaster. A total of 35 were built, powered by 6,500-shp T34 turboprops driving three-blade propellers of 18-ft (5.49-m) diameter. They could carry a cargo load of 100,000 lb (45,360 kg) or 200 troops, but it was soon evident that aircraft would be needed to carry the enormous Atlas, Titan and Minuteman ICBMs (p.107) from the factories to the silos. Accordingly Douglas delivered a further 15 C-133Bs, with 7,500-hp T34 engines and large clamshell doors at the rear. Unusually for a Douglas aircraft, they were retired in 1971 because of airframe fatigue.

In 1958 the Antonov bureau in Kiev, Ukraine, flew the An-12, in the class of the C-130 but with two 23-mm cannon in a tail turret. The An-12BP became the standard Soviet airlifter, 1,247 being produced. Many were later converted for other roles, such as electronic warfare. In 1965 the same design bureau produced the first An-22 *Antei* (Russian name for the giant Antheus). Powered by four NK-12MA turboprops of 14,995 shp, driving contra-rotating eight-blade AV-60N propellers of 20 ft 4 in (6.2 m) diameter, 66 of these 'carry anything' monsters were built. They performed tremendous service throughout the former USSR.

Rotating Wings

Above: The engineless Focke-Achgelis Fa 330 folded to fit in a box in Hitler's U-boats. With the submarine running on the surface, the Fa 330 could rise to 394 ft (120 m). The pilot could spot a ship over 40 miles (64 km) away.

Many 19th century inventors tried to create a flying machine lifted by various forms of rotating wing. In 1907 Igor Sikorsky tried, but he did not succeed for another 32 years. Meanwhile, in Spain Don Juan de la Cierva made his first autogyro in 1920. An autogyro has a tractor or pusher propeller, and the air flowing up through the free-spinning rotor causes the rotor to rotate and give lift. Cierva achieved success on 9 January 1923.

Cierva and licensees made many autogyros (registered name Autogiro), some of which had wings, while the British C.40 (Avro Rota) could pre-spin the rotor and make a 'jump' takeoff. The fastest (152 mph, 245 km/h) and most powerful (700 hp) autogyros were the Soviet A-7 and A-12 of 1934–36 which were armed for front-line observation roles. Today autogyros are small fun machines. Wg. Cdr. Ken Wallis's machines hold the international autogyro records.

In contrast, a helicopter has power-driven rotors. There are various configurations. Usually the drive torque is reacted by a smaller rotor at the tail, whose pitch can be varied to point the machine in different directions. The most common alternatives are to have two rotors in tandem, or two superimposed rotors turning in opposite directions.

A third approach is the 'eggbeater', with two intermeshing rotors, and this was adopted by German Anton Flettner for the Fl 265. This was flown in 1939 and six were built for the German navy in 1940–41. During one test a Bf 109 and an Fw 190 spent 20 minutes trying to capture an Fl 265 on their camera-gun film but were thwarted by the helicopter's agility. By 1941 Flettner was in production with the Fl 282 *Kolibri* (hummingbird), the first helicopter in shipboard service. The rival Focke Achgelis team used side-by-side rotors that did not intermesh. The Fa 61 of 1936 led to the first really capable helicopter, the Fa 223 *Drache* (kite). This had a 1,000-hp engine and could carry a load of 2,822 lb (1,280 kg), which during tests included two SC250 (551-lb) bombs. After the war the 14th production Fa 223, first flown in July 1943, was flown non-stop to, England.

PIONEERING SIKORSKY

In 1939 Sikorsky returned to the helicopter and began testing his VS-300 before the end of the year. This led to the XR-4 of January 1942 and to 233 production R-4s, with a single main rotor, the first of many famous Sikorsky helicopters. The S-56 of 1953, powered by two 2,000-hp Double Wasps, was the end of the road for piston engines.

Four years later Mikhail Mil in Moscow showed the way to go with the Mi-6. This was a major leap in helicopter technology, with two 5,500-hp turboshaft engines driving a rotor of 114 ft 10 in (35 m) diameter to carry 90 passengers or 26,455 lb (12 tonnes) of cargo. In 1977 Mil began testing the Mi-26, with two 11,240-hp engines and a payload of 48,500 lb (22 tonnes) Today the Mi-26 is still in limited production, together with advanced versions of the Mi-8/Mi-17 transport family (about 13,000 delivered), the Mi-14 amphibious naval helicopter (over 250) and the Mi-24/25/35 family of attack helicopters (over 3,000). All these are large, with paired engines in the 2,000-hp class.

On 29 December 1942 Bell flew the small Model 30. From this stemmed more helicopters than have been built by any other company (at least 33,600). Output began with over 6,000 Model 47s, followed by the 204/205 Huey family (13,000+) and the 206 JetRanger and derivatives (8,000+).

In 1941 Frank Piasecki began work which led in 1945 to a succession of large machines with rotors at nose and tail, initially with banana-like fuselages. In 1956 his firm became Vertol, flying the CH-46 in 1958 and the CH-47 Chinook in April 1961. Today the latter remains an active programme for Boeing, the T55 engine having doubled in power to nearly 5,000 shp. Boeing also took over the McDonnell Douglas plant in Arizona building the AH-64 Apache attack helicopter originally produced by Hughes. Hughes also developed an attractive range of

small helicopters with piston and (OH-6 Cayuse and Defender) turbine engines, and the latter continue in production by MD Helicopters.

In 1955 Sud-aviation flew the simple *Alouette* (Lark), the first production machine with a turbine engine. From this stemmed a vast range of Aérospatiale helicopters which continue to develop under the Franco-German banner of Eurocopter. Most powerful of the West European helicopters is the EH 101, jointly developed in several versions by Westland of the UK and Agusta of Italy, which has three engines in the 2,000 hp class.

SPECIFICATIONS

Boeing Vertol CH-47C Chinook

Type: twin-rotor medium transport helicopter

Powerplant: two 3,750-shp (2796-kW) Avco Lycoming T55-L-11A turboshafts

Performance: maximum level speed at sea level 178 mph (286 km/h); maximum rate of climb at sea level 2,045 ft/min (623 m) service ceiling 10,800 ft (3290 m); mission radius 115 miles (185 km)

Weights: empty 21,464 lb (9736 kg); maximum take-of 38,500 lb (17,463 kg)

Dimensions: rotor diameter, each 60 ft (18.29 m); length overall, rotors turning 99 ft (30.18 m); height 18 ft 7.75 in (5.68 m) to top of rear rotor head; rotor disc area, total 5,654.86 sq ft (525.34 m²)

Armament: provision for one door-mounted 0.30-in (7.62-mm) machine gun on flexible mount

Refuelling in Flight

I n World War I several visionaries suggested setting a distance or duration record by taking on fuel in flight, but with little official interest nothing was done. The only way aircraft endurance was actually increased was by seaplanes or flying boats landing alongside friendly warships and being refuelled via a hose. This was a purely experimental procedure, impossible except in a flat calm.

After the November 1918 Armistice many former military pilots, especially in the USA, sought to earn a living by barnstorming (putting on an airshow in one town after another). These daredevils were always looking for new ways to entertain, and a few would pass a hosepipe to a partner aircraft, or even lower a passenger on a rope carrying a fuel can.

Serious inflight refuelling was first practised by the US Army Air Service in 1923. On 25 August of that year a DH-4B 'Liberty plane', flown by Lts Lowell H. Smith and John P. Richter, took off from Rockwell Field, San Diego. It formated below a second DH-4B with its fuel tank connected to a hosepipe with a steel cable on the end. The cable was used to haul down the hose to feed fuel to the lower aircraft. This tricky procedure was accomplished 15 times. At last the long demonstration was halted

Above: On 7 August 1949 Pat Hornidge stuck the nose probe of Meteor F.3 EE597 into a Flight Refuelling Lancaster's hose ten times to remain airborne for over 12 hours.

by fog, but by this time Smith and Richter had set a duration record of 37 hours 15 minutes.

The next major series of trials took place over Southampton Water in England at the start of 1938. Pioneer aviator Sir Alan Cobham formed a company called Flight Refuelling Ltd with the objective of enabling Imperial Airways 'Empire' flying boats to fly greater distances, such as across the North Atlantic. He used the Armstrong Whitworth A.W.23 and a Handley Page Harrow as tankers, passing up to 920 gal (1,105 US gal, 4,182 litres) through a hose grabbed by a cable

Boeing and the USAAF (USAF from 1947) looked for a better way. By December 1948 they had adopted the Flying Boom. The tanker is equipped with a massive rigid telescopic tube mounted on pivots under the tail, which is 'flown' by a boom operator using a joystick driving 'ruddervators' on the end of the boom. The receiver formates close behind and below the tanker while the boomer aims carefully and then drives the extending boom into a self-sealing receptacle on top of the receiver. This puts the onus of a successful contact on the boom

operator. Though tricky and to a degree dangerous, the method was gradually perfected until air refuelling became a routine procedure in almost any weather or at night.

A major advantage is that the boom can transfer fuel at greater rates than a long hose. This was doubly important in the jet era, because the new engines consumed fuel much faster and fighters and bombers had far greater fuel capacity. For example, while the B-29 had a capacity of about 8,000 US gal, the B-47 jet bomber could take off with 14,600 US gal and the B-52 with over 48,000 US gal! Thus, the USAF Strategic Air Command built up an enormous tanker force. This started with 777 KC-97Gs, but these were piston-engined and the jets had to fly low and slow to refuel. From 1956 Boeing delivered 820 even larger KC-135 Stratotankers, based on the 707 airliner. Many of these, re-engined, are still in service.

The US Navy, and several other air forces including those of the former Soviet Union, adopted the British probe/drogue scheme. They also equipped many aircraft with 'buddy packs'. Attached like a bomb or drop tank, these enable one fighter or attack aircraft to refuel another of the same type. The latest fighter and attack aircraft have neat retractable probes. The pilot can at the touch of a switch extend these from beside the nose where he can see it as he guides his aircraft until the 'prod' into the drogue on the end of the tanker's hose. Many modern tankers can refuel three aircraft at once.

with a grapnel and winched in to the extreme tail of the receiver aircraft.

TESTS FOR THE BEST

Immediately after World War II the looped-hose method was overtaken by the far better probe/drogue system. Here the receiver thrusts a rigid probe into a 'basket' with a self-sealing coupling on the end of a hose trailed by the tanker. This was experimented with by Flight Refuelling using Lancasters, and by the USAAF, using KB-29 Superfortress tankers. Among receivers were F-84 Thunderjets with a probe on the wing and Meteors with a probe on the nose.

Above: The KC-10 Extender of the USAF has a three-man refuelling station under the rear fuselage from where an operator can 'fly' a boom over 60 ft (18 m) long to hit a socket on the receiver aircraft. It also has hose-reels under the outer wings.

Right: After serving as a bomber, this Handley Page Victor was rebuilt to K.2 standard as an air-refuelling tanker. Here one of its hoses is replenishing a Harrier GR.3.

The Aircraft Carrier

Farsighted people envisaged aeroplanes being operated from ships before World War I. Pioneer trials by the US and Royal Navies were from short runways built over gun turrets. Next came converted liners, such as the 20,000-ton *Campania* of April 1915 (p.26), which had a 200-ft (91-m) deck to allow ten seaplanes to take off from trollies. By 1917 a fast cruiser, HMS *Furious*, had been modified with a forward landing deck on which Sqn Cdr E.H.Dunning landed a Sopwith Pup on 2 August 1917 (the first on a speeding ship). This deck was only one-quarter of the ship's 786-ft (240-m) length, so sailors had to grab the landing aircraft and bring it to rest. On 7 August they failed and Dunning was drowned.

By March 1918 *Furious* had flight decks fore and aft, but separated by a towering superstructure in the centre. On 20 March 1922 the US Navy commissioned USS *Langley*, a former collier rebuilt with an unobstructed flight deck (her two funnels could be pivoted out horizontally).

Above: Originally designed in the 1950s as a supersonic bomber, the RA-5C Vigilante was the most capable reconnaissance aircraft ever to operate from a carrier. Its largest sensor was an APD-7 side-looking radar with a 'canoe' antenna along the underside of the fuselage. This RA-5C of RVAH-14 is about to be catapulted off USS *John F. Kennedy*.

Japan's first carrier, the *Hosho* of December 1922, had a miniature bridge and pivoting funnels. In March 1923 the 27,500-ton HMS *Eagle* was completed with an 'island' superstructure offset to starboard. This configuration has been followed ever since. Another idea standard since the 1920s is to bring landing aircraft sharply to a halt by fitting it with a hook to engage in any of several cables stretched across the deck.

In 1927 the French completed a carrier of similar size, *Bearn*, but she was too slow (21 kt). Late in the same year the US Navy commissioned the fast 39,000-ton *Lexington* and *Saratoga*, each with a complement of 90 aircraft. These were the most powerful and effective carriers in the world until World War II. By the end of that conflict the US Navy had over 100 carriers, ranging from the useful CVEs (escort carriers) in the 10,000-ton class to the 24 CVs of the 40,000-ton *Essex* class. The latter typically had 12 127-mm (5-in) guns, with blind-fire radar control, plus 68 40-mm (1.57-in) and 70 20-mm (0.78-in) to put up an almost impenetrable curtain of anti-aircraft fire. They carried 80 aircraft.

STILLBORN SUPER CARRIER

In 1949 the keel was laid of CV-58 *United States*, the first 'super-carrier' of 65,000 tons. It caused conflict with the newly formed Air Force, and in particular with Strategic Air Command, and the carrier was cancelled. The Admirals fought back, and CV-59 *Forrestal* was commissioned in October 1955. Her full-load displacement was 75,900 tons. As built she had eight 12.7-mm (0.5-in) guns, and carried 100 aircraft.

Among her features were three innovations pioneered by the British. One was the angled deck. In the traditional axial deck any aircraft that failed to pick up an arrester wire had to open the throttle smartly and overshoot or crash into a barrier. Even so, on many occasions the aircraft crashed into a closely packed mass of aircraft on the foredeck waiting to take off. The post-war position was even worse, because aircraft were heavier, they landed much faster and their turbine engines took longer to 'spool up' to maximum power. The angled deck made aircraft land 8° diagonally, so that they had a clear deck in front.

The second British idea was the mirror sight. An arrangement of bright lights and

mirrors carefully positioned beside the landing area, and stabilized against pitch or roll in a rough sea, gave landing aircraft accurate guidance to follow the correct glide path. The third invention was the steam catapult. Previous catapults had been driven by inconvenient and potentially dangerous energy systems, either hydraulic or cordite. By taking high-pressure steam from the ship's huge boilers it was possible to equip a super-carrier with four catapults powerful enough to fire off the heaviest aircraft, such as an RA-5C Vigilante (79,588 lb, 36,101 kg) or RA-3B Skywarrior (83,000 lb, 37,649 kg), and to keep on doing it as fast as the aircraft could be positioned for the shot. Originally aircraft were catapulted by a large 'bridle' of rope or cable, lost in the sea on each shot, but a US invention was the nose-towbar. The shuttle on the 'cat' picks up an arm pivoted to the super-strong nose landing gear and hurls the aircraft into the sky.

CV-59 has now been followed by CV-60 to CV-76 inclusive. These are by far the greatest warships ever built. Many have nuclear propulsion, displacements up to 102,000 tons, and a complement of (typically) 3,184 plus a further 2,800 aircrew. In 1966 the only new British carrier was cancelled, but France's nuclear-powered *Charles de Gaulle* was commissioned in 1999, and a second is planned, as in 1999 is a promised British carrier.

Above: CVA-59 USS *Forrestal* was the US Navy's first giant carrier. With a length of 1,068 ft (331 m) she dwarfed the S-3 seen landing. The four catapults on each CV may be replaced by a new pattern based on electric power.

Right: Powered by GE TF34 turbofans of 9,275 lb (4207 kg) thrust, the Lockheed S-3 Viking has served 27 years as the US Navy's carrier-based anti-submarine aircraft. Packaged into the fuselage are a mass of sensors and weapons as well as four men on ejection seats. To fit the ship, the wings and vertical tail all fold.

ASW

At the start of World War I the submarine was a feared but unproven weapon. Within a matter of weeks it was proved to have the capability of destroying the greatest ships, and ASW (anti-submarine warfare) became a subject of the most vital interest.

Throughout World War I submarines, and in particular German U-boats, wrought havoc among merchant vessels and warships alike. Their weapon was the torpedo, though where circumstances permitted they could rise to the surface and attack with a gun of about 3-in (76-mm) calibre. Others could lay mines. Surface propulsion was by diesel engine. When submerged it was possible to travel about 100 miles (161 km) on electric motors fed by batteries recharged on the surface. When submerged, the only visible part of the vessel was the tip of the optical periscope. This was hard to see, yet several U-boats were destroyed by Allied aircraft using A/S (anti-submarine) bombs of 65 or 230 lb (30 or 104.3 kg).

Between the world wars depth charges and other A/S weapons were improved, but the Asdic (an acoustic receiver of sound waves reflected off a submerged submarine) could not be used by aircraft. By 1943 this was being rectified in the sonobuoy, a tube containing powerful sonic emitters and sensitive receivers which, dropped into the ocean, gave the range of a hostile submarine and, in later types, even its direction. Passive sonobuoys do not emit, but listen for the sound of submarine propellers. By 1940 the first airborne radars capable of detecting a U-boat periscope were being perfected, and by 1942 large numbers of Allied aircraft were in service with effective ASW radar.

Despite bombing of German industry, 78 new U-boats joined the *Kriegsmarine* in the fourth quarter of 1943 alone, and by this time U-boats were fighting back. The *Schnorkel*, an air supply and exhaust tube, enabled them to run on diesel power when submerged. Better hydrodynamic shapes and enormous electric power enabled them to travel submerged not at the previous 8 knots but at 16 or 20. In 1953 USS *Albacore* showed that a submarine could travel underwater at 33 knots (over 38 mph,

Left: First flown over 40 years ago, the Lockheed P-3 Orion is proof that what matters in ASW is not so much the basic platform as what is packaged into it. Powered by 4,910-hp Rolls-Royce (originally Allison) T56 turboprops, repeated updates have introduced over 60 new items of electronics and equipment.

62 km/h) and manoeuvre in three dimensions like a fighter. In 1955 USS *Nautilus* showed that a submarine could have steam turbines driven by a nuclear reactor, giving limitless underwater capability.

MISSILE SUBS

Many submarines had been equipped to launch and retrieve small aircraft. By the 1950s US Navy submarines were firing various types of cruise missile, against strategic land targets if necessary. In 1960 the US Navy commissioned *George Washington*, the most significant warship of the century. She was armed with 16 vertical tubes each capable of firing, from deep underwater, a Polaris missile with a range of over 1,370 miles (2,200 km). This led to giant submarines with Trident intercontinental missiles able to deliver thermonuclear warheads to any point on Earth.

This transformed the threat posed by submarines. At first carrier-based aeroplanes could carry ASW sensors, such as radar and

sonobuoys, or weapons, such as A/S torpedoes and depth charges, but not both together. Such aircraft as the Grumman AF-1 Guardian therefore operated in pairs, one aircraft a hunter and the other a killer. The slightly larger Fairey Gannet (with a twin turboprop engine driving contra-rotating propellers) and the Grumman S-2 Tracker (with two piston engines) combined both functions.

Much larger land-based aircraft could carry all the weapons and sensors needed, the latter adding new devices such as a MAD (magnetic-anomaly detection) receiver able to detect the distortion caused by a submerged submarine to the Earth's magnetic field, a 'sniffer' for diesel exhaust in the atmosphere, and IR (infra-red) detectors able to spot anything warmer than its surroundings. The most widely used ASW aeroplane is the Lockheed Martin P-3 Orion, with four turboprop engines, based on the Electra airliner of 1957. Other aircraft in this class include the Franco-German Atlantique and the RAF's Nimrod, which is unique in

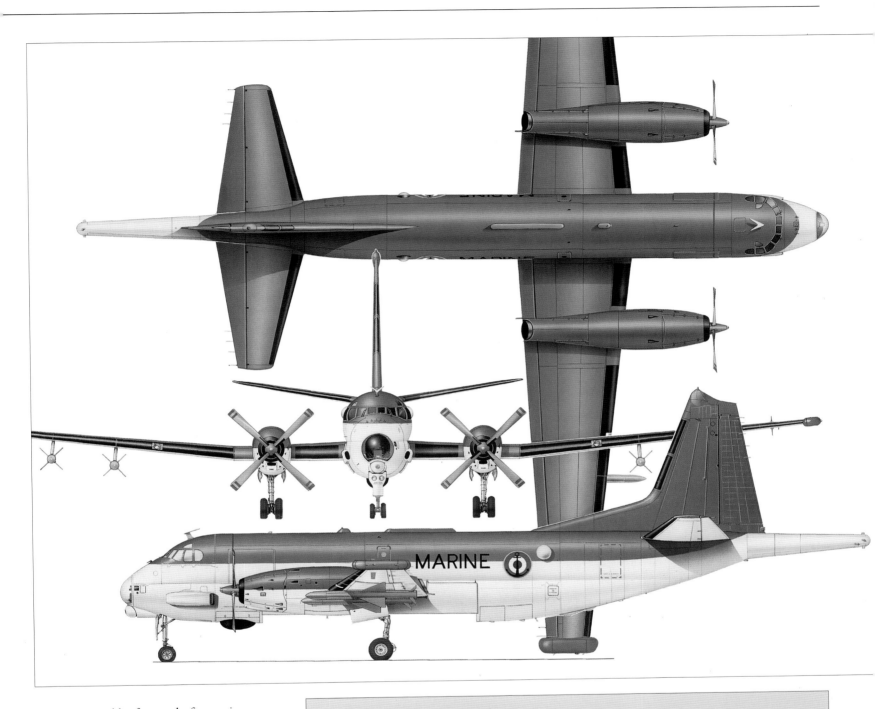

being powered by four turbofan engines.

In 1942 helicopters were studied as ASW aircraft. Gradually they became more powerful, and by 1961 the Sikorsky S-61 (US Navy SH-3) Sea King proved it could do both the hunter and killer tasks, the search being carried out with sensitive radar and with either sonobuoys or with a large and powerful sonar which is repeatedly dipped in the ocean, each immersion refining the target's position. The Russian Navy uses the coaxial-rotor Kamov Ka-27PL, operating in hunter/killer pairs. Today the most capable ASW helicopter is the Royal Navy's Merlin, a version of the EH 101 (p.127).

SPECIFICATIONS

Dassault Aviation Atlantique 2

Type: maritime reconnaissance/anti-submarine warfare aircraft

Powerplant: two Rolls-Royce Tyne RTy.20 Mk 21 turboprops each rated at 6,100 ehp (4549 ekW)

Performance: maximum level speed 'clean' at optimum altitude 402 mph (648 km/h); maximum rate of climb at sea level 2,900 ft (884 m) per minute; service ceiling 30,000 ft (9145 m); operational radius 2,071 miles (3333 km) for a 2-hour patrol in the anti-surface vessel role with one AM39 Exocet missile; endurance 18 hours

Weights: empty equipped 56,437 lb (25,600 kg); maximum take-off 101,852 lb (46,200 kg)

Dimensions: wing span 122 ft 9.25 in (37.42 m) including wingtip ESM pods; length 103 ft 9 in (31.62 m); height 35 ft 8.75 in (10.89 m); wing area 1,295.37 sq ft (120.34 m²)

Armament: maximum 7,716 lb (3500 kg); maximum internal 5,511 lb (2500 kg)

Anti-armour

Though they might be overturned or otherwise disabled by bombs, tanks and other AFVs (armoured fighting vehicles) were proof against most aerial weapons until World War II. Then the Soviet Union led the way with the Il-2 aircraft armed with the VYa-23, a very powerful gun firing armour-piercing ammunition, and the RS-82 rocket of 82-mm (3.23-in) diameter. Though unguided,

Above: Even burdened by the extra ton of 16 loaded launchers for Hellfire missiles, the Boeing AH-64D Apache retains a measure of agility, though not enough to dodge SAMs. This is the Longbow version, with surveillance radar above the main rotor.

the RS-82 (and, from 1941, the RS-132) was stabilized by spin induced by offset tailfins. It had a hollow (shaped) warhead (p.122) able to pierce most AFV skins, especially as pilots tried to attack from the rear.

By October 1942 No 6 Sqn RAF was in action in the Western Desert with the Hurricane IID, armed with two 40-mm (1.57-in) Vickers S guns. Each fired about two rounds per second of shells which could disable any tank in service at that time. The aircraft was aimed by the usual Mk II reflector sight, but two Browning machine guns were retained (10 being removed) so that with tracer ammunition they could help to hit the target. The only problem was that the recoil not only slowed the aircraft but also tended to tilt it nose-down, which at very low level was dangerous.

At the same time the RAF began to receive rocket projectiles. Like the Soviet RS-82 the British RP was stabilized by spinning. Its 76-mm (3-in) cordite motor was made by the million. On the front was attached either a 60-lb (27.2-kg) high-explosive warhead or a slimmer 25-lb (11.3-kg) armour-piercing head. After the Allied invasion of Europe on 6 June 1944 RPs were fired in large numbers from Hawker Typhoons, causing havoc among the normally victorious *Panzer* columns. Once a complete division was caught in the open in daylight; Typhoons flew sortie after sortie until the 2nd *SS Panzers* ceased to exist.

GERMAN HEAVY GUNS

The German Luftwaffe used a version of the *Stuka* dive bomber, the Ju 87G, with two 37-mm anti-tank guns. One Ju 87G pilot, Hans-Ulrich Rudel, was credited with the destruction of 519 Soviet tanks (he previously sunk the battleship *Marat* by dive-bombing). Other German anti-armour aircraft were the twin-engined Hs 129B and Ju 88P, both of which could be fitted with awesome guns of 75-mm calibre. In the final 18 months of the War the Germans tested numerous radical anti-armour weapons, such as downward-firing mortars with large armour-piercing shells.

Another German weapon was a primitive anti-tank missile fired by an infantryman and guided by him with the aid of aerodynamic control surfaces responding to commands transmitted along fine wires from spools in the missile. In 1947 the idea was taken up by France. By 1955 the SS.10 was in production and some were fired from helicopters, creating a powerful new anti-armour combination. From the SS.10 came the faster and heavier SS.11. Weighing 66 lb (29.9 kg), it had a hollow-charge warhead guaranteed to disable any tank in existence at that time. Over 179,000 were delivered, many being of the AS.11 type launched from a helicopter or slow aeroplane.

In 1965 Hughes in the USA began working on TOW (Tube-launched, Optically-tracked, Wire-guided) and this has since been made in numbers exceeding any other guided missile and exported all over the world. Upgraded versions still serve in large numbers on such helicopters as the Bell AH-1 Cobra and SuperCobra. Later missiles are the 101-lb (45.8-kg) AGM-114 Hellfire and several Russian equivalents, which need no guidance wires and thus can fly very fast. The aircraft or a co-operating soldier aims a laser at the target and the missile homes on (steers towards) the reflected signal.

Today the most important anti-armour helicopters are the Boeing (formerly Hughes, then McDonnell Douglas) Apache, the Soviet Mi-28 and Ka-50 and the newest designs, the European Tiger and South African Rooivalk. All are heavily armed with a powerful gun and various missiles and rockets and equipped with sensors and sighting systems for use at night or in bad weather.

The only modern specialist anti-armour aeroplanes are the Russian Su-25 and USAF Fairchild A-10A. Though both are jets, they are quite slow aircraft, designed to loiter over the battlefield looking for targets for their guided missiles, rockets, bombs and high-velocity 30-mm (1.18-in) gun. Every part of their structure, encompassing twin engines and duplicated systems, is designed to ensure survivability in the face of intense fire from the ground. Of course, the same can be said of today's tactical helicopters.

SPECIFICATIONS

Fairchild Republic OA-10A Thunderbolt II

Type: single-seat anti-armour/ (A-10A) or (OA-10A) forward air control aircraft

Powerplant: two General Electric TF34-GE-100 turbofans, each rated at 9,065 lb st (40.32 kN)

Performance: maximum level speed (clean) at sea level 439 mph (706 km/h); maximum rate of climb at sea level 6,000 ft (1828 m) per minute; combat radius 620 miles (1000 km) on a deep strike mission or 288 miles (463 km) on a close air support mission with a 1.7-hour loiter

Dimensions: wing span 57 ft 6 in (17.53 m); length 53 ft 4 in (16.26 m); height 14 ft 8 in (4.47 m); wing area 506.00 sq ft (47.01 m²)

Weights: basic empty 21,541 lb (9771 kg); maximum take-off 50,000 lb (22,680 kg)

Armament: one 1.18-in (30-mm) General Electric GAU-8/A Avenger seven-barrelled cannon with maximum capacity of 1,350 rounds; maximum ordnance 16,000 lb (7,258 kg); potential maximum load of 28 Mk 82 500-lb or 10 AGM-65 LDGP bombs, or 16 Mk 84 1,000-lb bombs, or eight CBU-87 cluster munitions, or 16 CBU-52/71 cluster munitions, two SUU-23/25/30/65 dispensers, practice bombs, assorted ECM pods; primary anti-armour weapon is the AGM-65 Maverick air-to-surface missile available in three versions (AGM-65B with TV scene magnification guidance and AGM-65D/G with imaging infra-red (IIR) seeker); twin-rail AIM-9L Sidewinder launcher for self defence; typical general-purpose load for the A-10 during Desert Storm comprised single Mavericks on each main wing pylon, and six SUU-30/64/65 cluster bombs on the unoccupied pylon; standard ordnance for the OA-10 is the LAU-68 rocket pod, with a maximum of seven rounds carried

French Colonial Wars

Above: Ancestor of the Chinook, the Vertol H-21 was powered by a 1,425-hp Cyclone piston engine and could airlift 20 troops.

Left: This T-6G was one of 450 upgraded and rebuilt Texans (Harvards) used by the Armée de l'Air and Aéronavale in the Algerian war. They carried bombs, rockets and gun pods.

After World War II Great Britain did its best to give independence to its former colonies. France did not, and instead fought bloody wars in two large countries on opposite sides of the world.

The first war took place in Indo-China, south-east Asia. In 1942 the colonial power had been swept away by the Japanese invaders and this proof that France could be defeated led to rapid growth in the Viet Minh, the nationalist political power. In 1946 French administrators returned, to find a situation very different from 1941. In December 1946 poor and ill-equipped Viet Minh tried to wrest control of Hanoi and other cities from French troops, this was the start of a bloody war.

The Viet Minh found an inspired leader in Vo Nguyen Giap, but in 1950 the French appointed Gén. de Lattre de Tassigny as commander in Indo-China and he restored French fortunes until his death in 1952. The Viet Minh fought in the jungles and paddy fields, offering difficult targets for attack by aircraft. The Armée de l'Air, organized into three tactical groups, started out with a motley collection of former World War II-era aircraft. From France came little but the AAC.1 Toucan (Ju 52/3m) transport. From the USA came a wealth of aircraft, including the P-63 Kingcobra, F6F Hellcat, F8F Bearcat, SB2C-5 Helldiver, SBD Dauntless, PBY Catalina, PB4Y Privateer and the B-26 Invader and C-47 transport. Britain supplied Spitfires and Mosquitos, and former Japanese aircraft put to good use were the Nakajima Ki-43 fighter and Aichi E13A seaplane.

By 1954 the transport fleet of over 120 C-47s was augmented by the new Nord 2501 Noratlas and by CIA-managed Fairchild C-119s of the USAF, which were flown with French markings by civilian US crews. Like the Germans at Stalingrad, the garrison of 11,000 at the vital fortress of Dien Bien Phu was sustained by a round-the-clock airlift in a long and bloody siege, but surrendered on 7 May 1954. The shock to France was cataclysmic. A cease-fire transferred Indo-China to the Viet Minh on 20 July 1954, the country then being divided into North and South Vietnam.

NEW THREAT

Within weeks, trouble broke out in Algeria. This was not regarded as a colony but as an integral part of France. Few people thought the diverse Arab nationalists could be more than a minor nuisance. However, they found a leader, Ahmed Ben Bella, and coalesced into the FLN (Front de Libération Nationale), with a military wing the ALN (Armée).

It was Indo-China all over again. In the mountains and deserts of North Africa the French suffered one reverse after another, and the original Armée de l'Air squadron (EC6, with Mistral jets [licence-built D.H. Vampires] at Oran-la-Sénia) grew over the bloody eight-year war into an air force of over 3,000 warplanes and helicopters, while over one million French troops were committed on the ground.

Among the aircraft involved were the Mistral, Ouragan, *Mystère* IIC and IVA jet fighters, B-26 Invader and AD-4 Skyraider heavy attack aircraft, and a huge assortment of Co-In (counter-insurgent) attack aircraft including the North American T-6 Texan and T-28 *Fennec*, Morane-Saulnier MS.500 and MS.733, Max Holste *Broussard*, and many SIPA S.12 variants derived from the Arado Ar 396. Among tactical twins were the NC.701 and 702 *Martinet* derived from the wartime Siebel Si 204 and various Dassault MD.311 and 315 *Flamants* with radar and Nord AS.11 missiles. These wire-guided missiles proved effective in killing ALN dug in among the mountains.

A huge transport fleet included a growing number of helicopters, beginning with the Bell 47G and Sikorsky H-19 (most of which bristling with rocket launchers and guns of 7.5, 12.7 and 20-mm calibre). From 1956 these were joined by units equipped with the Piasecki (Vertol) H-21 and Sikorsky H-34, the latter also being made under licence as the *Eléphant Joyeux* and the gunship *Pirate*. Under Gén. Maurice Challe the French adopted 'steamroller' tactics which forced the ALN into guerrilla operations.

The sheer cost of the war, in both money and French lives, gradually sapped the will of France. On 18 March 1962 the Accord de Evian was signed, establishing Algeria as a sovereign country.

No Pax Britannica

After World War II the impoverished United Kingdom dismantled the greatest empire the world had ever seen. However, that still did not stop bloody confrontations starting.

In 1946 Britain tried but failed to establish a Malayan Union comprising all the Malay States plus the Straits Settlements (basically, Singapore). Larger than England, this beautiful land was almost entirely tropical jungle, ideal for guerrilla warfare. During World War II Malayan Chinese Communists had been a thorn in the side of the brutal Japanese occupying power and after the war they tried to oust the British. They never numbered more than about 3,000, but from 1948 until 1960 they waged war against 40,000 troops, 61,000 armed police and 250,000 Malayan Home Guards. The 12-year campaign cost the lives of 519 troops, 1,346 police and 2,473 civilians, as well as 6,700 guerrillas.

By 1948 the huge wartime forces had been disbanded or returned home, and in South-East Asia there were almost no RAF assets apart from Beaufighters of No. 45 Sqn. and Spitfire 18s of No. 60 Sqn. These were almost useless against insurgent forces dispersed throughout dense jungle. By 1954 there were 242 aircraft in 14 squadrons, and under brilliant Gen. Sir Gerald Templer, they had learned how to fight over and in the jungles.

The types used were: the Avro Lincoln heavy bomber; Bristol Brigand tactical attack aircraft; Supermarine Spitfire 18, de Havilland Hornet F.3 and de Havilland Vampire F.B.5 fighters; de Havilland Mosquito P.R.34 and Spitfire 19 photo-reconnaissance aircraft; Handley Page Hastings, Avro York, Vickers Valetta and Douglas Dakota transports; Short Sunderland flying boats; Auster and Pioneer STOL aircraft and Westland Dragonfly and Whirlwind helicopters. The RAAF flew Lincolns and Dakotas, and the RNZAF Vampires and Bristol 170s. By 1960 the Lincolns had been replaced by Canberras and other new types included the Meteor P.R.10 and N.F.14, the Venom F.B.4 and Twin Pioneer.

UNEASY PEACE

By 1960 the insurgent threat had been overcome and an independent Malaysia was formed in 1963. The British had hoped that the Malaysian super-state would incorporate her previous colonies of Brunei and Sarawak in the north of the great island of Borneo. These were separated by an ill-defined 1,000-mile (1,609-km) frontier from Kalimantan, the former Dutch territory now forming part of Indonesia. Brunei was rich in oil and had no intention of joining Malaysia. Naturally, it was coveted by Indonesia. It was easy for Indonesia to foment rebellion, train guerrilla forces and even invade the British territory.

The Indonesian-trained guerrillas began their campaign in December 1962. The RAF had disbanded most of its Far East Air Force, leaving just No. 20 Sqn. (Hunter FGA.9), No. 45 Sqn. (Canberra B.2) and No. 60 Sqn. (Javelin FAW.9 all-weather and night fighters). The RAAF and RNZAF each had a Canberra squadron, and the RAAF also fielded the Sabres of No. 77 Sqn. The RAF rotated detachments of Vulcans and Victors equipped for conventional bombing, but the key units were those providing transport, using the Beverley, Argosy,

Hastings, Valetta and Beaver, and the Belvedere and turbine-engined Whirlwind 10 helicopters.

By carefully preventing the situation from escalating, and by winning 'the hearts and minds' of the local population, the confrontation was contained. It petered out in 1966.

The third conflict erupted in East Africa in 1952. In that year Jomo Kenyatta, the British-educated President of the KAU (Kenya African

Above: Powered by a 1,050-shp Bristol Siddeley (later Rolls-Royce) Gnome turbine engine, a Westland Whirlwind HC.10 alights in Borneo. In this theatre 110 Sqn.'s HC.10s flew 25,000 sorties in 1962–67.

Above: In true British style, after World War II little was done to re-equip the RAF. Then, in a panic, the Canberra B.2 was built by English Electric, Avro, Handley Page and Shorts, who delivered 430 in three years.

Union) was arrested on charges of inciting an uprising in the Kikuyu tribal area. This triggered a bloody campaign by a Kikuyu secret society called the Mau Mau. Its members murdered 95 white settlers, mostly isolated farmers and their families, but before the conflict ended in 1955 it had involved substantial air assets. These began in April 1953 when 12 Harvard trainers were moved up from Southern Rhodesia (where the author had flown them) to operate in Kenya as ground attack aircraft. Within a year they had flown 2,000 sorties, fired 750,000 rounds of

7.7-mm (0.303-in) ammunition and dropped 15,000 19-lb (8.6-kg) fragmentation bombs, but to little apparent effect. Far more impact was made by two Lincolns and so 1340 Flight was formed at Eastleigh (Nairobi airport) equipped with six Lincolns, eight Harvards, two Meteor P.R.10s, a Pembroke light transport, two Austers and a Sycamore helicopter. Ground forces were supported by supplies dropped from Valettas. By June 1955 the Mau Mau were no longer a menace. Kenya became independent in 1963 and a republic two years later.

Suez

In the 1950s Britain still had substantial seagoing airpower, embarked aboard the carriers *Albion*, *Bulwark*, *Victorious*, *Eagle* and *Ark Royal*. She also had RAF air bases in many parts of the world, which included a string extending through the Middle East from Malta and Cyprus to Egypt, Aden and the Persian Gulf. Used to playing the role of global policeman, in 1956 Britain found itself out of its depth.

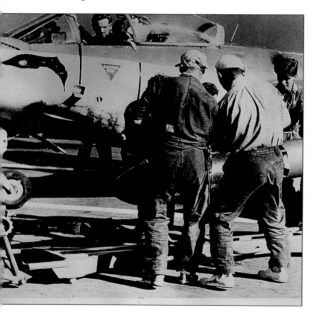

Above: Rearming an Armstrong Whitworth (Hawker design) Sea Hawk aboard HMS *Eagle* for a strike on Egyptian airfields. Six Sea Hawk squadrons operated from three carriers.

On 14 May 1948 Britain terminated its mandate to govern Palestine, which became an independent Jewish state called Israel. At midnight on the same day the new country was invaded by Egypt, Syria, Lebanon and Transjordan. The hastily arranged Israeli forces hit back, though they had no effective air force, and a truce was signed on 11 June. In January 1952 orchestrated mobs attacked foreign (especially British) assets in Egypt, and in November 1954 British forces began to withdraw from the Suez Canal Zone, which they had previously protected. On 26 July 1956 Col Nasser, President of Egypt, announced a decree nationalizing the Suez Canal, in effect stealing it from the Anglo-French company which had operated it since its construction.

By this time Egypt had a large and growing air force. At first most of its front-line assets were of British origin, including Vampires and Meteor N.F.13 night fighters. From October 1955 large batches of aircraft began arriving from the Soviet Union, the first types supplied being MiG-15 and MiG-17 fighters and Il-28 jet bombers. Taking over the Canal was just part of big changes; the ultimate goal being that, in concert with its Arab neighbours, Egypt would wipe out the state of Israel.

JOINT ACTION

A week after the takeover of the canal, Britain, France and Israel began planning military action against Egypt. On 24 October an agreement was signed at Sèvres in France under the terms of which the partners would start operations five days later. The RAF committed 120 Canberra and Valiant bombers, 20 reconnaissance Canberras and 100 Venom and Meteor fighters. The Fleet Air Arm provided 200 Sea Hawks, Sea Venoms, turboprop Wyverns and early-warning Skyraiders embarked in four carriers. The Armée de l'Air committed over 200 Mystère IVA, SMB.2 and F-84F Thunderstreaks as well as RF-84F Thunderflash reconnaissance aircraft. The Aéronavale provided a carrier with 50 Corsairs and Hellcats. Large transport forces included Yorks, Hastings, Valettas, Beverleys and even Shackletons and French Noratlas. The still

embryonic Israeli air force (Chel Ha'Avir) had 69 Meteor, Mystçre and Ouragan jets and 45 Mustangs, Mosquitos and B-17s.

The campaign began late on 29 October, when 1,600 Israeli paras dropped into the Mitla Pass, to be supplied with heavy equipment dropped by six French Noratlas. On the 30th an Egyptian Il-14 transport was shot down and an RAF reconnaissance Canberra was damaged by a MiG-15. An Egyptian destroyer bombarded Haifa, but was so damaged by Ouragans that she surrendered. Meanwhile a big battle developed over the Mitla Pass which ended with a Mystçre seriously damaged and two MiG-15s shot down.

On the 31st heavy ground and air battles took place over the Pass and the Sinai desert, while RAF Valiants and Canberras based in Malta and Cyprus bombed Egyptian airfields from 40,000 ft (12,192 m). A Valiant captain was disconcerted by being given accurate homings from the tower of the airfield he was about to bomb. Another Valiant was damaged by an Egyptian Meteor NF.13. Subsequent reconnaissance by Canberras confirmed only minor damage to the airfields and a Canberra was shot up by a MiG-15.

In the first days of November action intensified, liberally sprinkled by poor intelligence and 'own goals'. For example, Israeli forces advanced from opposite directions on Abu Ageila (whose garrison had departed) and bitterly fought each other until an Israeli pilot saw what was happening. On 2 November Israeli aircraft mistook the frigate HMS *Crane* for an Egyptian ship and accurately bombed it.

By 5 November British and French paras had dropped on Port Said and Port Fuad, and following seaborne landings on 6 November the Suez Canal was largely in the hands of the invaders. It was all for nothing, however, as UN (essentially American) pressure forced the parties to accept a cease-fire. Before the ill-starred campaign began Air Marshal Barnett had assured Prime Minister Eden 'Air power alone will topple the Nasser government'. The RAF and Fleet Air Arm lost six aircraft in action and about 20 more in accidents, many on crowded carriers.

SPECIFICATIONS

Westland Wyvern S.4

Type: single-seat carrier-based strike fighter

Powerplant: one Armstrong Siddeley Python 3 axial-flow turboprop, rated at 3,760 shp (2736 kW) plus 1,180 lb (536 kg) jet thrust for take-off

Performance: maximum speed 380 mph (612 km/h) at 10,000 ft (3048 m); initial climb rate 2,350 ft (716 m) per minute; service ceiling 28,000 ft (8535 m); maximum range 910 miles (1465 km)

Weights: loaded with torpedo 24,500 lb (11,113 kg)

Dimensions: wing span 44 ft (13.42 m); length 42 ft 3 in (12.88 m); height (wings spread) 15 ft 9 in (4.80 m); wing area 355 sq ft (32.98 m²)

Armament: four wing-mounted 0.79-in (20-mm) British Hispano Mk V cannon (one inboard and one outboard of each wing-fold) with 200 rounds per gun, plus underwing racks for sixteen 25-lb (11-kg) or 90-lb (41-kg) unguided rocket projectiles and bombs up to 1,000 lb (454 kg), centreline rack for a single bomb or one 2,500-lb (1134-kg) aerial torpedo

Cold War

it. For the US Central Intelligence Agency Lockheed developed the U-2. This equipped so-called 'weather reconnaissance' units based in the UK, Turkey, Germany, Japan and, later, other theatres. Flying at up to 80,000 ft (24,384 m) these sensor-carriers resembled jet-propelled sailplanes. On 1 May 1960 their cover was blown sky-high by the shooting down by a SAM of a CIA U-2B over Sverdlovsk. The pilot, Francis G. Powers, survived and appeared on Moscow TV. He had been briefed to fly from Peshawar in Pakistan to Bodø in Norway, photographing installations as they were on May Day.

This brought the Cold War to a worryingly warm level, and other factors kept the cauldron simmering. On 9 May 1955 West Germany had become a sovereign state, and joined NATO (the North Atlantic Treaty Organisation). The furious Soviet Union tore up treaties with its former Allies, and formed the Warsaw Pact to confront NATO by a military alliance in the East.

The Soviet Union exploded a fission nuclear weapon on 29 August 1949, and a fusion thermonuclear (hydrogen) device on 12 August 1953. From that date the so-called Cold War was on in earnest. For the first time, two superpowers possessed the means to destroy all human life. Both were also devising an unstoppable delivery system, the ICBM (intercontinental ballistic missile) with a range of over 6,300 nautical miles (11.675 km).

Both also constructed vast electronic defence systems, so that, even if an ICBM attack could not be stopped, about four minutes' warning would be given. Thus, a balance of terror ensued, with peace preserved by the belief that if either side annihilated the other, it would itself suffer equally in retribution. The USAF and RAF learned the new tasks Elint, Comint and Sigint (electronic, communications and signals intelligence).

During the Korean War RB-29s operated with new sensors. Next came the RB-50F and G. Later came the ERB-47H and RB-47K, while the US Navy operated VP (fixed-wing recon) and VQ (Elint) squadrons. In the 1950s Soviet fighters and SAMs shot down three RB-29s, two RB-50s and an RB-45, C-118A, C-130A and RB-47K of the USAF, and three P2V Neptunes, a PB4Y Privateer and two P4M Mercators of the US Navy.

The RAF also played a role, though the RB-45C squadron based at RAF Sculthorpe and wearing RAF markings was in fact a unit of the USAF. Its crews were drawn from both nations. Legitimate RAF units included No 192, with Elint Lincolns (in March 1953 a Lincoln was shot down by MiGs over Germany) and later B-29 Washingtons; Nos 97 and 151 with special Hastings and No 51 Sqn (No 192 renumbered) which for 45 years used special Canberras and three de Havilland Comet 2Rs, later replaced by Nimrod R.1s.

COVER BLOWN

By 1954 both superpowers were developing reconnaissance aircraft designed to fly so high that they could not be shot down. The Soviet Union fielded the Yak-25RV, but did not use

Above: Derived from the wartime B-24 Liberator, the Consolidated PB4Y-2 (from 1951 P4Y) Privateer was equipped with Elint receivers, often carrying a crew of up to 14. One was shot down and two others damaged in 'eavesdropping' missions.

Matters came to a head in 1961 when the Soviet military budget was increased by 25 per cent, and newly installed President Kennedy mobilized the Reserve and National Guard. On Sunday 13 August 1961 the frontier between the two Germanys was sealed, and construction began of a huge wall dividing East and West Berlin. Then a crisis appeared in a totally different theatre.

After a bitter guerrilla campaign Fidel Castro overthrew the corrupt government in Cuba. Supported by the Soviet Union, he was suddenly seen as a danger in the USA's 'own backyard'. Matters came to a head when, in March 1961, a US-supported invasion by Cuban exiles at the island's Bay of Pigs failed ignominiously. Then in 1962 U-2s of the CIA and USAF photographed rapid construction of SAM sites, as well as large new airfields. The culminating shock came on 14 October 1962 when a U-2E took 928 photographs showing installation of what the USA called 'SS-4 Sandal' missiles. Actually designated R-12, these Soviet weapons could deliver nuclear warheads to targets in the USA.

This seemed only a tit-for-tat response to the siting of much larger US-made Thor missiles in England and Jupiter missiles in Italy and Turkey to menace the USSR, but President Kennedy ordered his forces to blockade Cuba. Strategic Air Command went on full alert and the world held its breath. On 28 October the USSR backed down, and agreed to remove the missiles and Il-28 jet bombers. It was the turning point in the Cold War.

Above: Powered by four General Electric J47s, the North American RB-45C Tornado was a camera-packed derivative of the USAF's first jet bomber. It flew many clandestine missions, many of them wearing British markings.

The Deterrent

Left: In 1954–57 the Weybridge factory of Vickers-Armstrongs (Aircraft) delivered 108 Valiants. Their career was cut short because the wrong version was ordered.

As noted on the previous pages, the advent of nuclear weapons made the prospect of all-out war essentially unthinkable, so to that degree they deterred conflict. At first there was only one nuclear power, but the USA was soon joined by the Soviet Union. Britain and France followed, and today some nuclear capability is possessed by India, Israel, China, Pakistan, Iran, Iraq and possibly other countries. The situation has not been helped by fragmentation of the Soviet Union. Ukraine ranks third among nuclear powers, and several former Soviet republics in central Asia are hosts to giant nuclear-tipped missiles.

Until the end of the 1950s the only delivery system was the manned bomber. The B-29, the only aircraft to drop nuclear bombs 'in anger', was replaced by the B-50 and the gigantic B-36, both of which later had their piston engines boosted by added jets. Strategic Air Command next received the graceful six-jet 600-mph (966 km/h) B-47, 1,590 of the principal B-47E version being delivered in three years along with 820 KC-135 tankers to stretch their otherwise limited radius of action. Limited radius was also a problem with the first supersonic bomber to enter service, the Convair B-58, which set a shoal of records cruising at Mach 2 (1,322 mph, 2,127 km/h).

In 1952 Boeing flew the first B-52 Stratofortress. Powered by eight of the most powerful turbojets then available, this at last combined 600 mph 966-km/h speed with all the radius of action SAC needed. Over seven years from 1955 Boeing delivered 744 of successively improved versions, the final B-52H having a 'wet' (integral tank) wing and 18,000-lb (8,165-kg) thrust TF33 turbofan engines. What nobody expected was that at the Millennium these aircraft would still be in service, older than the crews who fly them.

In December 1974 Rockwell flew the first B-1, with variable-sweep wings. From this was developed the B-1B Lancer, able to carry 75,000 lb (34,020 kg) of conventional weapons internally or 59,000 lb (26,762 kg) externally at subsonic speed 'under the radar' at treetop height. In October 1981 President Reagan ordered 100, and these have been cleared to drop or launch many types of weapon. The B-2 (pp.178–179) followed.

TRIO OF 'V' BOMBERS

In January 1947 Britain went ahead with an indigenous nuclear weapon and bombers to carry it. Today, with only a single type of British military aircraft (the Hawk trainer), it is difficult to believe that contracts were placed for four types of large jet bomber: the Short

Left: Capable of Mach 2 at high altitudes, the Dassault Mirage IVA carried its nuclear bomb semi-externally. The flight-refuelling probe on the nose was essential. The engines were SNECMA Atar 09K afterburning turbojets rated at 7000 kg (15,432 lb).

Above: Seen here with its pivoted wings at maximum sweep, the Rockwell B-1B Lancer has gradually matured in what is now USAF Air Combat Command, with progressive clearance to use a wide range of weapons. In theory it can drop 128 500-lb (227-kg) bombs.

Sperrin, Vickers-Armstrongs Valiant, Avro Vulcan and Handley Page Victor. All these so-called V-bombers were excellent aircraft. The Sperrin remained prototypes, and 108 Valiants were quickly delivered, but the chief types were the Vulcan, a tailless aircraft powered by Bristol Olympus engines whose thrust was developed from 10,500 to 21,000 lb (9,526 kg), and the 'crescent-winged' Victor powered at first by Armstrong Siddeley Sapphire engines and in the B.2 version by Rolls-Royce Conway turbofans.

A foolish mistake was not to order the Mk 2 version of the Valiant, which had a structure strengthened for full-throttle flight at low level at 552 mph (888 km/h). Instead the Mk 1 was ordered, with a structure designed for high altitudes, so that at sea level speed was limited to 414 mph (666 km/h). After 1960 it was belatedly realized that bombers had to fly low; cracks soon appeared in the Valiants, which had to be grounded.

Another was to pay for complex rocket-boost systems, to enable all three V-bombers to make short takeoffs from tropical runways and then decide such equipment was not needed. Another was to develop large supersonic cruise missiles, such as the Blue Steel, switch to the proposed American Skybolt and then decide that the Vulcan and Victor would be used only to drop conventional bombs. Yet another was to start withdrawing the Vulcans and removing their flight-refuelling probes, while converting the Victors into tankers. The Falklands (pp.168–169) showed this to have been folly.

France determined to have a deterrent at the earliest possible date. Unlike Britain, France organized a US-style Triad of nuclear-armed bombers, submarine-launched missiles and silo-emplaced land-based missiles. The bomber was the Dassault Mirage IVA, 62 of which were delivered in 1963–66 to form the *Force de Frappe* (strike force). To reach targets in the Soviet Union they had to operate in pairs, one with overload fuel to top up the other, which carried a 60-kilotonne bomb. Later 18 were converted into the Mirage IVP, carrying an ASMP cruise missile with a 150-kilotonne warhead.

Vietnam: the US Air Force

Above: Gunners firing a broadside from a AC-47 gunship. They operated mainly at night.

Top: Fewer than 1,400 F-100 Super Sabres flew more sorties over Vietnam than the same maker's P-51 (11 times as numerous) flew in World War II.

The large French forces in Indo-China were defeated by peasants armed with rifles and sharpened bamboo stakes. The Geneva accord of July 1954 divided the country into North and South Vietnam, Laos and Cambodia. The grip of the Communist Viet-Minh on North Vietnam was already unshakeable. In May 1959 their leader, Ho Chi Minh, announced the objective of re-unifying the four territories. The other three were propped up by the South East Asia Treaty Organization and a US Military Assistance Advisory Group. US President Eisenhower chillingly made the prediction that all three would 'fall like a row of dominoes'.

South Vietnam was already infested by Communist guerrillas called the Viet-Cong (VC). Little by little the US was sucked into increasing support for the unpopular regime of Ngo Dinh Diem. From 1960 the USAF sent in forces: H-21, H-34, H-1 and H-3 helicopters, B-26 Invaders, T-28D light attack aircraft, Mach-2 RF-101C Voodoo photo aircraft and C-123 transports equipped to spray defoliation chemicals to deny the VC their jungle cover. The situation became worse each day, and the final straw, on 2 and 4 August 1964, were attacks by three tiny North Vietnamese boats on two US destroyers (see pp.148–149). This triggered open war with the United States.

Though enormous, the US forces were mostly in other theatres, and designed for a totally different kind of war. Orders were quickly placed for more helicopters for special forces and for a new kind of aircraft called COIN (counter-insurgency), able to operate from short unpaved airstrips. Scores of millions of dollars were spent in the construction of gigantic airbases and then in expanding them to accommodate larger numbers of aircraft. Week by week the USAF in Vietnam was built up, occasionally punctuated by daring airfield attacks by VC infiltrators. At the same time, the US tried to build up an effective VNAF (Vietnam Air Force), with such aircraft as the A-1 Skyraider, Cessna Bird Dog and A-37B Dragonfly, Caribou and later, the C-130 and F-5 Freedom Fighter.

THUNDER OVER THE NORTH

In 1965 the US launched a campaign called Rolling Thunder, to break the will of the VC by heavy bombing. It was misconceived: targets were selected in Washington, which also dictated every detail of the attack and its timing (a nonsensical procedure). Many industrial targets were obscured, while the obvious ones, such as airfields and SAM sites, were deemed off-limits, for fear of killing a Soviet or Chinese advisor. Not least, the will of the VC was far stronger than that of the South Vietnamese.

Rolling Thunder attacks were begun by the Navy. The USAF started on 2 March 1965 with Martin B-57s and Republic F-105s escorted by North American F-100s, losing three F-105s and two F-100s to anti-aircraft guns. Henceforth, the USAF was engaged in a bitter struggle, crippled by limitations and direction from the other side of the world. The only people who benefited were the plane-makers, enormous orders being placed for the F-4 Phantom and UH-1 Huey helicopter in particular.

North Vietnam gradually acquired modest fighter assets, notably the MiG-17 and MiG-21, as well as thousands of anti-aircraft guns. Their trucks kept up a ceaseless supply of war material along a network of jungle and mountain pathways called the Ho Chi Minh Trail. To try to stop this traffic the USAF devised new methods involving thousands of air-dropped sensors called Adsid, Acoubuoy and Spikebuoy to detect passing trucks. The difficulty then was how to hit the trucks. Even assisted by a FAC (Forward Air Controller) in a Cessna it was exceedingly difficult. Just one type alone, the F-100, flew over 300,000 sorties, more than the total flown in World War II by almost 16,000 P-51 Mustangs!

By 1965 other new weapons were in use. One was the gunship, a transport aircraft designed to circle round a suspected ground target whilst blasting it with the fire from an array of guns arranged like the 'broadside' of a warship. First came the AC-47 nicknamed 'Puff the Magic Dragon'. Next came the AC-130 Spectre and finally the AC-119 Shadow and Stinger. The AC-130 Spectre was armed with a battery of guns of 7.62, 20, 40 and even 105-mm (0.3, 0.79, 1.57 and 5.9-in) calibre firing up to a total of 500 rounds per second – possibly against a non-existent target.

Another weapon was the B-52, called the Buff (big ugly fat feller). Rebuilt to carry enormous loads of conventional bombs, they flew gruelling missions of up to 15 hours from Guam and later Okinawa. More bomb tonnage rained down on South-east Asia than on Germany in World War II, but to no avail.

Below: Likewise, B-52s dropped a heavier load of bombs on South-East Asia than fell on Germany in World War II. These B-52Ds were among those converted to carry enhanced loads of conventional bombs, something never thought of when they were designed. One mix was 84 bombs of 500 lb internally plus 24 of 750 lb under the inboard wings.

Vietnam: other US Forces

Left: When Bell designed the 'Huey' in 1955 it was hoped orders might reach 500. The actual run exceeded 15,000, of which many hundreds were lost in South-east Asia. These are early UH-1B versions, powered by a 960-hp T-53 engine.

From 1963 giant US carriers patrolled off the coast of the two Vietnams. From their decks RF-8A Crusaders flew photo missions over North Vietnam. They were often fired upon, and on 6 June 1964 (the 20th anniversary of D-Day) Lt Charles F. Klusmann was shot down. As noted previously, on 2 August 1964 three small North Vietnamese torpedo boats purportedly attacked the USS *Maddox*. The attack was never fully proven but the destroyer called up the carrier *Ticonderoga*. Four of her F-8E Crusaders of VF-53 were already airborne. They attacked the small craft with cannon and Zuni rockets, sinking the third. A long and bloody war had started.

Three days later Douglas A-1 and A-4 aircraft from *Ticonderoga* and *Constellation*, with F-4B Phantoms providing top cover, attacked the torpedo-boat bases and oil storage tanks. From then on, US airpower was to fly several million sorties against targets which were seldom seen and were possibly elsewhere or purely imagined. The piston-engined A-1 'Spad' and jet A-4 'Scooter', both designed at Douglas El Segundo by Ed Heinemann, headed the attack campaign throughout the early phases, later being joined by the two-seat Grumman A-6 Intruder and the Vought A-7 Corsair II 'Sluf' (Short little ugly feller).

At the start the Navy fighter was the F-8 Crusader, but this gave way to the F-4; 22 Navy and one Marine F-4 squadrons made 84 war cruises to the Gulf of Tonkin, 51 with F-4Bs, one with the F-4G (B plus a data-link) and 32 with F-4Js. The Navy F-4s were credited with 42 air-combat victories, for the loss of 71 in action (5 in combat, 13 to SAMs and 53 to ground gunfire) and 54 in accidents. Later Air Force F-4s outnumbered the Navy/Marines versions, experience showing the need for a slatted wing and a gun.

HUEYS AND LOACHES

An aircraft flown only by the Marine Corps was the North American OV-10A Bronco, a STOL (short takeoff and landing) twin-turboprop designed to find and attack ground targets, and also double as a Casevac (casualty-evacuation) transport carrying litter (stretcher) casualties in the rear fuselage. Another Marines' attack aircraft was the Bell AH-1J SeaCobra, a twin-engined development of the slim-bodied HueyCobra, which in turn had been derived from the UH-1. Enormous numbers of many UH-1 versions also served in Vietnam, some as assault transports and others as heavily armed gunships which operated close in amongst the VC in the jungle.

The main user of the Huey was the Army. This service also operated the most powerful helicopters, such as the CH-47 Chinook and the 'flying crane' CH-54 Tarhe, which among other things picked up and brought back over 380 downed aircraft. At the other end of the scale Army squadrons also operated the OH-6A Cayuse, better known as 'Loach', from its designation as an LOH (light observation helicopter). Often heavily armed, this fast and agile little helicopter operated right in the jungle drop zones and landing zones. That the job was dangerous is shown by the fact that one Loach pilot was rescued and airlifted back *six times* after having been shot down by point-blank fire.

Among Army fixed-wing aircraft were the C-7A Caribou STOL assault transport (in 1967 the 134 survivors were transferred to the USAF). Another was the Grumman OV-1 Mohawk, about the size of a jet fighter but with two crew side-by-side in the bug-eyed nose, with bullet-proof transparencies and flak curtains, and a variety of surveillance devices.

Other important Navy/Marines types included the EF-10B Skyknight ECM aircraft, EA-6B Prowler EW (electronic-warfare) platform, RA-5C Vigilante supersonic strategic reconnaissance aircraft, various types of A-3 Skywarrior, the E-1 Tracer and later the E-2

Hawkeye early–warning radar platforms, and the H–2 Seasprite, H–3 Sea King, H–34 Sea Bat, H–46 Sea Knight and H–53 Sea Stallion helicopters.

One of the lesser-known types was the Lockheed Neptune, flown as the OP–2E and AP–2H on special reconnaissance/attack missions. Another was the same maker's Super Constellation, derived from the famed airliner, flown in many EC–121 Warning Star versions on Elint (electronic-intelligence) and reconnaissance versions by both the Navy and Air Force. Early in the conflict P–5 Marlin flying boats patrolled offshore, C–1 Traders flew COD (carrier on–board delivery) missions throughout, and right at its conclusion on 30 April 1975 the F–14 Tomcat interceptor flew its first combat missions from the nuclear-powered USS *Enterprise* to cover the final panic–stricken evacuation of Saigon.

SPECIFICATIONS

McDonnell Douglas F-4B Phantom II

Type: two-seat carrier-based multi-role fighter

Powerplant: two General Electric J79 turbojets, each rated at 17,110 lb (7761 kg) thrust with afterburning

Performance: maximum speed 1,485 mph (2389 km/h) at 48,000 ft (14,630 m); initial climb rate 40,800 ft (12,436 m) per minute; service ceiling 62,000 ft (18,898 m); normal range 1,610 miles (2590 km)

Weights: empty 27,897 lb (12,654 kg); maximum take-off 54,600 lb (24,766 kg)

Dimensions: wing span 38 ft 4.75 in (11.71 m); length 58 ft 3.75 in (17.77 m); height 16 ft 3 in (4.95 m); wing area 530 sq ft (49.24 m²)

Armament: standard intercept load of four AIM-7E Sparrow semi-active radar-homing medium-range air-to-air missiles and four AIM-9B Sidewinder infra-red-guided short-range air-to-air missiles, maximum weapons load of 16,000 lb (72,578) kg, typical ordnance including 750-lb (340-kg) M117 and 500-lb (227-kg) Mk 82 freefall 'iron' bombs in slick or Snakeye retarded form

The United Kingdom

Above: Beloved by its pilots, the Lightning could have been a valuable multi-role aircraft, but in 1958 the British government's attitude was 'It has unfortunately gone too far to cancel it'. Nearest the camera is a T.5 two-seater.

Left: Even though the years 1952–55 were wasted, by the 1960s the Sea Vixen was maturing as a useful carrier-based all-weather interceptor and attack aircraft. Then the government took away the carriers.

Until 1960 the Britain had a powerful aircraft industry. Every year it held a great trade show at Farnborough, naturally open to British Empire aircraft only. In 1958 the new types on display, in flight and on the ground, numbered 59, from 20 companies.

At that time the Hawker Hunter was well established in service and in large-scale production for customers all over the world. Powered by a Rolls-Royce Avon engine of 10,050 lb (4,559 kg) thrust, it had the devastating inbuilt armament of four 30-mm (1.18-in) guns, and could also carry substantial loads of bombs and rockets. The Avon also powered the Valiant strategic bomber, Supermarine Scimitar naval fighter-bomber and de Havilland Sea Vixen naval all-weather fighter. All were totally British, apart from the fact that the Scimitar could launch US-supplied Sidewinder and Bullpup missiles. The Sea Vixen carried British missiles, Firestreak on the Mk 1 and Red Top on the Mk 2.

The same two types of air-to-air missile armed successive versions of the English Electric Lightning. Powered by two advanced Avon engines with afterburners, this all-weather interceptor had limited internal volume, which translated into short radius of action and primitive avionics, but it did had tremendous flight performance. It was the aircraft every RAF pilot wanted to fly, and when it was replaced in 1988 by the Tornado F.3 there was a palpable feeling of loss.

The first Lightning made its first flight on 4 April 1957. The same day the British Minister of Defence, Duncan Sandys (pronounced 'sands'), proclaimed that manned military aircraft were henceforth obsolete, and would be replaced by missiles! In 1940 Major Sandys had commanded a Z-battery, the name given to totally ineffectual anti-aircraft rockets. By 1957 he believed that rockets and missiles should somehow replace fighters and bombers. He was piqued at the existence of the Mach-2 Lightning, which had 'already gone too far to cancel'.

NO 'SUPER LIGHTNING'

Among programmes that were cancelled were an advanced Lightning with new engines and radars and much greater fuel capacity, developments of the Vulcan B.2 and Victor B.2 strategic bombers (which would have transformed the Falklands conflict, p.168), the Avro 730 supersonic bomber and multi-sensor reconnaissance aircraft, and the Gloster G.50 'thin-wing Javelin' and Saunders-Roe SR.177 all-weather interceptors. Powered by an afterburning turbojet and a powerful booster rocket, the SR.177 would have had a flight performance at extreme altitudes never before approached, and it excited intense interest among NATO air forces. The Luftwaffe sent over an evaluation team, but were thwarted when their hosts said 'We have cancelled it, because fighters are obsolete, but you are welcome to have it'. The Luftwaffe bought the F-104 instead.

Some people refused to believe in the new policy. At Kingston, Hawker Aircraft spent over £1.5 million developing the P.1121, a Mach-2 multi-role tactical aircraft. They gave up when told such a disagreement with the Government would have 'unfortunate repercussions'. The Chairman of the entire Hawker Siddeley Group, former Avro designer Sir Roy Dobson, told the author 'I have instructed my public-relations manager at Avro never to give the slightest hint that we disagree with Government policy'. He personally thought it was madness.

There were many spin-off effects. One was the cancellation of the Canadian Arrow (pp.116–117). Another was that the Vulcan and Victor might not be obsolete, provided that they carried Blue Steel cruise missiles (p.122). Another was the development of British SAMs, Bloodhound for the RAF, Thunderbird for the Army and Seaslug for the Navy. What was not explained was how these could actually replace RAF Fighter Command, because the only SAMs in Britain were Bloodhound batteries defending V-bomber bases. Hostile aircraft merely had to avoid going within 40 miles (64.3 km) of them. Moreover, once fired, a SAM cannot be used again. Fortunately, after a decent interval of about ten years the 'missiles instead of aircraft' policy was quietly forgotten. The pendulum perhaps swung too far the other way, because SAMs do have a role, and nothing has been done to replace the Bloodhounds which were made 35 years ago. Another problem was the radical idea of jet lift.

151

France

In World War II the French aircraft industry built German aircraft for the Luftwaffe. Some factories merely contributed parts, but the Morane-Saulnier plant built the Fi 156 Storch, a group managed by Amiot built the Ju 52/3m with assembly by Breguet, SNCA St Nazaire produced the Ar 196 cannon-armed seaplane, and SIPA built the Ar 396 trainer, continued after the war as the S.11 and S.12. The Bf 108 was built by Nord and gave rise to a profusion of post-war versions, the Ju 488 was assigned to Latécoère and the huge He 274 to the Farman group. Production of the Fw 189 was assigned to SNCASO plants in the Bordeaux area. The Fw 190 fighter was produced by the SNCAC at Cravant, and after the war this briefly continued in production as the NC.900. The SNCAC's Bourges factory made all versions of the Si 204, and these continued post-War as

the NC.701 and 702 *Martinet*. German factories also received French engines, such as the GR14M for the Hs 129 and GR14N for the Me 323, while Renault mass-produced German Argus engines for the Fi 156, Fw 189 and Ar 396

A few brave engineers refused to work for the Germans, and migrated south into the Unoccupied Zone to form the Groupe Technique de Cannes. Here several important aircraft were designed, notably the S.O.30 and S.O.90 transports. On 16 August 1943, by which time Cannes was under Italian occupation, Maurice Hurel made the first takeoff of the S.O.90 under the noses of Italian guards and, with six companions, boldly flew to Philippeville in Algeria.

In 1944 work began at Suresnes on a small jet aeroplane, the S.O.9000 *Triton*. Powered by a German Jumo 004B, it made its first flight on

11 November 1946 at Orleans-Bricy. Four days later it had a place of honour in the first of the great post-war Paris airshows. By this time the Hispano-Suiza company had a licence for the Rolls-Royce Nene turbojet, and over the next 15 years the French *motoriste* made thousands of Nenes, and more powerful Tay and Verdon engines derived from it. Meanwhile, a former senior engineer on BMW turbojets, Dr Hermann Oestrich, had formed a group called ATAR, and in turn used this as the name of an axial turbojet for France. The SNECMA Atar gradually supplanted the Rolls-derived centrifugal engines.

BLOCH'S EMINENCE

The most important post-war firm was that of Marcel Bloch, who changed his name to Marcel Dassault. His first post-war product was the M.D.315 *Flamant* (flamingo) light military transport, but on 28 February 1949 flight testing began of the M.D.450 *Ouragan* (Hurricane). This Nene-engined fighter was a great success, and led to the swept-wing *Mystère* (mystery) and transonic *Super Mystère* SMB.2, with an afterburning Atar. These sold to many countries, and provided a basis for future developments. What Dassault never expected was that the much bigger British industry would be forbidden to compete!

In 1954 Dassault took the plans of the Fairey F.D.2, a tailless delta-winged research aircraft designed for Mach 2 and, with Fairey's assistance, used this as the basis of a fighter to be called *Mirage*. First came a simple research aircraft, the Mirage I, flown on 25 June 1955. The twin-engined Mirage II was discarded on 30 January 1956. Within nine months Dassault created the Mirage III, powered by an afterburning Atar. It could have a rocket to boost performance. Without this, on 24 October 1958 Roland Glavany in a Mirage IIIA reached over Mach 2 in level flight, the first time this had been achieved in Europe.

From the IIIA Dassault developed many versions of the Mirage III, 5 and 50, selling 1,422 to customers worldwide, including 19 air forces which had previously bought British jet

Above: Emerging at a time when Britain thought manned fighters obsolete, the Mirage III sold all over the world. This early IIIC has a Matra R.530 missile.

fighters. The same design was scaled up to produce the twin-engined Mirage IVA (p.145). In
1956, to meet a NATO requirement, Dassault
produced the *Etendard* (standard, or flag) light
fighter, which was developed into various
Etendard IV and Super Etendard missile-armed
naval attack aircraft (see p.168), while a totally
fresh start in 1966 resulted in the Mirage
F1, with a fuselage and afterburning Atar
engine similar to the delta Mirages but with a
much smaller high-mounted swept wing and
horizontal tail.

On 10 March 1978 Dassault flew the first
Mirage 2000, which looks like a Mirage III but
is actually a totally upgraded design powered by
a SNECMA M53 engine. A total of 574 had
been sold by late 1999. Even more important is
the *Rafale* (p.184).

SPECIFICATIONS

Dassault Mirage F1.E

Type: single-seat multi-role fighter

Powerplant: one SNECMA Atar 9K-50 turbojet rated at 11,023 lb st (49.03 kN) dry and 15,785 lb st (70.21 kN)
with afterburning

Performance: maximum level speed (clean) at 36,090 ft (11,000 m) 1,453 mph (2338 km/h); maximum rate of climb at sea
level 41,930 ft (12,780 m) per minute with afterburning; service ceiling 65,615 ft (20,000 m); combat radius 324 nm; 373
miles (600 km) on a lo-lo-lo attack mission with six 551-lb (250-kg) bombs and two drop tanks; endurance 2 hours
15 minutes on a combat air patrol with two Super 530 AAMs and one drop tank

Weights: empty 16,314 lb (7400 kg); normal take-off 24,030 lb (10,900 kg); maximum take-off 35,715 lb (16,200 kg)
Dimensions: wing span 30 ft 6.75 in (9.32 m) with tip-mounted Magic air-to-air missiles; length 50 ft 2.5 in (15.30 m);
height 14 ft 9 in (4.5 m); wing area 269.11 sq ft (25.00 m²)

Armament: two fixed 1.18-in (30-mm) DEFA 553 cannon with 125 rounds per gun, maximum ordnance 13,889 lb
(6300 kg); standard intercept load of two MATRA Magic 2 or AIM-9J Juli IR-guided air-to-air missiles and two MATRA
Super 530D semi-active radar-homing medium-range air-to-air missiles

The Soviet Union

On 20 June 1945 the 37-strong Normandie-Niemen fighter wing arrived back in its native France, with a proud record of fighting on the Eastern Front. Stalin had said 'You have a choice of any Allied fighter, we have them all'. They chose the Yak-3.

This would have amazed the Anglo-Saxons, whose only knowledge of Soviet aircraft was that they must be inferior copies of Western designs. Such a stupid assessment was rudely shattered by the MiG-15 (p.109). The MiG bureau subsequently maintained a pace of development no other design team could match, with the 60°-swept MiG-19 (the first supersonic fighter in

Above: Following a disappointing prototype, the Sukhoi T-10 was totally redesigned. The result was the Su-27, an aircraft of such brilliance it has awed every pilot who has flown it. Today several derived versions are finding customers in many countries. This example was sold to the Ukraine.

service), the delta-plus-tailplane MiG-21 selected by a record 56 air forces (a configuration also used for larger all-weather interceptors), the 'swing-wing' MiG-23 and MiG-27, and the Mach-2.82 MiG-25 family made mainly of welded steel.

In the 20 years from 1950 the total number of MiG fighters produced in the USSR exceeded 50,000, with many more made in other countries. The current family is the MiG-29, which since 1977 has been equipped with excellent radar, passive infra-red, a laser ranger, wide-angle head-up display and helmet-mounted sight, which Western pilots should get on Eurofighter 25 years later. Next came the 1-44 (p.184).

The rival Sukhoi bureau provided the IA-PVO (manned interceptor force) with the Su-9, Su-11 and twin-engined Su-15. In 1975 the

Su-25 appeared, to fight limited wars (p.170), followed in 1981 by the Su-27. It is sufficient to say that this superb aircraft and its many successors are the yardstick against which today's fighters are measured. Even the original Su-27, powered by two AL-31F turbofans of 27,557 lb (12,500 kg) thrust, combines outstanding sensors, a weapon load of 13,668 lb (6,200 kg) of 42 types of store including eight species of guided missile, the best gun in the world, and agility unrivalled by any Western aircraft (the amazing Cobra and *Kulbit* have tactical significance). Derivatives include naval versions, tandem-seat interceptors with trans-Siberia range, and side-by-side-seat heavy attack aircraft. A customer option is vectored thrust (p.184).

TUPOLEV'S GIANTS

Specializing in large aircraft, the long-established Tupolev bureau provided the ADD (strategic aviation) and AV-MF (naval aviation) with 25 versions of Tu-16 twin-jet, with maximum weights heavier than the British four-engined Valiant, and 27 versions of the Tu-95 and Tu-142 swept-wing turboprops, the only military aircraft in the world able to fly from anywhere to anywhere else without using their inflight-refuelling probe. Tupolev also supplied the IA-PVO with a powerful long-range interceptor, the Tu-128.

In 1958 came the first flight of the prototype Tu-105, from which were derived 11 versions of Tu-22 supersonic bomber, which despite having only two engines were heavier and more capable than the US counterpart, the B-58. Unlike the Convair bomber, the Tu-22 also had a 30-year service career, and from it was derived the 'swing-wing' Tu-22M family which still has an important range of roles in the former Soviet air forces. Many impressive Tupolev designs never got built, but in the Tu-160 Russia has the most powerful warplane ever put into service. It looks like the USAF's B-1B, but it has a smaller radar cross section, lower aerodynamic drag, and 79 per cent more installed thrust. Shortage of funds resulted in fewer than half the production batch of 100 being completed.

In January 1953 testing began of the enormous Myasishchev M-4 jet bomber, and this led

to 17 production versions, later types being designated as variants of 3MS, 3MN or 3MD.

The Soviet helicopter industry produced more heavy machines than any other in the world. The Mil bureau designed a succession of machines which achieved enormous production runs, and whereas the Mi-4 looked like a S-55 and the Mi-8 looked like an S-61 they were, in fact, far more powerful than the Sikorsky machines. The Mi-6 and Mi-26 are more powerful than any Western counterparts.

The Kamov bureau specializes in helicopters with superimposed coaxial rotors, but today also produces what might be termed conventional machines. One of its more remarkable creations is the Ka-50 *Chernaya Akul* (black shark) and the two-seat Ka-52*Alligator*. These compete with the Mi-28 family in the anti-armour market.

SPECIFICATIONS

Mikoyan-Gurevich MiG-21FL (India Air Force)

Type: single-seat interceptor

Powerplant: one MNPK 'Soyuz' (Tumanskii) R-11F2S-300 turbojet rated at 8,600 lb st (38.26 kN) dry and 13,613 lb st (60.57 kN) with afterburning, and provision for two SPRD-99 solid-propellant booster rockets each rated at 5,511 lb st (24.50 kN)

Performance: maximum level speed (clean) at 36,090 ft (11,000 m) 1,320 mph (2125 km/h); maximum rate of climb at sea level with two missiles and 50 per cent fuel more than 24,600 ft (7500 m) per minute; service ceiling 62,335 ft (19,000 m); ferry range more than 808 miles (1300 km) with 211-US gal (800-litre) drop tank

Dimensions: wing span 23 ft 5.75 in (7.15 m); length 51 ft 8.5 in (15.76 m) including probe; height 13 ft 6.2 in (4.125 m); wing area 247.5 sq ft (23.00 m²)

Weights: empty 11,795 lb (5350 kg); maximum take-off 20,018 lb (9080 kg), or 19,400 lb (8800 kg) on rough strip

Armament: standard intercept load of two K-13 (R-3S) infra-red-guided short-range air-to-air missiles; maximum ordnance of 1,102 lb (500 kg) includes provision for GP-9 gun pack containing a twin-barrelled 0.90-in (23-mm) GSh-23L cannon with 200 rounds

Italy and Sweden

In World War II Italy had a large aircraft industry, and a proud heritage of records and headlines around the world. It suffered from the fact that many of its most important aircraft had out of date structures, and from an absence of powerful engines. By 1942, to achieve an output of 1,500 hp Italy's fighters had to use the German DB 605 engine, made by Fiat.

After World War II Fiat hitched its wagon to the de Havilland star and made the Vampire and Venom fighters under licence, together with the Venom's Ghost engine. In 1954 NATO issued a specification for a 'light strike fighter' able to operate from unpaved airstrips. To the disgust of the French the winner was the Fiat G.91, powered by a Bristol Orpheus turbojet of 5,000 lb (2,268 kg) thrust.

France said 'Non', and this excellent tactical attack and reconnaissance aircraft was adopted only by Italy, and by the reborn West German Luftwaffe which received 282 made by the resurgent Dornier company. These were later passed on to Portugal. Fiat made 370, and from 1966 followed with 72 G.91Y upgrades powered by two General Electric J85s. Fiat Aviazione became Aeritalia, which then merged into today's Alenia.

In 1957 the famed Macchi company flew the prototype M.B.326, a tandem-seat trainer powered by an Armstrong Siddeley Viper turbojet. Many were sold globally, including light attack versions. From them was developed the MB-339 (originally M.B.339), with a more powerful Viper and many options. By 1999 214 had been sold to nine air forces and the Argentine Navy. Aermacchi and Alenia collaborated with Embraer of Brazil to produce the AMX attack aircraft, powered by a Rolls-Royce Spey turbofan.

GHOST IN THE BARREL

Sweden's Saab company made various aircraft under licence before itself designing the Saab-17 and Saab-18 piston-engined reconnaissance bombers and Saab-21A fighter. The latter had a pusher DB 605 engine, the tail being carried on twin booms. This was ideal for conversion to jet propulsion, and 60 of the 299 were rebuilt as the J21R powered by a Goblin built either by de Havilland or by SFA (Svenska Flygmotor).

Left: If Britain had bothered to continue development of the Hunter it would rapidly have evolved into something like the AMX, developed jointly by Italy and Brazil. This pair of the *Aviazione Militare* have served in Balkan operations under UN command. On the wingtips are self-defence Sidewinders.

SFA also had a licence to make the Ghost, of 5,000 lb (2,268 kg) thrust, and this was used to power the Saab-29 *Tunnen* (barrel). This was an outstanding design, and when the prototype flew on 1 September 1948 it was far in advance of any fighter in Britain! Saab delivered 661.

Next came the Saab-32 *Lansen* (lance), the prototype of which flew on 3 November 1952. Though this looked rather like a Hunter, it had a loaded weight 80 per cent greater. Powered by an SFA-made Avon with a Swedish afterburner and nozzle, and supersonic in a shallow dive, 450 Lansens were built in attack, night fighter and reconnaissance versions. They were outstanding aircraft, and in 1999 several still served after conversion into J32E electronic-warfare platforms.

One of the most striking aircraft in the sky, the Saab-35 *Draken* (dragon) first flew on 25 October 1955. Its equipment was packaged front-to-rear along the inboard wings, which had the incredible sweep angle of 80°. A night and all-weather interceptor, with a more powerful SFA-built afterburning Avon engine, and armed with two 30-mm (1.18-in) guns and two Swedish-made Sidewinder missiles, the J35A entered service in 1959. Subsequent versions carried heavy bomb loads or reconnaissance sensors, but could still reach Mach 2 in clean condition. Total production was 606, foreign customers including Denmark, Finland and Austria. The upgraded J35J multi-role fighter was still in Swedish service in 1999.

Next came the Saab-37 *Viggen*, with large canard foreplanes and a Volvo Flygmotor RM8 augmented turbofan derived from the Pratt & Whitney JT8D, fitted with a reverser to assist operation from short icy stretches of roadway. Saab delivered 180 attack and reconnaissance versions, followed by 149 of the more powerful JA37 interceptor version. These impressive aircraft have a powerful 30-mm (1.18-in) gun, and carry a wide range of missiles.

The latest Swedish warplane, the Saab JAS 39 *Gripen* (griffin) is again a 'double delta' with a canard foreplane. It is powered by a single RM12 (F404 made by Volvo under GE licence). Saab is delivering 204 to Sweden's air force, 28 will be built for South Africa, and British Aerospace shares in manufacture and is assisting in sales. Since 1945, of Britain's military prototypes, 18 per cent reached squadrons, but Sweden's figure is 100 per cent.

SPECIFICATIONS

Saab JA 37 Viggen

Type: single-seat interceptor

Powerplant: one Volvo Flygmotor RM8B turbofan (Pratt & Whitney JT8D-22 turbofan with Swedish-designed afterburner and thrust reverser) rated at 16,200 lb st (72.06 kN) maximum military dry and 28,110 lb st (125.04 kN) with afterburning

Dimensions: wing span 34 ft 9.25 in (10.60 m); canard foreplane span 17 ft 10.5 in (5.45 m); length 53 ft 9.75 in (16.40 m) including probe; height 19 ft 4.25 in (5.90 m); wing area 495.16 sq ft (46.00 m²); canard foreplane area 66.74 sq ft (6.20 m²)

Weights: normal take-off 33,069 lb (15,000 kg); maximum take-off 37,478 lb (17,000 kg) interceptor, or 45,194 lb (20,500 kg) attack

Performance: maximum level speed (clean) at 36,000 ft (10,975 m) more than 1,321 mph (2126 km/h); climb to 32,800 ft (10,000 m) in less than 1 minute 40 seconds from brakes-off with afterburning; service ceiling about 60,000 ft (18290 m); combat radius

Armament: one integral high-velocity 1.18-in (30-mm) Oerlikon KCA revolver cannon (offset to port) with 150 rounds mounted in a ventral pack; maximum weapons load 13,000 lb (5897 kg); standard beyond visual range weapon is the medium-range,semi-active radar-guided, all-weather BAeD Rb 71 Sky Flash (now being replaced by AIM-120 AMRAAM weapon) plus Rb74 (AIM-9L) IR-homing Sidewinders for short-range engagements; other weapons include four pods each containing six Bofors 5.3-in (13.5cm) rockets for air-to-surface role

Vertical lift

The gas turbine offered such an increase in power for a given weight that it became possible to imagine aeroplanes able to rise vertically and hover, as well as to fly at high speed. There were many possible routes to VTOL (vertical takeoff and landing).

One was to fit powerful turboshaft engines geared to two large propellers arranged to tilt through 90°, so that an otherwise conventional aeroplane could rise vertically. Another was to fit turboprops on a wing mounted on pivots, to the same end. Another was to drive two or four propellers inside swivelling ducts, or to make them blow against enormous flaps depressed to 90°. Another was to fit powerful jet engines with a switch-in deflector, so that for VTOL the jet blasted downward. Another was to fit a powerful jet engine with rotating (so-called vectoring) nozzles. Another was to fit an otherwise conventional jet aircraft with an extra battery of simple jet engines used only for VTOL.

The most dramatic idea was to tilt the whole aircraft nose-up, but in fact the first jet VTOL was hardly an aircraft at all. Called a TMR (thrust-measuring rig), it comprised two Nene turbojets pointing towards each other, with the jetpipes turned down through 90°. Compressed air bled from the engines could be blasted through down-pointing nozzles to tilt the TMR in any direction or make it pirouette. Clearly dangerous, it was handed to Sqn Ldr Ron Harvey to test. He completed the test programme from 3 July 1953. It was then handed to the maker, who crashed it fatally.

SNECMA, the French engine firm, flew an Atar turbojet mounted vertically, and then wrapped a circular wing round it to produce the *Coléoptère*. In the USA Bell made the first takeoff of a 'flat riser' aeroplane when the Model 65 lifted off on 16 November 1954. It had two J44 turbojets mounted on pivots. Ryan built the delta-wing X-13 Vertijet, with a Rolls-Royce Avon engine. In 1955 it was flown conventionally, followed in May 1956 by testing in which, like a moth on a wall, it hooked on and off a large upright platform.

NAVY TAIL-SITTERS

The US Navy thought a turboprop fighter standing on its tail might operate from a small area of deck. Convair and Lockheed built machines powered by a 5,850-hp Allison T40. Convair's 'Skeets' Coleman rose vertically on 1 August 1954, and then transitioned to wing-supported flight and back to a VL, but the idea was obviously a non-starter.

The US Army funded the Bell XV-3, with a 23-ft (7-m) prop-rotor on each wingtip, arranged to pivot 90° for VTOL, tested from 23 August 1955. There followed a wealth of other strange flying machines which explored every possible route to VTOL. Lockheed's XV-4A had the central fuselage occupied by a vertical duct which, when the blowing was turned on from multiple air jets, entrained a huge airflow through doors on top to augment the lift. The Ryan XV-5A had large lift fans inside the wings, normally covered by doors for flight at 547 mph (880 km/h).

In 1957 the Short SC.1 began testing what could be done with a battery of simple lift jets. This idea was taken further in Dassault's Mirage III-V. Powered by eight Rolls-Royce RB.162 lift jets and an augmented turbofan propulsion engine, it reached Mach 2.04 on 12 September 1966, and was sponsored by British Aircraft Corporation and Boeing to meet NATO Basic

Below: Here seen in the vertical-flight mode, the Bell-Boeing V-22 combines the ability to hover with the efficiency (and thus speed and range) of an aeroplane. It can carry 24 combat-equipped troops at 316 mph (509 km/h). Its unique qualities finally overcame the scepticism and hostility of Congress and should now lead to delivery of many versions to many customers.

Military Requirement No 3. This called for a jet-lift tactical fighter.

A rival was Britain's Hawker P.1127. This was much simpler, having only one engine, a Bristol BE.53 turbofan with four nozzles able to rotate down through about 98°. As British military aircraft were forbidden it had to be presented as a pure research aircraft, funded by the USA and the Bristol company. It worked so well that by stages it was developed into the Harrier GR.1, which entered service with the RAF in 1969. This in turn was developed with much more powerful Rolls-Royce Pegasus engines into today's family of Harrier, Sea Harrier and US Marines AV-8B tactical multi-role aircraft.

The only other vertical-lift idea in service is the tilting prop-rotor. The LTV XC-142 was powered by four GE T64 turboprops on a wing pivoting through 90°, and after a VTO one reached 430 mph (692 km/h) in September 1964. Bell decided it was better to fix the wing and tilt the tip-mounted prop-rotors, as they had done with the XV-3. After testing the XV-15, they went into partnership with Boeing to produce the V-22 Osprey. On each wingtip is a 6,150-hp Rolls-Royce T406 driving a massive 38-ft (11.6-m) prop-rotor. The Osprey is in production for the US Marines, Navy and Air Force as a multi-role airlifter.

Left: Also seen in the vertical-fight mode, the XC-142 pivoted its entire wing, on which were four 3,080-hp turboprops. Able to carry 32 troops or 8,000 lb (3629 kg) of cargo, it was one of countless aircraft which did everything asked of it yet was taken no further.

Above: In contrast, the Ryan X-13 was never more than a purely experimental vehicle. Test pilot Pete Girard had a seat which slightly eased the problems of tilting through 90°.

New Wings

Above: First flown in 1964, the F-111 failed to replace all the USAF and USN's tactical aircraft, but 556 were built as all-weather bombers. This example, carrying triplets of bombs, is an F-111A of the 366th Tactical Fighter Wing.

As related on p.114, swept wings are not essential for supersonic aircraft, but they do help to reduce drag at high subsonic Mach numbers. The MiG-19 and British Lightning had a leading-edge angle of around 60°, and Sweden's Draken hit 80°. Inevitably, such aircraft are penalized at low speeds, when the need is for a 'straight wing' with a wide span and effective high-lift devices such as leading-edge slats or flaps and trailing-edge flaps. In 1944 the German Messerschmitt company began building an aircraft with variable sweep, to try to get the best of both shapes.

Early VG (variable-geometry) aircraft, such as the Bell X-5 (based on the Messerschmitt) and Grumman XF10F, had complicated wings, with roots that had to slide to front and rear. Vickers-Armstrongs in Britain discovered how wings could be pivoted well out from the aircraft centreline on a fixed portion called a glove. When Britain abandoned fighters (p.151), it handed the 'swing wing' to the USA, where it was at once used in the General Dynamics F-111. This low-level attack bomber was intended also to be a fighter for the Navy, but failed in this role. Instead Grumman produced the F-14 Tomcat, an excellent aircraft which again had a VG wing.

VG wings were also used in such aircraft as the Rockwell B-1B, the Tu-22M and Tu-160, the Su-24 (a more powerful counterpart to the F-111), the MiG-23 and MiG-27, and the

Panavia Tornado (all described on other pages). These have wings which are hardly swept back at all for takeoff and landing, fitted with powerful high-lift devices so that, despite having a very high wing loading, the aircraft can use ordinary runways. Wing loading is the aircraft weight divided by the wing area. It went up from the 15 lb/ft³ of the Fairey Swordfish (p.76) to 46 lb/ft² in the Lancaster and 77.6 lb/ft² in the B-29, but the Tornado can take off with each square foot having to lift over 215 lb!

MANNED BULLET

This makes an enormous difference to how well the aircraft can attack at low level. With the wings swept back at the maximum angle of 67° – which reduces the available area, and thus increases the loading even further – the Tornado, and any other VG aircraft, can fly 'clean' (no bombs or tanks) in full afterburner much faster than sound. It becomes a projectile, able to cut through low-level turbulence whilst still proceeding in a straight line, whereas a long-span aircraft with a lower wing loading,

such as the F-15 or F/A-18, would 'shake the crew's eyeballs out' unless it slowed down.

On the other hand, the F-15 gains in air-combat manoeuvrability. It has a simple wing, with a fixed leading edge and plain hinged trailing-edge flaps, because it has such a large area. The F-15 wing has an area of 608 ft² (56.5 m²), compared with only 286 ft² (26.6 m²) for the Tornado, so in a close combat between the two it would be 'no contest'. Such aircraft as the Eurofighter and F-22 again have large fixed-geometry wings, and therefore are primarily air-combat aircraft rather than hedge-hopping bombers.

Sweptback wings suffer from various aerodynamic problems which are absent from an FSW (forward-swept wing). On the other hand an FSW is torsionally divergent. To understand what this means, hold a cardboard wing out of a speeding car. If it is swept back, no problem, but if it is swept forward the result will be obvious. In 1944 the German Junkers firm built a jet bomber with an FSW, but at high speed such a wing made with traditional structure would be torn off. A safe FSW can now be built, using layers of resin-bonded carbon fibre with the fibres arranged for maximum stiffness and strength, to put torsional divergence beyond the maximum speed attainable.

To prove it could be done Grumman built the X-29 research aircraft, flown in December 1984. Then the FSW appeared to sink without trace until, in September 1997, Sukhoi in Moscow flew the S-37 *Berkut* (Golden Eagle). This impressive technology demonstrator is powered by two Aviadvigatel D-30F6 turbofans, each with an afterburning thrust of 34,170 lb (15,500 kg). From it could be derived a formidable fighter.

In stark contrast to the F-15, the S-37 and the rival MiG 1-44 have a profusion of control surfaces. Almost all recent Russian fighters and projects feature the 'integrated triplane' formula, with a powered foreplane and tailplane, as well as powered wing edges. Some designers have even looked again at the variable-incidence wing, as used on the Vought F-8 Crusader of 1955.

Below: Perhaps the most striking shape in the sky, Sukhoi S-37 *Berkut* (Golden Eagle) is expected to lead to a multi-role fighter. Powered temporarily by D-30F6 engines, it has 14 fight-control surfaces. Length is 74 ft (22.6 m).

Avionics

Left: By 1944 US designers had put the big APS-20 surveillance radar into aircraft. Here APS-20 is airborne in a Douglas AD-4W Skyraider of Britain's Fleet Air Arm. They were later fitted in Gannets, and when the FAA lost its carriers the 20-year-old radars were bolted under RAF Shackletons.

The first electronic device in aviation was the radio. Clumsy and unreliable sets were used in World War I to transmit or receive (or both) using either Morse signals or direct voice speech, but speech was distorted and often rendered unintelligible by interference. In World War II v.h.f. (very high frequency) radios working on shorter wavelengths brought clarity to speech and replaced long wire antennas by a rod or blade. The shorter wavelength enabled the number of channels (frequencies used) to be increased from a dozen or so to thousands. Today's u.h.f. (ultra-high) is even better, but like v.h.f. the signals travel in straight lines. Thus, to speak to a pilot making a distant low-level attack one has to use long h.f. waves, which are reflected by electrically charged layers above the atmosphere and so can travel round the Earth.

In 1928 American pilots began using radio as a navaid (navigation aid). Signals were sent out like fixed-direction beams from a lighthouse. On the left of the beam pilots heard a Morse letter A • - and on the right an N - • while, if they flew carefully along the centre, the two signals merged to give a continuous note. Next came the D/F (direction-finding) loop, an antenna which indicated the direction of the ground station being received. The Americans developed the system of

beams into VOR (v.h.f. omni range), which in 1959 was bulldozed through as the world standard navaid in preference to the dramatically better area-coverage Decca system which had the misfortune to be British.

Other radio beams were devised to guide aircraft down to runways in bad weather. In 1954 Marconi produced Green Satin, a navaid for the RAF V-bombers operating on the doppler principle (familiar as the change in pitch of a horn or whistle as it rushes past). By 1958 American aircraft, such as the B-58 and A-5, were fitted with the first inertial systems in which position and velocity are known by measuring with incredible accuracy the accelerations along all three axes imparted from the moment the aircraft starts to move. More recently navigation has been assisted by satellites.

BIRTH OF RADAR

In 1935 Britain began developing radar (RAdio Detection And Range) to defend itself against oncoming bombers by making them reflect back radio signals. A year later it was realized that radars might be made small enough to fit into aircraft, and the results included forward-looking radars for fighters and down-looking radars to paint pictures of the ground. It was at once recognized that it

would also be possible to design aircraft to be less detectable (p.177).

Moreover, to every new device there is a countermeasure. In World War II ECM (electronic countermeasures) became vitally important. One of the simplest is jamming; communications, or any other electronic transmission, can be interfered with by sending out high-power obliterating signals on the same frequency, or swept over a frequency band. Alternatively, from 1943 the RAF used German-speaking operators to overcome the Luftwaffe controllers and order the defending night fighters to go to the wrong places.

The simplest and commonest ECM is chaff. Most chaff consists of billions of strips of reflective foil cut to a length matching hostile radars. With the sky covered in reflections the defenders cannot see any targets. Chaff is dispensed as a cloud, or exploded from ejected cartridges. Internal jammers transmit from antennas on the aircraft. The B-1B's ECM occupies 108 boxes weighing over 5,400 lb (2.5 tonnes), plus over a ton of cables, consuming 120 kW! The antennas cover all wavelengths, and point in all directions.

Another range of detectors operate on much shorter wavelengths to detect IR (infra-red) such as the heat from engines. Many kinds of

anti-aircraft missile, fired from aircraft, the ground or ships, rely on a seeker able to home on the IR from the target. The obvious IRCM is to eject from the aircraft a large cartridge called a flare, presenting the missile with a much juicier target. Helicopters usually have a permanently installed IRCM radiator, which like a lighthouse sends out strong heat pulses. These are modulated to confuse the missile seeker, and make it 'break lock' and fall away harmlessly.

EW (electronic warfare) is a vast subject. Some aircraft, such as the Grumman EA-6B Prowler and the Tornado ECR (electronic combat and reconnaissance) carry nothing but devices for EW missions. Having retired the EF-111A Raven, the USAF was in 1999 realizing that it should have done something to provide a successor.

Above: Though known best for its Mach-3 speed, the USAF's Lockheed SR-71 carried a unique array of reconnaissance sensors. These included a choice of palletized cameras, Elint receivers and synthetic-aperture radar.

In the cockpit

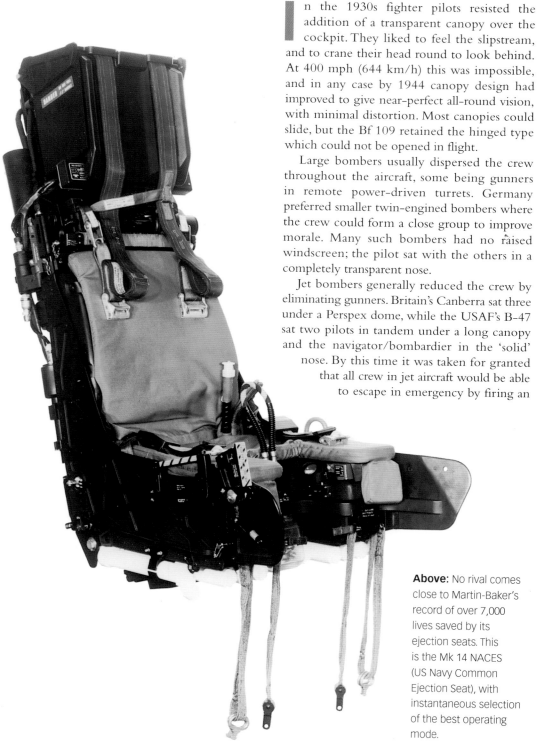

Above: No rival comes close to Martin-Baker's record of over 7,000 lives saved by its ejection seats. This is the Mk 14 NACES (US Navy Common Ejection Seat), with instantaneous selection of the best operating mode.

In the 1930s fighter pilots resisted the addition of a transparent canopy over the cockpit. They liked to feel the slipstream, and to crane their head round to look behind. At 400 mph (644 km/h) this was impossible, and in any case by 1944 canopy design had improved to give near-perfect all-round vision, with minimal distortion. Most canopies could slide, but the Bf 109 retained the hinged type which could not be opened in flight.

Large bombers usually dispersed the crew throughout the aircraft, some being gunners in remote power-driven turrets. Germany preferred smaller twin-engined bombers where the crew could form a close group to improve morale. Many such bombers had no raised windscreen; the pilot sat with the others in a completely transparent nose.

Jet bombers generally reduced the crew by eliminating gunners. Britain's Canberra sat three under a Perspex dome, while the USAF's B-47 sat two pilots in tandem under a long canopy and the navigator/bombardier in the 'solid' nose. By this time it was taken for granted that all crew in jet aircraft would be able to escape in emergency by firing an ejection seat. The first such seats were devised in Sweden and Germany during World War II, and often caused crushed vertebrae and other injury. By 1950 designs were refined, with a predictable acceleration applied by carefully designed cartridges or, later, rockets.

Disgracefully, many British aircrew were killed in such aircraft as the Vampire, Venom, Valiant, Victor and Vulcan by the absence of an ejection seat. Sometimes the decision was taken to make a seat fire downwards. This was acceptable for the man in the nose of a B-47 while it was a high-flying bomber, but not after more deadly SAMs forced it to come down to tree-top height. Another aircraft with a downward-ejecting seat was the Lockheed F-104. This also became a low-level bomber, and so when many pilots were killed it had to be redesigned with an upward-fired seat. Casualties continued at an unacceptable level until an improved seat was fitted, supplied by the British Martin-Baker company.

LIFE-SAVING SEAT

Today the number of aircrew (mostly pilots) whose lives have been saved by Martin-Baker seats has reached 7,000, but Russian *Zvezda* (star) seats have also gained a high reputation. Today's seats have zero/zero capability: they can be safely used with the aircraft at rest on the ground. They are complex systems, which once triggered follow an automatic sequence matched to the circumstances. A few aircraft have even seated the crew inside an ejectable capsule which can subsequently serve as a shelter or boat.

Once aircraft began operating above about 30,000 ft (say, 9.1 km) it became essential to provide an auxiliary supply of oxygen for the crew, and in World War II most pilots used oxygen even in low-level missions. Above about 40,000 ft (say, 12 km) it is necessary to seal the cockpit or cabin and supply air under pressure. Modern fighters typically pressurize the cockpit to a maximum of some 6 lb/in^2 (0.4 bar) above that outside at high altitude (though the pressure is still less than at sea level) and, of course, the cockpit is comfortably heated and air-conditioned.

Early aircrew wore a simple overall, and leather helmet. The latter gradually acquired earphones and an oxygen mask incorporating a microphone, while the flight suit itself could be plugged in for electric heating. The first anti-g suits were also issued to fighter pilots. By 1946 pilots of US jet fighters wore 'bonedomes' (light but rigid protective helmets), and in the 1950s they were issued with partial-pressure suits for high-altitude flight, and improved anti-g suits which in violent manoeuvres apply pressure round the lower abdomen.

Early cockpits had an instrument panel on which might be an ASI (airspeed indicator), altimeter, engine rpm (revolutions per minute) indicator, compass, a simple bubble-in-tube lateral level indicator and ignition switches.

By 1935 there might be 30 or more instruments, nearly all with a needle moved round a dial or vertical scale. The RAF grouped six primary flight instruments – ASI, VSI (rate of climb/descent), directional gyro, altimeter and the vital artificial horizon and turn/bank indicator – in a BF (blind flying) panel, and this remained almost unchanged for 40 years. A World War II pilot would have been at home in the cockpit of an early RAF jet such as a V-bomber.

Then a revolution happened: the dial instruments vanished. Today's warplanes confront the pilot with up to three large coloured multi-function displays. Each has a TV-like screen surrounded by buttons on which the pilot calls up any information he wants.

Below: Ejection seats are tested on rocket-propelled sledges running along railed tracks and subsequently in flight. Here a NACES seat is fired from a Meteor test aircraft.

8 RECENT CRISES

India's Frontiers

Above: By 2000 the Indian Air Force operated 80 MiG-29s of various sub-types. This example serves with No 28 Sqn. at Pune. Though all superb aircraft, the Indian MiG complex of factories is tooling up instead to manufacture the Su-27 family.

Left: Pakistan managed to acquire a batch of 40 General Dynamics F-16 fighters, equipping Squadrons 9, 11 and 14, but a further 28 have never been delivered. Whether, with equally skilled pilots, a PAF F-16 could beat a Mirage IIIEP remains to be seen.

In August 1947 Britain handed over India to self-rule, but the predominantly Muslim north-west and north-east became new countries, Pakistan and East Pakistan (now Bangladesh). Thousands died in riots between the different religions. Eventually these died down, but the borders were places of friction, and Kashmir was claimed by both.

Britain supplied Tempests and Vampires to India, and Furies and Attackers to Pakistan. Pakistan then bought Sabres and Martin B-57s from the USA, while India bought Dassault Ouragans and Mystères, as well as Hunters and Canberras. India also made the British Folland Gnat light fighter, later developing it into the Hindustan *Ajeet* (invincible). When fighting over Kashmir erupted again in 1965, Hunters and Gnats fought Sabres.

The US temporarily cut off supplies to Pakistan. This caused the Muslim country to turn to China, starting with 140 J-6s (Chinese-made MiG-19SFs). Pakistan also bought the Mirage III, but went to the UK for an air-defence system. Even before Pakistan bought Chinese weapons, India's relations with China had been frosty, and in 1962 Chinese troops invaded India's mountainous north-east border, so this also became a troubled region.

In August 1971 India signed in Moscow for an agreement to produce the MiG-21F and its R-11F engine. Ever since, India has had a large aerospace industry, which went on to mass-produce later versions of MiG-21 and the MiG-27M, and their powerful engines. Airframe factories are at Ojhar, near Nasik, other large plants in the MiG Complex being at Bangalore, Lucknow and Hyderabad. The engine works is at the new town of Koraput

In 1968 the IAF began receiving the Su-7BM attack aircraft, imported from the Soviet Union. By December 1971 nearly 100 equipped four squadrons, while nearly 400 of the smaller MiG-21s were at readiness in eight squadrons. War erupted again on 3 December 1971, when India invaded East Pakistan. Air combats took place on both fronts, and the fact that the two Pakistans were separated by over 1,000 miles (1,609 km) of India was a handicap.

STARFIGHTERS DOWNED

In assessing the 1971 war one cannot help being struck by the disparities between the accounts of it written by experienced professional journalists who viewed from one side only. One of the lessons of this war was that Pakistani F-104s – perhaps the fastest and, seen from astern, the smallest targets in the sky – were vulnerable to both missiles (Soviet K-13A copies of the Sidewinder) and guns. Another was that the PAF's J-6 was, despite having been designed in Moscow in 1952 and made in China, a formidable dogfighter, rated superior to the later Mirage III. The F-86F, an even older design, also showed that combat agility can be more important than Mach 2.

India subsequently placed other large orders with the Soviet Union. It has numerous airlift squadrons equipped with the An-12BP, the An-32 and the outstanding Il-76, named *Gajaraj* (king elephant), including the Il-78 tanker and an AWACS conversion. Strategic reconnaissance squadrons have flown the Mach-2.8 MiG-25R and RU, while very large numbers of Mil helicopters serve in many roles. To increase industrial strength, in the 1970s Pakistan planned an aircraft industry, the PAC (Pakistan Aeronautical Complex), at the city of Kamra. First to open, in 1978, was the Mirage Rebuild Factory, followed two years later by the F-6 Rebuild Factory. In 1981 the Aircraft Manufacturing Factory began licence-production of the Saab Supporter light-plane in various *Mushshak* (Proficient) versions. Clearly the Pakistan Ministry of Defence would like to see a factory building something more powerful. After all, India is buying the formidable Su-30MKI, and intends to manufacture it under licence. Meanwhile, Pakistan purchased 40 F-16As, though a second batch of 28 was embargoed by the USA.

Today the rugged frontiers remain uneasy. Tension rose sharply on 10 August 1999 when an IAF MiG-21 fired an R-60 missile to shoot down an Atlantic of the Pakistan Navy, all 16 crew being killed. Arguments raged over on which side of the frontier it had fallen. What makes it even more worrying is that both countries are nuclear powers.

The Falklands

Many people ask 'Why do we waste money on arms? Who are we going to use them against?' The answer is 'We cannot predict what will happen tomorrow'. On 1 April 1982 nobody in Britain knew that on the following day the Falkland Islands would be invaded.

Over 8,000 miles (12,874 km) from Britain in the remote South Atlantic, the islands had never been part of Argentina, but that country claimed them and named them the *Islas Malvinas*. On 2 April the first of over 9,000 troops landed at the capital, Port Stanley. There seemed to be little the British could do except bluster before the United Nations.

Argentina had misjudged Prime Minister Margaret Thatcher. On 3 April she called the House of Commons to its first Saturday sitting since Suez, and announced that a Task Force

would be organized to expel the invaders. A few months later this would have been impossible. The carrier *Hermes* would have gone to the scrapyard, the new *Invincible* would have been sold to Australia, and the last Vulcan bomber would have been withdrawn.

Even as it was, many decisions were now seen to have been stupid. Vital items had either been scrapped or never ordered. The persistent request for a suite of ECM (electronic counter-measures) for British aircraft – which in 1944 led the world in ECM – had been ignored, so Harriers had to jam bundles of chaff under their airbrakes, so the pilot had to remember not to touch the airbrake until he needed ECM protection! Flight-refuelling probes had been removed from the Vulcans and thrown away (one was found on a rubbish tip in Canada). The last Gannet AEW.3 carrier-based airborne early

warning aircraft had been scrapped, so the Task Force had no advance warning of hostile attack.

After frantic activity, most of the Task Force sailed from Portsmouth on 5 April. By this time Hercules transports had flown round the clock to set up provisions for flight-refuelling Victor tankers to be positioned at Wideawake airbase on remote Ascension Island, 4,000 miles (6,437 km) from the UK and the same distance from the Falklands.

LONGEST SORTIES

The first mission was flown on 20 April by a Victor SR.2 of No 55 Sqn RAF (Sqn. Ldr. John Elliott and crew) which made a radar reconnaissance of the southern ocean around South Georgia. Covering 7,250 miles (11,667 km) in 14 h 45 min, it was the longest reconnaissance mission ever flown. On the following day, 1 May, Fl. Lt. Martin Withers of No 101 Sqn and crew left Ascension in Vulcan B.2 XM607 on a mission called Black Buck 1. Refuelled five times, they flew to Port Stanley and dropped 21 1,000-lb (454-kg) bombs across the island's single runway. They refuelled once on the way back, to complete a round trip of 7,860 miles (12,650 km), the longest bombing mission in history.

On 4 May the absence of AEW aircraft enabled an Argentine Navy Super Etendard to launch an Exocet missile against HMS *Sheffield*. This was the first of several major British ship losses, one being the container ship *Atlantic*

Left: This Boeing Chinook HC.2 of RAF No 18 Sqn was the only one available throughout the campaign, the rest being sent to the sea bed by an 'Argy' missile. After the break-out from the San Carlos beach-head it operated round the clock in support.

Conveyor which sank with three Chinooks, a Lynx and six Wessex helicopters. One Chinook had already been assembled and flown off, and it subsequently flew night and day. Surviving Lynx and Sea King helicopters also flew round the clock, on transport, casevac and anti-submarine missions.

The most important British aircraft were the ten RAF Harrier GR.3s (four of which flew out from the UK!) and 20 Sea Harriers of the Royal Navy. Lacking almost everything except capable pilots and ground crews plus AIM-9L Sidewinder AAMs, the Sea Harriers not only took on the 256 land-based Argentine aircraft but were also configured for ground attack missions (later taken over by the RAF Harriers). The main Argentine aircraft were the A-4B and C Skyhawk and Dagger (Israeli-built Mirage 5) of the air force, and the A-4Q Skyhawk and Exocet-armed Super Etendard of the navy. Also feared was the locally-made Pucará twin-turboprop, with guns, bombs (including napalm) and rockets, but nearly all were destroyed on the ground.

On 21 May British troops landed at San Carlos and following a hard land campaign Argentine General Menendez surrendered on 14 June. The RAF and Royal Navy had lost 10 Harriers and 24 helicopters, while Argentina had lost 102 aircraft. This was the first conflict in which every aircraft either could operate without a runway or else needed repeated flight refuelling in order to reach the war zone. It was also the first land campaign supported entirely by helicopters and the first war involving sea-skimming missiles.

Above: During the hectic operation to retake the Falklands in 1982 the Harrier had to take on the entire Argentine AF and Navy. Here steam pours from the catapult of HMS *Invincible* as it launches a Royal Navy Sea Harrier FRS.1, with underwing Sidewinders. In the foreground is an RAF Harrier GR.3.

Afghanistan

Above: Factories at Kazan and Ulan-Ude delivered no fewer than 13,000 helicopters of the Mi-8 and Mi-17 families. Here an Mi-8T utility transport, equipped with either 26 seats or 12 stretchers (litters), is seen in rugged Afghan terrain.

Rugged Afghanistan has for centuries been the abode of fierce tribesmen who are crack shots from childhood. Policed by the RAF between the world wars, a succession of bloody 'palace fights' culminated in King Zahir Shah granting a measure of democracy in 1963, but in 1973 he was deposed. In 1978 the Communist *Khalq* (masses) party seized power, triggering full-scale war between the Government and the *Mujahedeen* Islamic rebels.

In November 1979 the Soviet Union was so concerned that it began sending in ground and air forces. On 25 December three airborne divisions were flown in, while four motor-rifle divisions invaded by road. Moscow should have looked further ahead, because this was the start of a 'Soviet Vietnam'. An immediate result was that President Carter imposed a grain embargo on the USSR and withdrew the USA from the Moscow Olympics.

Afghanistan's border on the West was with Iran, and on the South and East with Pakistan, both well-armed warlike states which were to fly many combat missions against Soviet and Afghan aircraft. Moreover, the civil war in Afghanistan resulted in thousands of refugees fleeing into Pakistan, where many acquired arms. Several thousand returned as fanatical Muslim guerrilla fighters, often with anti-aircraft guns and surface-to-air missiles. Most of these weapons had been supplied from the Soviet Union to Egypt, whose President, Anwar Sadat, sold them on to the US Central Intelligence Agency. The CIA distributed them to the Afghan rebels. By 1986 the USA was supplying arms directly.

At first the Soviet commanders regarded the Afghan campaign – officially the OKSV, standing for 'limited contingent of the Soviet Forces' – as a useful 'opportunity to test new equipment under real combat conditions so that any necessary modification and refinements can be made'. The aircraft types initially involved were the An-12BP, An-26 and An-30 transports, the MiG-21bis, MiG-23MLD, MiG-27D, Su-7BM and Su-25 tactical aircraft and the Mi-6, Mi-8, Mi-17 and Mi-24 helicopters.

MAPPING MISSIONS

The first thing to do was to produce accurate maps, and this involved cartographic and EW (electronic warfare) missions by An-30s, backed up by the MiG-21R, Yak-28R and Su-17M3R photo and EW aircraft. A No 2 Sqn of Special Aircraft was formed equipped with the An-26M, An-26RR and An-26TR for EW surveys, while construction regiments built six major and 11 minor airfields. In this work the Mi-6, with its payload of some 10,000 lb (4,500 kg) in summer and up to 15,432 lb (7 tonnes) in winter, played a crucial role.

Throughout, the *Mujahedeen* were never far away. By day they fired on the Government and Soviet forces from craggy hillsides, while at night they mined the landing strips. In 1984 several regiments of the Soviet DA (long-range aviation) equipped with the Tu-16 were committed. Like the B-52 over South-east

Asia, it was hoped that these would simply demolish the opposition with heavy loads of conventional bombs.

By 1985 Soviet units were flying advanced Su-25s, the Su-22M4, Mi-25 and 35, the Il-76 airlifter, the Mi-26 heavy-lift helicopter with a 44,090 lb (20 tonne) payload, MiG-29 fighters and even the Tu-22M2 supersonic bomber. Bringing in the Tu-22M was a risk, because such expensive aircraft were having to operate in a perilous environment.

Soviet losses mounted alarmingly, and one of the main tasks of the Mi-6 and Mi-26 was to bring back the remains of shot-down aircraft. Several combats took place with the Pakistan Air Force, especially against their newly acquired F-16s (one of which was believed to have been shot down by his own wingman). No engagement took place between MiG-29s and F-16s, but the superior Soviet missiles were judged to have more than compensated for the marginally inferior agility of the MiG-23. During an operation against a *Mujahedeen* base in April 1982 a helicopter landed its troops by mistake in Iranian territory. Most were recovered, but an Mi-8 was shot down by an Iranian F-4D, while another F-4D was shot down by two MiG-23s.

In February 1989 the Soviet Union had had enough and, like the USA in Vietnam, decided to pull out. In April 1992 Communist President Najibullah was overthrown. Since then Afghanistan has been fought over by several factions. With Pakistani support, the Taliban, a hardline Islamic sect, had by 1999 defeated opposition except in northern areas. They are rebuilding an air force with MiG-21s, Su-22s, L-39Cs, An-26s and Mi-17s.

Left: Self-protection flares were a vital part of the kit carried by the superb Ilyushin Il-76 heavy airlifters, to protect them against heat-seeking missiles.

More Gulf Wars

Yet another war around the Persian Gulf began on 9 September 1980 when, thinking Iran (Persia) weak in the aftermath of the revolution which overthrew the Shah, Iraq invaded. Their army soon penetrated 30 miles (48 km), later capturing the city of Khorramshahr. There followed eight years of pointless bloodshed, reminiscent of World War I.

Both sides had large air forces. Iran's assets included 225 Phantoms (mainly F-4Es), 140 F-5s, 80 F-14 Tomcats, 202 AH-1J SeaCobras and large transport forces. Iraq fielded 108 Mirage F1.EQs armed with Exocet missiles, 220 assorted MiGs, 111 Sukhoi attack aircraft and over 300 helicopters. These were used sporadically, and played a minor role in a brutal war which saw the frigate USS *Stark* hit by an Iraqi Exocet and an Iranian Airlines Airbus mistakenly destroyed (with 290 killed) by a SAM from the American cruiser USS *Vincennes*. Warweariness prompted both sides to accept a UN-brokered ceasefire in August 1988.

On 2 August 1990 Saddam Hussein, President of Iraq, ordered his forces to invade Kuwait. The UN passed five Resolutions, while Iraq and Kuwait were plastered with posters celebrating Saddam's triumph in the war with Iran (the fact that it had been a total failure, and an appalling waste of human life, was overlooked). On 17 January 1991 a campaign to free Kuwait was begun by a UN coalition of 21 countries. They faced 550,000 troops in 42 divisions, with 4,200 tanks and 180 helicopters, plus some 550 combat-ready aircraft. Operation Desert Storm was the biggest multi-national campaign since World War II.

Many air forces were involved. Some, such as the USAF squadrons equipped with the B-52, F-111, MC-130 gunship and F-4G Wild Weasel and EF-111A Raven EW (electronic-warfare) aircraft, the US Navy/Marines EA-6B Prowler EW platform, F-14 Tomcat fighter and A-7 Corsair II attack aircraft plus the RAF's Tornado, Buccaneer and Jaguar attack aircraft, used technology only one generation later than World War II. Others, such as the F-117A 'stealth' attack aircraft, the E-8 J-STARS, able to detect and order the destruction of the smallest

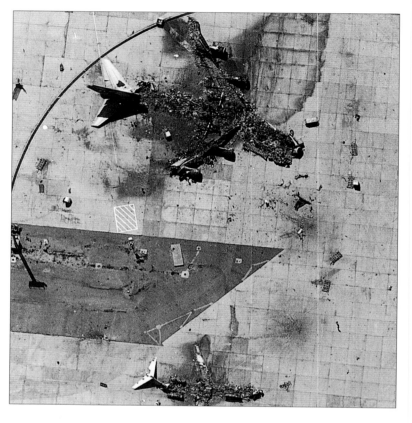

Left: Large numbers of Iraqi aircraft fled to Iran, their erstwhile enemy. Two that did not are seen in this reconnaissance photo of a devastated airfield. Both appear to be US-built civil transports.

vehicle within vast areas of territory, and the E-3A AWACS (airborne early-warning command and control system), able to co-ordinate missions by 1,000 aircraft simultaneously, represented technology never used before.

LASER-GUIDED MUNITIONS

Even the older aircraft had new weapons. Many dropped laser-guided Paveway and GBU-15 EO/IR (electro-optical and infra-red) homing bombs. RAF and Saudi Tornados ejected runway-cratering bomblets and anti-personnel mines from capacious JP233 dispensers, and fired over 120 Alarms (air-launched anti-radiation missiles). Powered ASMs (air/surface missiles) included the long-range Harpoon and SLAM (stand-off land attack missile). Apache helicopters fired Hellfire laser-guided missiles against armour. Combat Talon MC-130s dropped BLU-82 blast bombs weighing 15,000 lb (6,804 kg).

An enormous airlift which included USAF C-5 Galaxies, KC-10 Extenders, C-141 StarLifters and many US civilian transports (mainly 747s and DC-8s) supported the 525,000 US troops on the ground. RAF transport/tankers included the VC10, Victor K.2 and TriStar. Many coalition air forces operated C-130s. Tactical aircraft included USAF F-15 Eagles and A-10s, USN/USMC F/A-18 Hornets and AV-8B Harrier IIs, French Mirage 2000s and Jaguars with C-135FR tankers, Canadian CF-18s with CC-137 tankers, Italian and Saudi Tornados, UAE and Qatar Mirages, and many kinds of helicopter. Argentina sent a Fokker F28 and a destroyer. The sky was controlled by USAF and NATO AWACS and US Navy E-2C Hawkeye surveillance aircraft. Among Elint (electronic intelligence) assets were the USAF RC-135V and RC-135W, the RAF's Nimrod R.1 and French EC.160 Gabriel.

A few Kuwaiti aircraft (A-4 Skyhawks and Mirage F1s) managed to escape the Iraqi invasion and fought with the coalition. In the same way 148 Iraqi aircraft escaped to Iran, their former enemy, where they were interned. The land campaign lasted a mere 100 hours. At least 48,000 Iraqi troops were killed, and over 60,000 captured. Coalition casualties amounted to 95 killed and 20 missing. Saddam Hussein proclaimed a great victory.

He was allowed to continue his reign of terror, attacking his own dissident minorities, notably the Shi'ites and Kurds in northern Iraq. Following repeated provocations, his regime was again attacked on 16 December 1998 in Operation Desert Fox. This time previously unused weapons included the B-1B Lancer bomber, F-14B and F-14D 'Bombcats', AGM-130 and T-LAM missiles and new tactical decoys.

SPECIFICATIONS

Panavia Tornado GR. 1

Powerplant: two Turbo-Union RB.199-34R Mk 101 turbofans each rated at 8,475 lb st (37.70 kN) dry and 14,840 lb st (66.01 kN) with afterburning or, in later aircraft, Turbo-Union RB.199-34R Mk 103 turbofans each rated at 8,650 lb st (38.48 kN) dry and 16,075 lb st (71.50 kN) with afterburning

Performance: limiting Mach No. 1.4 with LRMTS, M1.3 with intakes deactivated (all RAF aircraft); limiting indicated air speed 921 mph (1482 km/h); maximum level speed (clean) at 36,000 ft (10,975 m) 1,453 mph (2338 km/h); climb to 30,000 ft (9145 m) in less than 2 minutes from brakes-off; service ceiling more than 50,000 ft (15240 m); combat radius 863 miles (1390 km) on a typical hi-lo-hi attack mission with a heavy warload

Dimensions: wing span 45 ft 7.5 in (13.91 m) minimum sweep (25°) and 28 ft 2.5 in (8.60 m) maximum sweep (67°); length 54 ft 10.25 in (16.72 m); height 19 ft 6.25 in (5.95 m); wing area 286.33 sq ft (26.60 m²)

Weights: basic empty about 30,620 lb (13890 kg); maximum take-off about 61,620 lb (27951 kg)

Armament: fixed armament comprises two 27-mm IWKA-Mauser cannon, with 180 rounds per gun; nominal maximum ordnance more than 9000 kg (19,841 lb); weapons specific to RAF Tornados include the 950-lb (431-kg) WE177B nuclear bomb (withdrawn 1998 but remaining in the inventory until 2007), JP233 airfield-denial weapon, 1,000-lb (454-kg) freefall, retarded and Paveway II LGBs and (from 1991) BAe ALARM anti-radar missile, AIM-9L/M AAMs for self-defence, Sea Eagle anti-ship missile; GBU-28 laser-guided bomb in 2,000-lb (9907-kg) class, Brimstone laser-guided anti-armour missile

More Balkan Wars

Between the World Wars Yugoslavia, first a kingdom and then a republic, was held together with difficulty by a federal government in Belgrade. Sadly, old tensions, religions and ethnic hatreds festered until the uneasy federation split apart.

First to go was Slovenia, on 20 June 1991. Federal forces hit back at once, the JRV (Yugoslav air force) being given a new commander, replacing a Slovene. Faced by nothing more than small arms, the JRV used MiG-21, J22B *Orao* (Eagle), J-1 *Jastreb* (Hawk) and G-4 Super *Galeb* (Gull) jets and Mi-8 and Gazelle helicopters to hit Slovene targets with impunity – though one Gazelle landed on a Slovene hill and changed sides. Slovenia declared independence on 8 October 1991. Later in the year Yugoslavia was racked by civil war, and Croatia and Bosnia-Herzegovina proclaimed their own independence.

Over the next five years Slovenia, Croatia and Macedonia all built up their own armed forces, with upgraded MiG-21s, ex-Turkish F-5s and, in prospect, used F-16s. Yugoslavia itself (effectively now just Serbia) became a Federal Republic with Montenegro, and in 1999 began sending troops and 'special police' into the republic of Kosovo. It was soon obvious that this was an 'ethnic cleansing' operation, with the objective of either killing or forcing from their homes all non-Serbs. The action naturally caused a storm in the United Nations, but Russia adopted a pro-Serb posture and ignored what was happening.

Eventually NATO issued an ultimatum to Serb President Milosevic in Belgrade, saying 'Stop the killing and withdraw, or we will attack you'. For the first time, the large high-tech forces of the united NATO countries were in a difficult position. Shrinking from

Left: The F-15, originally a product of McDonnell Douglas, is today a Boeing aircraft. Top of the range, and the final production version, the F-18E Strike Eagle can carry a weapon load of no less than 24,5000 lb (11,113 kg). It formed the backbone of the Allied precision-attack force over the Balkans, hitting numerous infrastructure targets.

Above: Ultimate version of the B-52, the B-52H force were nevertheless nearly 40 years old in 1999. They operated from RAF Fairford in England.

Above: Festooned with stores, this Dassault Mirage 2000D will have left the ground at well over 300 mph (482 km/h). The attack weapons are Matra laser-guided bombs, steered by the Atlis designator in the tubular pod ahead of the drop tank. Outboard are Magic 2 self-defence missiles. Note the projecting flight-refuelling probe.

committing ground troops, the NATO command had to rely on air power only, and this time they were up against a well-armed, cunning and resourceful foe.

SPIRIT'S COMBAT DEBUT

Several new weapons were deployed, including the Northrop B-2A Spirit strategic bomber. On the first day of Operation Allied Force, 24 March 1999, two B-2s each dropped 16 heavy precision-guided weapons in a flight-refuelled 15-hour round trip from Whiteman AFB. Further heavy loads were put down by six B-52H bombers launched from RAF Fairford. Other missions were flown by RAF Harrier GR.7s and French Mirage 2000Ds, while Tomahawk cruise missiles were fired from US warships and a Royal Navy submarine.

On 27 March it was estimated that 40,000 Serb 'ethnic cleansers' were in Kosovo, with over 400 armoured vehicles and 400 pieces of artillery. Some 500,000 Kosovo Albanians had fled or been killed. On the same day Belgrade TV showed the wreckage of an F-117 (whose pilot was rescued) and later said pieces would be handed to Russia. In fact, this was one of only two NATO aircraft shot down (the other was an F-16), but it was an embarrassment. On the political front, while Russia's Foreign Minister said NATO was 'committing unconcealed genocide against the people of Yugoslavia', the Secretary-General of the UN declared his 'outrage at Serbian atrocities in Kosovo'.

Among Dutch aircraft were the CH-47D Chinook, P-3C Orion and KDC-10 tanker, as well as the F-16, which was also flown by the USA, Belgium, Denmark and Norway. Germany's units included the ECR (electronic combat and reconnaissance) version of the Tornado, while Italy operated attack and interceptor Tornados as well as the AMX attack aircraft p.156). Canada and Spain partnered the US Navy/Marines with versions of the F/A-18 Hornet. Among the huge USAF commitment was an F-15C, 84-0014, the pilot of which added a second kill marking under the cockpit for a MiG-29, having shot down an Su-22 in Desert Storm.

Prolonged peace talks led to air strikes being suspended on 10 June (Day 79), while the Serbs withdrew from Kosovo. Some 1.8 million ethnic Albanians had been displaced or killed, while 855,000 (mainly Serbs) had left after the air campaign began. Yugoslavia was estimated to have lost 102 aircraft. This was the first war governed by a need to avoid casualties, and major use was made of UAVs (p.188) for Elint and targeting. The only NATO casualties were two fatalities in an AH-64A Apache on a training mission.

Despite such care, NATO aircraft attacked several targets in error, notably the Chinese Embassy in Belgrade and fleeing refugees. Moreover, Serb air defences were formidable, even with archaic missiles. USAF Secretary Whitten Peters said 'If they had had S-300MPU or S-300V it would have been very different'.

Tomorrow's Technology

Above: Sweden's brilliant Saab team once more produced a winner in the JAS 37 *Gripen*, which does what other fighters do but on half the power. Nearly 80 had been delivered by 2000.

Left: Powered by two new General Electric F414 augmented turbofans, of 22,000 lb (9979 kg) thrust, the Boeing (previously McDonnell Douglas) F/A-18E/F Super Hornet may at first glance look like the original versions but is larger and totally different in detail. At least 548 are being bought, despite the unit price of over US$76 million. This total ignores the planned F-18G electronic-warfare version and probable exports.

Half-way through the 20th century it was easy to predict the future of combat aircraft. Jet propulsion had removed the previous limit on speed, so future fighters were expected to have sharply swept-back wings and fly at Mach 1.5, then 2, then 3 and perhaps Mach 5. Guided missiles appeared to have made guns obsolete, and the idea of fighters dogfighting seemed ridiculous.

50 years on, fighters have wings which may be large, and probably tapered mainly on the leading edge, but they are *not* swept back. Few fighters are designed to fly faster than Mach 2, and the Super Hornet and Raptor have brochure limits around 1.8. One of the main reasons for speed is that it provides energy which can be temporarily exchanged for extreme altitude. Not least, guns are a vital part of the armament, and dogfighting forms an essential part of every fighter pilot's training.

Indeed, agility, loosely defined as rate of turn (instantaneous or sustained) and rate of roll, is far more important to a modern fighter than sheer speed. Air forces and aircraft designers are increasingly recognizing the human pilot as a limiting factor (p.188). Reaching this manoeuvre limit has demanded not only a strong airframe structure and powerful aerodynamics to provide lift equal to up to ten times the aircraft's weight, but also new flight-control systems and a bold fresh approach to aircraft design.

An important influence has been the development of AAMs (air-to-air missiles) for BVR (beyond visual range) engagements. A quantum leap was provided 30 years ago by the US Navy's Phoenix, which can lock on to the correct aircraft in a close pair and destroy it from a range of 124 miles (200 km). Impressive, but its high cost restricted procurement, and this missile is carried only by the US Navy's F-14 Tomcat. Today smaller and lighter AAMs can achieve BVR, and Russian firms make the world's best fighter missiles and guns.

Back in the 1950s such interceptors as the F-106 and Arrow carried their missiles in internal bays, like those of traditional bombers. This went out of fashion, and today we see fighters and attack aircraft ploughing through the sky festooned with bombs, guided missiles, rockets, fuel tanks, ECM containers, reconnaissance pods and anything else needed for the mission. Eurofighter, for example has attachments for 13 large external stores. With plenty of engine power this is no problem, but it dramatically increases the RCS, making the aircraft more vulnerable. Future aircraft will probably carry all weapons and other paraphernalia internally.

CONTRASTING WINGS

Two of the best fighters of the 1970 era show startling differences. The F-15 manoeuvres well because it has a wing area of 608 ft² (56.5 m²), even though the wing is simple. The F-16 has a wing less than half as large, but computers vary the camber by pivoting the leading and trailing edges to increase lift. The Swedish *Gripen* (Griffin) has a big wing with automatic leading-edge flaps in two sections with a 'dogtooth' discontinuity at the joint to generate a strong vortex to keep flow from breaking away across the wing. The MiG 1-44 has no fewer than 16 control surfaces, and like all the latest Russian fighters has a 'triplane' layout with both foreplanes and tailplanes.

All such 'superfighters' (p.184), are designed with RSS (relaxed static stability). Traditional fighters were naturally stable, with the centre of gravity well forward, and a big tail to keep them pointing in the right direction, like a weathercock or dart. Thus, the pilot had to force them to change direction. It was discovered that modern computers, working essentially with the speed of light, can be programmed to keep an *unstable* fighter pointing the way it is going. Such a fighter can outfly any older aircraft, because any commanded manoeuvre is obeyed instantly. For safety it must have three computers, in what is called a triplex fly-by-wire system. With only a single computer, its failure at high airspeed would probably cause catastrophic in-flight breakup.

On p.160 it was explained how fighters need a big wing for manoeuvring, and for STOL (short takeoff and landing), yet a small one for low-level attack. A canard (foreplane) can help here in automatically countering the effect of turbulence.

Stealth

An 1935 the invention of radar naturally spurred LO (low observables, or stealth) technologies to help aircraft escape detection. Amazingly, except for a small group in California, this vital subject was given only cursory attention until the 1980s!

The small group was Lockheed's secret 'Skunk Works', which studied radar signature in designing the U-2, followed by the SR-71 (pp.180–181). In 1974 DARPA (the Defense Advanced Research Projects Agency) began a study into how to make aircraft almost invisible to radars. To investigate LO, Lockheed and Northrop built the XST (experimental survivable testbed) followed in 1977 by Lockheed's Have Blue. Both HB1001 and 1002 were lost, because they were difficult to fly, but these amazing aircraft proved the basic principles.

They looked like paper-dart models, with a leading-edge sweep of 72.5°, twin small J85 engines discharging through a narrow horizontal fishtail slit along the back of the wing, and twin powered rudders sloping sharply inward. The skin was made up of flat surfaces with sharply defined angles at the joints, and it was covered in special RAM (radar-absorbent material), even the engine air inlets being covered by a RAM-treated grid.

This made it possible to design an operational USAF aircraft, the Senior Trend, better known as the Lockheed F-117 Nighthawk. Powered by two GE F404 turbofans without the usual afterburners, each rated at 10,540 lb (4,781 kg), it closely followed Have Blue principles but was larger and much more powerful, and the rudders were canted outwards. Intended purely for attack, it was fitted with passive (non-emitting) sensors comprising a FLIR (forward-looking infra-red) above the nose and a DLIR (downward) underneath. These cued laser-guided bombs carried in the two large weapon bays.

LOCKHEED'S BLACK JET

Again, all skin panels were flat, making for long takeoffs and landings and rather tricky handling. The entire aircraft was covered in black RAM, and the edges of all doors and other joints were zigzags with precisely chosen angles. Thus, the F-117 became popularly 'the black jet', and officially it was one of many 'black' (secret) programmes. The F-117 first flew on 18 June 1981 at remote Groom Lake, Nevada. In 1982 the first unit, the 4450th Tactical Group, moved to equally remote Tonopah Test Range. Lockheed delivered five pre-series and 59 production F-117As, the last in 1990. Many F-117As saw action in Iraq, and one was shot down over Yugoslavia on 27 March 1999.

In 1978 DARPA and others began work on a high-altitude LO strategic bomber, the B-2. In 1983 it was accepted that even this had to operate at low level, and that its primary weapons would be conventional (non-nuclear). After a gigantic development programme the first B-2A Spirit flew on 17 July 1989. Prime contractor Northrop Grumman was assisted by Boeing and Vought on the airframe. GE supplied the unique F118 unaugmented turbofan engines, each rated 'in the 19,000-lb (8,618-kg) class'.

Like the F-117 the B-2 is almost all-wing, has engines buried on each side of the swollen centreline, internal stowage of laser-guided bombs or cruise missiles, and a black RAM covering. Important differences are that there are no rudders, the crew number two seated side-by-side, the exterior is not made up of flat surfaces but has smooth curves, and there are two pairs of engines discharging through channels above the wing. Normal takeoff weight is given as 336,500 lb (152,636 kg) but the speed (said to be 609 mph, 980 km/h, at low level) is highly classified. Weapon loads can include 80 bombs of 500-lb (227-kg) or 16 Advanced Cruise Missiles or 16 B61 or B83 nuclear bombs.

Left: The wierdest aircraft in the sky, the Northrop-Grumman B-2A Spirit puts two men in charge of a vehicle with a unit price (1996) of $2,114,000,000. Possibly even more unusual than it looks, many aspects of this aircraft remain classified.

There has been much speculation that the B-2 is as strange as it looks. The author has a file of openly published accounts of its anti–gravity 'electrogravitics'. Diagrams show how electro-static generators charge the jets from the engines negatively, while the wing leading edge acquires a strong positive charge. No comment.

Originally the USAF planned to buy 132 B-2s, but this was scaled back to 75 and finally to only 20. The first to be delivered, Air Vehicle 8, named *Missouri*, reached the 509th Bomb Wing at Whiteman AFB in that state on 11 December 1993. The last, AV-21 *Louisiana*, was delivered on 10 November 1997. Two flew the first combat mission on 24 March 1999, each dropping 16 Joint Direct Attack Munitions on Yugoslav targets.

SPECIFICATIONS

Lockheed Martin F-117A Night Hawk

Type: single-seat low-observable attack aircraft

Powerplant: two General Electric F404-GE-F1D2 turbofans each rated at 10,800 lb st (48.04 kN)

Performance: maximum level speed at high altitude possibly more than Mach 1; normal maximum operating speed at optimum altitude Mach 0.9; combat radius about 700 miles (1112 km) with maximum ordnance

Weights: empty about 30,000 lb (13608 kg); maximum take-off 52,500 lb (23814 kg)

Dimensions: wing span 43 ft 4 in (13.20 m); length 65 ft 11 in (20.08 m); height 12 ft 5 in (3.78 m); wing area about 1,140 sq ft (105.9 m²)

Armament: maximum weapons load 5,000 lb (2268 kg); standard ordnance is the 2,000-lb (9,072 kg) laser-guided bomb, either in GBU-10 Paveway II or GBU-27 Paveway III form, each comes with two warhead options, the standard Mk 84 or the BLU-109 penetration with thicker, straight-sided walls, weapons bay can also reportedly accommodate B61 tactical free-fall nuclear weapon, AGM-65 Maverick air-to-surface missile, AGM-88 HARM anti-radar missile and AIM-9 Sidewinder air-to-air missile

Reconnaissance

Above: Though early examples were limited in capability, the Boeing AWACS gave battle commanders a totally new level of information. The original USAF E-3A versions have been repeatedly updated, and this photo shows a Sentry of the USAF, with TF33 engines, no wingtip pods, a FR probe and EW (electronic-warfare).

Reconnaissance was the first task performed by military aircraft. Today it is a specialized mission, for which many air forces operate dedicated aircraft (unable to do anything else). At the same time, tactical (battlefield) reconnaissance is often performed by a fighter or attack aircraft to which a special 'pod', a sensor container, has been attached.

A typical reconnaissance pod is a streamlined box about 10 ft (say, 3 m) long and weighing upwards of 250 lb (113 kg). It could contain framing cameras taking individual pictures on 70 or 126-mm film (with forward motion compensation to give sharp pictures at Mach 1 at low level), or panoramic cameras taking a continuous strip of film (vertical or diagonally on either side), or a FLIR (forward-looking infra-red) receiver giving images based on the precise temperature of everything in the FOV (field of view), or IRLS (IR linescan) the thermal equivalent of a panoramic camera, or any of many kinds of radar or receivers to pick up all sorts of electronic signal. Some Sigint (signals intelligence) platforms are covered in antennas.

Such equipment can be larger and more powerful if it is permanently installed in a dedicated aircraft. Some reconnaissance aircraft are designed to fly very high, either to avoid being shot down or in order to see further into hostile territory without crossing a frontier. Famous examples include the Lockheed U-2 and TR-1, which relied on great height, and the Lockheed SR-71A which relied on altitude and Mach 3. The RAF has only the venerable Canberra PR.9, but from 2005 it will operate five ASTOR (airborne stand-off radar) aircraft based on a Canadian business jet. Prime contractor in the $800 million deal is Raytheon, the US electronics giant. The main sensor will be a synthetic-aperture radar with its antenna in a large 'canoe' under the fuselage.

VARIETY OF PLATFORMS

A similar aircraft is now competing in an AGS (Alliance ground surveillance) NATO competition. A rival is an improved version of Northrop Grumman J-Stars (Joint surveillance target attack radar system). The USAF J/Stars is the E-8, based on the Boeing 707, but if this system wins the NATO competition it will be packaged into the Airbus A321, which offers many advantages. In contrast, Australia has chosen a similar kind of radar mounted above the rear fuselage of Boeing 737s, which might have been thought the optimum worst location!

The Boeing 707 was also the platform chosen for the USAF E-3 AWACS (airborne warning and control system), with the main sensor the APY-2 radar with an enormous slotted-waveguide antenna 30 ft (9.1 m) across inside a discus-shaped fairing rotating every ten seconds. The RAF version, the Boeing Sentry, has Elint receivers on the wingtips and a probe instead of a flight-refuelling receptacle. The main task of such aircraft is to keep control of air operations and direct friendly aircraft.

Sensing a large global market for a less costly AEW&C (airborne early-warning and control) system, Ericsson of Sweden has developed Erieye. This radar uses a phased-array antenna which can 'look' in any direction. Thus, it does not need to rotate, and resembles a giant plank carried above the fuselage.

Special sensors are needed to find submarines, which in a war are important targets able to travel deep underwater at remarkably high speed. Maritime reconnaissance aircraft are usually large, in order to have long range and

endurance. The most widely used is the Lockheed P-3 Orion turboprop, while the most advanced is the RAF's Nimrod MRA.4, which will replace earlier Nimrods from 2002. Powered by Rolls-Royce turbofan engines, it will be equipped with radar, a FLIR turret, a MAD (magnetic-anomaly detector) in the tail to sense the distortion in the Earth's magnetic field caused by a deeply submerged submarine, EO (electro-optical) sensors and sonobuoys which are canisters dropped into the ocean to detect submarines by listening for sound waves, either those caused by the target, or the buoy's own sounds reflected from it. Alternatively, ASW helicopters can 'dunk' sonars into the ocean and listen in the same way. As a sonar is non-expendable, it can be more powerful and effective than sonobuoys.

SPECIFICATIONS

Lockheed U-2R

Type: single-seat strategic/battlefield reconnaissance aircraft

Powerplant: one Pratt & Whitney J75-P-13B turbojet rated at 17,000 lb st (75.62 kN)

Performance: never exceed speed Mach 0.8; maximum cruising speed at 70,000 ft (21,335 m) over 430 mph (692 km/h); maximum rate of climb at sea level about 5,000 ft (1525 m) per minute; climb to 65,000 ft (19,810 m) in 35 minutes; operational ceiling 80,000 ft (24,385 m); maximum range about 6,250 miles (10,060 km); maximum endurance 12 hours

Dimensions: wing span 103 ft (31.39 m); length 62 ft 9 in (19.13 m); height 16 ft (4.88 m); wing area about 1,000.00 sq ft (92.90 m²)

Weights: basic empty without powerplant and equipment pods less than 10,000 lb (4536 kg); maximum take-off 41,300 lb (18,733 kg)

Airlift III

On p.124 the point is made that aircraft designers were slow to create a sensible airlifter. Such aircraft need a capacious unobstructed interior, with a flat level floor at a convenient 'truck bed' height, strong enough not to be damaged by tanks, and a full-section rear door that can be opened in flight. After World War II pressurization was a requirement, to enable gas-turbine engines to operate at high altitude for minimal fuel consumption.

The Lockheed C-130 was the first airlifter to meet all these requirements, and the Lockheed C-141 StarLifter was the first with turbofan engines. In 1968 the same factory produced the huge C-5A Galaxy, which was the

first airlifter to have a full-width door at both ends. It was powered by General Electric TF39 engines, each of 41,100 lb (18,643 kg) thrust. This was the first turbofan to have a high bypass ratio (8, at a time when civil jets had a bypass ratio around 1), which dramatically reduced fuel consumption and noise. The wings suffered fatigue problems, and the C-5As had to be expensively re-winged. A second batch called C-5B have engines of 43,000 lb (19,505 kg) thrust and other upgrades.

Today the most capable airlifter is the Antonov An-124, of Ukraine. This resembles the C-5 in layout and size, but has D-18T turbofan engines of 51,590 lb (23,401 kg) thrust, and

Above: Best of the West's airlifters is the Boeing (previously McDonnell Douglas) C-17 Globemaster III. This has matured as a superb aircraft, but few can afford its cost, both to buy and to operate.

Above: Powered by 15,000-hp propfans, Ukraine's An-70 is a next-generation airlifter. Capable of airlifting 300 troops, 206 stretcher (litter) casualties or large vehicles, it cruises at up to 497 mph (800 km/h). Meanwhile the West Europeans continue to argue over a proposed airlifter with less power, less load, a smaller hold and slower speed.

this is a conventional large airlifter, powered by four Pratt & Whitney F117 turbofans each of 40,700 lb (18,462 kg) thrust. Maximum interior width is 18 ft (5.49 m), only 1 ft (0.3 m) less than the C-5, and maximum cargo load is 169,000 lb (76,655 kg). At first there were problems with output and cost, but the Long Beach plant (now part of Boeing) got their act together and are delivering 120 on time and cost (unit price about $190 million).

In order to replace the mass-produced An-12, and possibly also some C-130s, in 1975 the Antonov design bureau began studying a completely new aircraft. At an early stage it was decided to use propfans, turboprops with a new kind of propeller giving high efficiency at cruising speeds up to 500 mph (800 km/h). The result is the An-70. The first was lost in a mid-air collision, but a second flew on 24 April 1997. Its four 13,800-hp D-27 propfans each drive contra-rotating propellers, with eight thin scimitar-like blades on the front unit and six on the rear. The capacious hold can carry a load of 103,615 lb (47 tonnes) or air-drop a single item weighing 44,092 lb (20 tonnes). With seats or litter (stretcher) racks installed the An-70 can carry 300 troops or 206 casualties.

In 1982 British Aerospace, Aérospatiale of France, MBB of Germany (now Daimler-Benz Aerospace) and Lockheed decided to build a new airlifter to replace the C-130 and Transall C-160. Since then the only tangible result is that Lockheed Martin has produced the C-130J, and partnered Alenia of Italy on the C-27J Spartan, an upgraded version of a long-established airlifter powered by two 4,200-hp Rolls-Royce turboprops, as fitted to the four-engined C-130J and driving the same six-blade Dowty propeller.

In Europe 19 years of talk has produced various changes of propulsion (from turboprops to jets and then back to conventional turboprops), changes of organization (the project is now part of Airbus) and a consistent refusal to go ahead. The 1999 idea was to build an aircraft called A400M, which according to the brochures would be less capable than the An-70, and powered by engines which do not yet exist.

wing fuel tanks holding 76,714 Imp gal (348,740 litres), compared with the C-5B capacity of 42,591 gal (193,624 litres). The An-124 also has a wider and more capacious cargo hold, and can carry loads up to 330,700 lb (150 tonnes), compared with the USAF aircrafts's limit of 291,000 lb (131,995 kg). To increase 'flotation' (ability to use unpaved airstrips) both these monster aircraft have a row of four nose-wheels and, while the C-5 has four six-wheel main bogies, the An-124 has five pairs of main-wheels along each side with the ability to 'kneel' to bring the floor close to the ground. Antonov has managed to find customers for over 50, most of them now being commercially operated.

HERCULES REPLACEMENTS

In the late 1960s the USAF studied how to replace the C-130, and ordered prototypes of the Boeing YC-14 and McDonnell Douglas YC-15. The former had two turbofans blowing across the top of the wing, which was fitted with large flaps which could generate tremendous lift for STOL (short takeoff and landing). This idea was adopted by Antonov for the An-72 and An-74, which serve in large numbers. The YC-15 had four engines into whose jets could be depressed large flaps of heat-resistant material.

McDonnell Douglas used this idea later in the C-17 Globemaster III. Apart from the flaps,

Superfighters

There is no precise definition of a Superfighter, except that such aircraft are characterized by a range of capabilities beyond those of previous fighters. One is so-called active flight controls, which 'think' and interpret the pilot's demands to give him the maximum of what he wants without ever endangering the aircraft, or overstressing it, or losing control. A second is the ability to make post-stall manoeuvres, in other words to get into previously impossible attitudes, with the nose pointing in any direction and the wing perhaps encountering the air at an angle (called angle of attack) of over 60°, yet with the aircraft *still under perfect control*. A third is the ability to 'supercruise', to fly for extended periods faster than sound in dry thrust (without using afterburner). A fourth is the provision of vectoring engine nozzles, to give extremely powerful control in pitch, yaw or roll at any airspeed. A fifth is so much engine thrust that tight turns can be sustained with no falling-off in airspeed. A sixth is the maximum degree of stealth, and a seventh is the incorporation of advanced electronic-warfare systems with antennas all over the aircraft.

Examples of Superfighters now flying are the Lockheed Martin F-22 Raptor and Sukhoi S-37 *Berkut* (Golden eagle). Another is the MiG 1-44,

but in late 1999 this impressive aircraft had still not flown, and its future appears doubtful. Near-Superfighters include the Saab JAS39 *Gripen* (Griffin), Eurofighter Typhoon and Dassault *Rafale* (squall), which incorporate limited Stealth technology and have fixed-axis nozzles.

These aircraft are among the most exciting aeroplanes ever created. They are quite large, very powerful, and able to do manoeuvres never seen before. On the other hand, they are also exceedingly costly, and another adverse factor is that in general they have taken 20 years to develop. So far, the best brains in governments and industries have failed to find a formula which reconciles large numbers of aircraft manufactured at a high rate, whilst at the same time saving money by keeping down the numbers ordered. Making fewer, at a lower rate, dramatically increases the cost of each aircraft.

RETRO CAPABILITY

Moreover, the long development period means that to some degree the new fighter is obsolete before it even enters service. In 1999 Air Commodore Rick Peacock-Edwards, who is overseeing the entry of the Eurofighter (actually the name of the company) into the RAF, said 'It is the future of the RAF....it has to beat the

threat, such as MiG-29s and Flankers' (Flanker is a NATO name for the Su-27). The obvious problem is that this suggests that the RAF is looking forward to receiving, long after the Millennium, a fighter which will be able to beat aircraft designed in 1972.

Before selecting the F-22 the USAF conducted a flyoff competition against a rival, the Northrop Grumman YF-23. Each had good points, and in the author's view such competitions with real flight articles will eventually become financially not worth while. At the same time, future fighter pilots, whose lives depend on their employer making the right choice, may be uneasy at the choice being based entirely on computer simulations.

Unquestionably, it makes sense for several nations to collaborate. Eurofighter GmbH is a German company, but its first product meets the carefully defined needs of four very capable air forces — the UK, Germany, Italy and Spain — and is already finding other air forces queueing up to fly it and sign contracts. France pulled out, partly because it wanted a carrier-based version. Today the plan for a future Royal Navy carrier has triggered Eurofighter to work on a possible naval Typhoon. Pity this was not thought about earlier. As it is, Europe has two

Left: This Eurofighter Typhoon development aircraft was the first to be fitted with both the EJ200 engines and the ECR90 radar. It is rumoured to be testing radar-absorbent materials, to give the aircraft better 'stealth qualities'. By 2000 the factories were in production with the first batch, though some of these may not be up to operational standard.

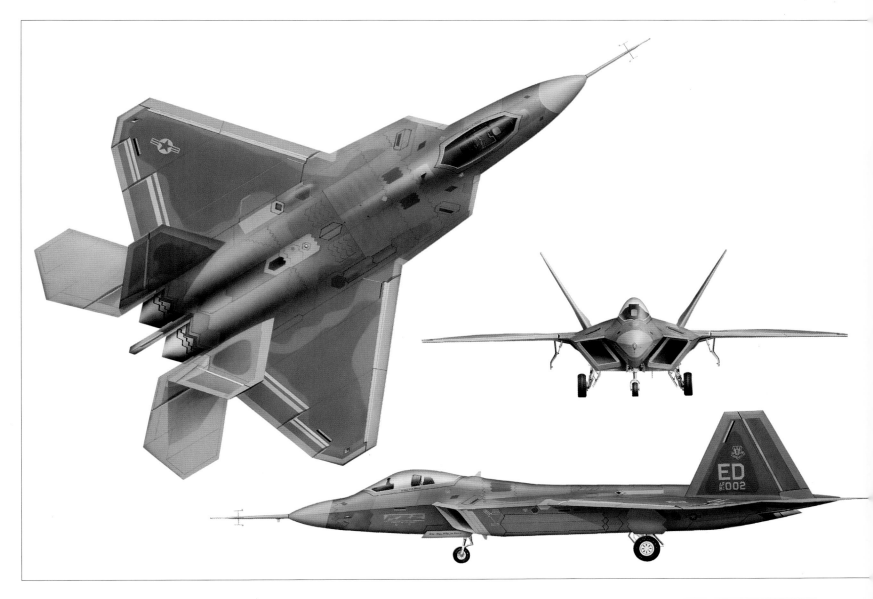

near-rivals competing for the same market (again). France is for the first time seriously thinking of making Dassault collaborate, and talks on a next-generation aircraft began with British Aerospace in 1998.

The sheer cost of modern warplanes makes the existence of near-rivals, such as *Rafale* and the Typhoon, nonsensical. Including RDT&E (research, development, test and engineering), and assuming a full 339-aircraft programme, each F-22 for the USAF was calculated in 1998 to cost $187,300,000. With inflation, this is bound to rise, and it will increase sharply if the total buy is cut. For example, launch of JSF (next page) would almost certainly cut the F-22 buy to 200, resulting in a unit price of around $220 million! The mind boggles at such figures and one begins to wonder whether it might not be a good idea for all nations to try to live together in harmony.

SPECIFICATIONS

Lockheed Martin F-22A Raptor

Type: single-seat air superiority fighter

Powerplant: two Pratt & Whitney F119-PW-100 turbofans each rated at around 35,000 lb st (158 kN) with afterburning

Performance: (estimated): maximum speed (design target) 921 mph (1482 km/h) at sea level, maximum level speed around Mach 2.0 with afterburning at high altitude and over Mach 1.5 in 'supercruise' mode (without afterburning) typically at altitudes around 50,000 ft (15,240 m)

Weights: empty (design target) 31,670 lb (14,365 kg); maximum take-off around 60,000 lb (27,216 kg)

Dimensions: wing span 44 ft 6 in (13.56 m); length 62 ft 1 in (18.92 m); height 16 ft 5 in (5.02 m); wing area 840 sq ft (78.00 m²)

Armament: one fixed 0.79-in (20-mm) M61A2 long-barrel cannon with 480 rounds; internal weapons load consists of AIM-9M Sidewinder or next-generation AIM-9X missiles in side weapons bays and six AIM-120C AMRAAM AAMs and/or 1015-lb (460-kg) JDAM precision-guided munitions in main weapons bay; wing mounted stores include JDAM, BLU-109 Penetrator, AGM-88 HARM anti-radar missile and GBU-22 laser-guided bomb with Paveway III guidance head

The Next Generation

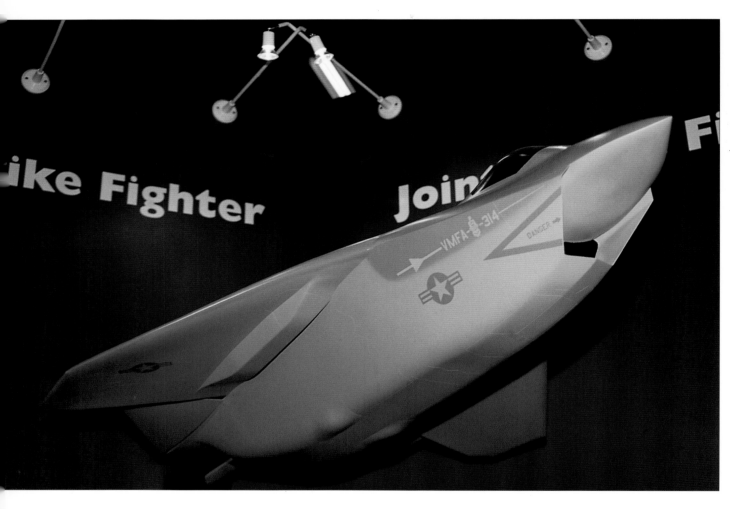

Left: Boeing's X-32 is a distinctive aircraft, its stumpy look belying its tremendous all-round performance. Like its rival, initial versions are all powered by a Pratt & Whitney JSF-F119 engine. At a late stage Boeing added horizontal tails.

Right: In contrast Lockheed Martin's X-35 has lateral inlets and in some respects draws on experience with the F-22. Like its rival, there are versions for each mission, differing in size, weight and propulsion. Whether or not the 'winner takes all' philosophy prevails, there seems little doubt that by 2020 one of these aircraft (or a merged version) will equip more than 20 air forces.

Today, with no feared enemy in sight, Western nations are discarding the previous secrecy surrounding future weapons. One has only to pick up *Aviation Week* or *Flight International* to read what the US and British air forces expect to operate 30 years hence.

In previous pages we have seen how often preconceived notions have been unfounded. What may be harder to believe is the extent to which the design of warplanes – the most high-tech life-and-death business imaginable – appears to be subject to the whims of fashion. Today swept wings are out, canards are in and so are twin fins or powered rudders. Among other things, tall centreline fins make it harder to eject safely. The next fashion will probably be no vertical tail.

Obviously, a lot depends on how far stealth qualities are allowed to rule the design. With the *Gripen*, Eurofighter and *Rafale* the basic philosophy was 'Design the best fighter possible, and then see how far the RCS can be reduced by local modifications'. This is a compromise, which might be justified in order to get a new aircraft into production quickly, but the time taken to develop new aircraft has become unacceptable. So, most observers would agree, is the price. Common sense suggests that we cannot go on taking over 20 years to develop fighters that then cost over $187 million each.

In the late 1950s the US Department of Defense tried to force through a single basic design (the F–111) that would fly both fighter and bomber missions for the USAF and Navy. The result was a bomber (only) for the USAF (only). Today Boeing and Lockheed Martin are building competing versions of JSF (Joint Strike Fighter), which should far surpass the versatility of the F–111. JSF's genesis was the Marine Corps' need for a STOVL (short takeoff, vertical landing) multi-role aircraft to replace the Harrier. This grew into a programme involving 1,763 for the USAF, 480 modified aircraft for the Navy, 609 STOVL for the Marines and 60 STOVL to replace the Sea Harrier in the Royal Navy. In late 1999 the RAF thought it might need 90 to replace the Harrier, making the launch total 3,002.

SUCCESS INDICATED

In contrast to the F-111, there is every indication that the JSF will be a resounding success. Both competitors expect to fly both conventional and STOVL demonstrators in 2000, with a view to service entry in 2008. All versions have a single main engine, the Pratt & Whitney JSF-F119, in the 40,000 lb (18,144 kg) class. From the 72nd aircraft an alternative engine, the even more powerful GE JSF-F120, could be fitted.

Lockheed Martin's X-35 demonstrator has side inlets to a normal engine in the USAF version, and a wing area of 412 ft² (38.3 m²). The Navy version has carrier equipment and a wing of 600 ft² (55.74 m²), while the Marines' and British versions have a small wing but a 25,000-hp shaft drive from the engine to a fan behind the cockpit to generate a huge lifting airflow

through doors in the top and bottom of the fuselage, while the main nozzle pivots down 90°. Boeing's X-32 versions instead have a chin inlet, and in the STOVL version the main engine is fitted with a large valve to deflect the entire jet out through left and right downward-pointing nozzles on the centre of gravity. In normal flight these nozzles are retracted. All versions carry a gun (yet to be chosen), missiles and bombs internally.

In late 1999 it was possible that, instead of 'winner takes all', the rivals might both build the selected aircraft, or somehow produce a combined design. Congressional pressure to cut funding for the F-22 is unlikely to hurt that programme, as it is the future core of the USAF. However, the fact that it is closer in timing, and an extremely expensive aircraft, has tended to divert attention from the fact that

the planned F-22 buy is 339, while the planned USAF buy for the JSF is more than five times that number. Moreover, while few air forces could consider the costly F-22, several have already expressed urgent interest in JSF, which could be the biggest Western warplane programme since 1945.

In Britain the Defence Evaluation Research Agency has organized studies, and British Aerospace has published a picture of an FOAS (future offensive air system). Perhaps more credible are possible successors to the B-2, proposed by Northrop Grumman for use from 2030. One is subsonic, one a supercruise type, and the third a hypersonic wave-rider like an updated version of the Antipodal Bomber of 1938. At Langley AFB the Global Attack Arm of USAF Air Combat Command is living in the far future.

Dropping the pilot

In 1927 a small aeroplane took off from HMS *Stronghold* and flew 100 miles (161 km) down the English Channel. Later examples carried 250-lb (113-kg) bombs on tests over the desert in Iraq. What was unusual was that this machine, the Larynx, carried no pilot. Since then countless thousands of pilotless aircraft have flown, some with engines resembling those of motorcycles and others with rocket or jet engines.

Most have been targets for guns or missiles. Some have carried cameras, IR, EW, Sigint, synthetic-aperture radar or other sensors, in order to fly reconnaissance missions. Today the USAF's Global Hawk, a product of Northrop Grumman's Teledyne Ryan, carries a ton of sensors to high altitude and can then stay there, almost invisible on hostile radars, for *almost two days and nights*.

Today a further revolution is taking place. Recognizing the fact that the limiting factor in the manoeuvrability of military aircraft is any humans that may be on board, the obvious thing to do is to remove them. This is not yet a factor in the design of oceanic ASW aircraft, airlift transports or helicopters, but it is an immediate and pressing consideration for any aircraft intended to operate over a battle area. This is doubly important in a world in which the media love to draw attention to body bags, to the extent that any serious battle casualties could be calculated to provoke a giant political storm.

While the Global Hawk is an example of a UAV (uninhabited air vehicle), new acronyms are emerging with confusing frequency. The URAV (uninhabited reconnaissance air vehicle) is already showing that it can be a valuable partner to SBSS (space-based surveillance systems, or spy satellites), which often in practice are not in quite the right place or are finding it difficult to see through cloud. The SUAV (support UAV) is intended to fly over-the-horizon targeting missions, as well as airborne early warning and weather monitoring (if necessary over enemy territory) and act as a backup to communications satellites, should they fail.

Left: A Lockheed Martin image of future warfare, using naval UCAVs. The ship would not be a traditional carrier but a multi-role surface combatant. On deck are UCAVs with wings folded, while another makes a vertical takeoff and others recover to the ship. Such vehicles would fly the missions of manned aircraft whilst weighing one-quarter as much and occupying one-third of the deck space.

PILOT-FREE FLIGHTDECKS

The big challenge is the UCAV (uninhabited combat air vehicle). Many companies around the world cannot afford to do more than carry out studies on paper and with computers, but in the USA two major programmes exist. Boeing Military Aircraft and Missile Systems are working on a UCAV for the Air Force, while Lockheed Martin is under contract for a UCAV for the Navy. While a UCAV is expected to be able to sustain an acceleration of about 20 g in previously impossible manoeuvres, close air combat is not expected to be the most important mission. The first priorities are precision attack on high-value surface targets, SEAD (suppression of enemy air defences) and battlefield air interdiction.

A rash of exciting artists' impressions of UCAVs has emerged, mainly from the two US companies actually working on such vehicles, but also from Northrop Grumman and others. All clearly show the influence of stealth technology, and several put the engine air inlet where the canopy used to be in order to reduce the radar cross-section. Some artworks show formations in which one of the aircraft has a human pilot, acting as a mission manager. Of course, all UCAVs are combat aircraft which happen not to have a cockpit. They are designed to return to base to be serviced for the next mission.

One of the interesting concepts being studied by the Navy is the VATOL UCAV (vertical attitude take-off and landing). This capability would enable the vehicle to be fired like a missile from a Trident launch tube in a submerged submarine. An obvious problem is how a submarine might recover its UCAV after each mission. Studies suggest that it is not beyond the bounds of possibility for the UCAV to tilt nose-up and descend under computer control back into its launch tube, the submarine being on the surface.

Some observers have noticed a cultural reluctance on the part of existing armed forces to replace manned systems by completely pilotless ones. One cannot help drawing a parallel with 'the Sandystorm' (p.151). At that time, in

Left: Powered by a Rolls-Royce AE3007H turbofan of 8,290 lb thrust the USAF's RQ-4A Global Hawk is designed to fly for up to two days at 70,000 ft (21,335 m). To operate at this height with infra-red, electro-optics and synthetic-aperture radar, plus ground and satcom data links, this vehicle has a wing span of 116 ft (35.36 m).

1957, there were essentially no computers, the whole subject of automatic control was in its infancy, and even flight at night or in bad weather still posed problems, yet Her Majesty's Government adopted the official position that they would buy no more combat aircraft with human pilots. Today the idea of dropping the pilot appears much less nonsensical, and many aircrew may have to spend their later years sitting in what will look like a TV programme control room, staring intently at numerous colourful screens.

Index

Page numbers in *italics* refer to illustrations.

Acknowledgements

Acknowledgements in Source Order
A Hamlyn History of Military Aviation

Aerospace Publishing Ltd Front Cover top, Front flap, Back flap, Back Cover top, 23, 31, 41, 45, 49, 55, 57, 61, 65, 67, 75, 79, 83, 89, 95, 99, 109, 113, 117, 127, 133, 135, 141, 143,149, 153, 155, 157, 162,173, 179, 181, 185

Aspect Picture Library 7

Corbis UK Ltd Back Cover bottom

Frank Spooner Pictures 171

Philip Jarrett 25, 111, 114, 115 Top

Courtesy Lockheed Martin 124, 188

Mary Evans Picture Library 8, 15

Peter R. March 161

REX Features 103

Russian Aviation Research Trust 16–17

Salamander Picture Library 74, 97 Bottom

Sygma 13

Topham Picturepoint 11

TRH Pictures 9, 18, 19 Bottom, 20, 21, 22, 24, 27, 29, 30, 34, 39, 40, 42, 44, 46, 50, 51, 52, 53, 54, 63, 64, 66, 69, 77, 78, 82, 84 Top, 85, 87, 90 Top, 90 Bottom, 91, 93, 97 Top, 100, 102, 105, 107, 112, 115 Bottom, 116, 118 Top, 118 Bottom, 121, 122, 126, 128, 129 Bottom Right, 131 Top, 136, 137, 140, 142, 144 Top, 144 Bottom, 150, 151, 159 Top, 159 Bottom, 166, 168, 170, /Aermacchi 156, /AMD-BA 152, /Martin Baker 164, 165, /BAE Systems 169, /Bell 158, /Boeing 134, 174, 176, 178, 182, /H.W. Cowin 12, 26, 48, 59, 60, 73 Top, 80, 98, 138, /Daimler-Benz Aerospace/ B. Tounel 184, /Dassault Aviation/ Aviaplans 175 Bottom, /E. Nevill 175 Top, 183, 186, /FMU K Dahlberg 177, /Imperial War Museum 19 Top, 28, 32, 33, 35, 43, 56, 58, 68, 70, 71, 76, 81, 84 Bottom, 86, /Lockheed Martin 2–3, 101, 131 Bottom, 132, 187, MOD 36, 37, /NASA Front Endpaper, Back Endpaper, 1, 4–5, 163, /NATO 104, /QAPI 108, 125, /RAF Museum 62, 106, 139, /M. Roberts 119, /The Science Museum 6, 14, /Teledyne Ryan Aeronautical 189, /US Air Force 72, 129 left, 145, 146 Top, 146 Bottom, 147, 160, 180, /US DOD 120, 123 Bottom, /US National Archives 88, 92, 94, 96, 110, /US Navy 10, 38, 73 Bottom, 130, 148, 172, /J. Widdowson 47, /Dave Willis 123 Top, /Kevin Wills 154.
Simon Watson 167

Quadrant Picture Library Front Cover bottom